Scale Aircraft
DRAWINGS

by PETER M. BOWERS

D1608972

ABOUT THE AUTHOR

Peter M. Bowers began to build model airplanes soon after Lindbergh flew across the Atlantic in 1927. He began to write for publication in the mid-1930s when the editors of model aviation publications, including Model Airplane News, asked him to write articles and draw up plans for his outstanding models.

From 1940 to 1942, he studied aeronautical engineering at the prestigious Boeing School of Aeronautics, and he began to amass one of the largest, most comprehensive, private collections of airplane photos in the world. Scale Aircraft Drawings—Volume II: World War II draws extensively on this collection.

After five years in the U.S. Army Air Forces as a Maintenance and Technical Intelligence Officer, he joined the Boeing Airplane Company as an engineer, and he retired in 1983 after 36¹/₂ years. Meanwhile, his model building had expanded to include the design and construction of pilot-carrying, "home-built" airplanes. His single-seat Fly Baby won the national EAA design contest in 1962, and he has been selling plans to amateur builders ever since.

Over the years, his many books and magazine articles have led to his worldwide recognition as an aviation historian, model builder and airplane designer.

★   ★   ★

Scale Aircraft Drawings—WW II—Volume II

Group Publisher: Louis V. DeFrancesco Jr.
Publication Director: Ed Schenk
Book Design: Alan J. Palermo
Publication Coordinator: Sally Williams
Copy Director: Lynne Sewell
Copy Editor: Karen Jeffcoat
Art Assistants: Allyson Nickowitz, Walter Sidas
Cover Photos: Budd Davisson

Published by Air Age Publishing, Inc.
251 Danbury Road
Wilton, CT 06897
PRINTED IN THE USA.

CONTENTS

INTRODUCTION

by PETER BOWERS

This book, Volume II of the Air Age Scale Aircraft Drawings series, covers 37 representative WW II airplanes. Some are prewar service models that served at the beginning of hostilities but were soon replaced, while others are more modern types that, with continual upgrading, were able to serve until the end. It's interesting that very few of the models that originated after the onset of the war actually saw combat.

Some of these drawings were made during the war when data was scarce or even restricted, but they're as accurate as possible under the circumstances. In fact, artist William Wylam drew some of them so well that the U.S. Army took him to task for being *too* accurate in depicting designs that were still classified. As a result, he deliberately included minor discrepancies in some subsequent drawings, notably the vertical tail of the B-29.

Some of these discrepancies are mentioned in the text that accompanies each airplane; each includes a brief history and details of the plane's development and operational use. With modelers in mind, I carefully selected the photos from my collection, and they combine the best views of the airplanes' structural detail and markings.

It should be noted that the drawings and photos in this book are, at best, rather general, and serious modelers who build

■ *Above:*
Me 262 nose details. At left, an Me 262A-2a with two 250kg (550-pound) bombs under the fuselage. At right, an Me 262A-1a fighter. Note the ports for the 30mm cannon in the upper nose.

■ *Below:*
One of six PBM-3Bs sent to England as "Mariner I," painted in the British Coastal Command's white and gray color scheme. The Mariners didn't meet British requirements and were returned to the U.S. Navy. Note the powered two-gun tail turret.

for scale competition will need additional supporting data to verify their efforts.

The most common errors found on models, illustrations and even restored military airplanes are national insignia of incorrect proportions, and incorrect markings for the period of aircraft operation being depicted. Accurate data on this complicated subject isn't generally available to modelers, so I've devoted a section to these markings (as obtained from official markings charts).

I've also included a section on designations, which discusses the basics of the various national designating systems. It also explains why an American-built airplane like the Douglas DB-7 (factory designation) was operated as a "DB-7" only by France; while Great Britain called it either a "Boston" or a "Havoc;" the U.S. Army called it an "A-20" or a "P-70;" and the U.S. Navy used it as a "BD."

Finally, I explain why different designations were used on otherwise identical U.S. Navy airplanes (such as the SB2C-4 and the SBW-4), as well as the meaning of "B-17G-BO," "B-17G-VE" and "B-17G-DL."

WORLD WAR II COLOR AND MARKINGS

The enormously complex subject of WW II markings and insignia fills many books. The best that can be done to address the subject in this limited volume is to present an outline of the basic colors used, the proper proportions and placement of national insignia, and the time during which these markings were used.

AIRPLANE COLORING

Most military airplanes were not camouflaged after the end of WW I, but, as WW II approached, "war paint" gradually came back into use: in England and Germany in 1937; in France in 1939; in the U.S. Army in 1940; and in the U.S. Navy in 1941. In general, European airplanes used a combination of several earth tones on the top and sides, and a light shade, such as sky blue,

(Figure 1) The early Curtiss P-40 (shown) and Douglas A-20A were the only camouflaged U.S. Army airplanes delivered with the distinctive Army rudder stripes and star insignia on both wing tips. Rudder stripes were eliminated from camouflaged airplanes in February 1942, and the star configuration changed to one on the upper left wing, one on the lower right wing and one on each side of the rear fuselage.

below. These changed extensively during the war according to theater of operation, season, mission, etc.

U.S. ARMY—In 1940, the U.S. Army adopted olive-drab coloring for the top and sides and light gray for the undersurfaces of the first Curtiss P-40s and Douglas A-20As. These planes carried the then-standard insignia arrangement of stars on both wings (top and bottom), and the distinctive rudder stripes used only by the Army since

1927 (Figure 1). Starting in February 1941, the same coloring was extended to other Army tactical models, and the insignia were rearranged (as described later).

From mid-1941 through 1943, many U.S. Army airplanes appeared in British camouflage because they had been appropriated by the Army through British contracts with U.S. manufacturers. Other basic colors for Army airplanes were matte black for night fighters (later changed to glossy black) and a light shade (almost pink) for planes flying in North African desert operations. Early in 1944, it was decided that camouflage wasn't really necessary for most combat types; it

was costly to apply and maintain, and it decreased airplane performance. Camouflage was eliminated from most subsequent production, though some metal-finished B-24s and B-29s were painted glossy black underneath when they were used for night bombing.

Until early 1942, primary trainers (like the Stearman/Boeing Kaydet) and basic trainers were delivered in prewar yellow and blue with rudder stripes. They were subsequently delivered in overall silver dope or natural metal. Some yellow and blue planes were repainted silver, but others survived the war in their original prewar colors.

U.S. NAVY—Prewar U.S. Navy airplanes were silver, with chrome yellow on the uppermost wing surface. In February 1941, overall light-gray camouflage was adopted for fleet-type airplanes, and the stars were placed as on the camouflaged Army planes. Late in 1941, tactical models operating over water adopted a dull blue-gray for the top and sides and retained the gray undersides. Planes with folding wings, on which the underside of the wing was visible from above when

folded, had the topside coloring applied to the undersurface of the folded wing. A few Navy fleet airplanes retained the overall gray into early 1942.

Early in 1943, the camouflage was changed to dark sea-blue on top surfaces, graduating through lighter shades to glossy white undersurfaces.

Early in 1944, glossy sea-blue was adopted as camouflage for carrier-based fighters. Soon afterward, this coloring was extended to all other fleet models. There were other special camouflage schemes for specific missions, such as the dull-gray top surfaces on otherwise all-white planes, which were used on sea-search and anti-submarine missions, and overall matte black on planes used for night missions, etc.

NATIONAL MARKINGS

The following drawings and photos are presented to give model builders the correct proportions and locations of the national markings used by the warring powers. Although there have been many variations and exceptions, these can be regarded as "standard."

WORLD WAR II COLOR AND MARKINGS

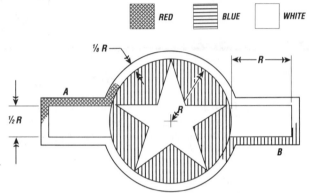

RED   BLUE   WHITE

UNITED STATES—From 1919 through 1942, the U.S. Army and Navy (which included the Marine Corps) used two separate national markings for their aircraft: the common star-in-circle markings on the

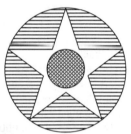

(Figure 2) An American Star-in-Circle insignia as used from May 1917 through January 1918, and September 1919 through May 15, 1942.

wings (and later, on the fuselages), and the red, white and blue stripes on the rudders. Each marking will be described separately.

Stars—Until May 15, 1942, the star marking had three colors: a red center disc inside a white, five-pointed star against a blue circle (Figure 2). (The very dark shade called "Insignia Blue" came into use

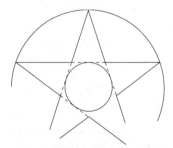

(Figure 2A) This enlarged detail of Figure 2 shows that the red center circle is tangent to projections of the star arms across the center of the star.

(Figure 3)The red center was removed from the U.S. insignia on May 15, 1942. The insignia remained in this form through June 1943.

in the late 1920s and early '30s, and replaced the brighter "True Blue" shade). As shown in Figure 2A, the red center was tangent to projections of the star arms across the center of the star. The most common error made when this marking is applied to models occurs when the center is made too large, and sometimes actually touches the blue circle.

In February 1941, the star was removed from the upper right and lower left wings of camouflaged Army and Navy planes, and one was added to each side of the rear fuselage (or to the noses of flying boats). The purpose of this arrangement was psychological. Tests showed that a gunner aiming at an airplane with two bright insignia on it would tend to sight between the bright spots, or right on the cockpit, when the markings were on the wing tips. By having one insignia on a wing tip and the other on the fuselage, the gunner—it was hoped—would center his aim on the empty space between the wing tip and the fuselage.

To avoid possible confusion

(Figure 4) A directive of June 28, 1943 added white rectangles to the U.S. insignia and surrounded the entire marking with a red border in the proportions shown(A). On September 4, 1943, it was directed that the red border be changed to blue(B).

with the red disc of the Japanese insignia, the red disc was removed from the American star insignia on May 15, 1942 (Figure 3). At the end of June 1943, the insignia was made more visible when white rectangles were added to each side of it, and the whole marking was surrounded by a red border (in the proportions of Figure 4). In the heat of combat, however, a glimpse of red could be mistaken for the Japanese marking, so the red border was changed to blue in September 1943. The blue border is still in use today.

This use of a blue border around a blue circle has always been a major source of confusion. Blue-around-blue made sense only for the pe-

riod when an existing red border was painted over with blue. I am not alone in believing that the blue border should have been retained only around the white rectangles, and not around the blue circle. Many modelers, artists and even some airplane manufacturers believe that the marking should be made that way, and they paint their aircraft accordingly.

The other major application error is made when the rectangles are the wrong proportion and misaligned; the tops of the rectangles should line up with the sides of the upper star points (Figure 4).

After Pearl Harbor, the Navy put the stars back on both wings of all its airplanes to

(Figure 5) Gray-painted Douglas SBD-3 Dauntless dive bombers onboard a U.S. Navy aircraft carrier early in 1942. Note the return of stars to both wings, and the variation in sizes used—even on the same airplane.

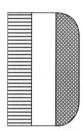

(Figure 6) Vertical rudder stripes as used by the U.S. Army and Navy from May 1917 through January 1918, and from September 1919 through 1926. Navy and Marine Corps made decreasing use of this arrangement up to WW II.

increase visibility for positive identification. It also increased the stars' size (previously limited to 60 inches for wing stars and not allowed to overlap the ailerons) to cover the full chord of the wing and the full depth of the fuselage. This size increase was only for camouflaged aircraft to be used in combat areas (Figure 5); others retained standard-size markings. Early in 1943, both services standardized the arrangement: one star was placed on the upper left wing tip, one was put on the lower right, and one was positioned on each side of the fuselage.

Stripes—From late 1919

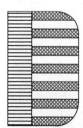

(Figure 7) The U.S. Army adopted this new rudder stripe arrangement in November 1926. It was eliminated from camouflaged airplanes in February 1941, and from all others on May 15, 1942.

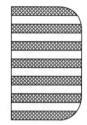

(Figure 8) On January 5, 1942, the U.S. Navy adopted this red-and-white variation of the Army rudder stripes for use on camouflaged airplanes, but used it only until May 15, 1942.

through 1926, the Army and Navy used the same rudder markings: three vertical stripes of equal width with red at the trailing edge, then white and blue forward (Figure 6). This duplicated the French and British markings.

After 1926, the Army deleted the vertical red and white stripes and replaced them with 13 alternating red and white stripes, as used on the American flag (Figure 7). This marking was eliminated from camouflaged Army planes in February 1941, and from all other Army planes on May 15, 1942.

The most common error in present-day model and real airplane restorations occurs when the vertical blue stripe is made the same width as the horizontal stripes. Whatever the shape of the rudder, the width of the vertical blue stripe should be one-third the maximum chord of the rudder.

After 1926, the Navy used rudder stripes less often, and they were eliminated by 1941. In January 1942, the Navy adopted a variation of the Army rudder stripes for camouflaged airplanes by deleting the vertical blue stripe and

running the horizontal stripes full-chord of the rudder (Figure 8). This marking was eliminated on May 15, 1942, along with the red center of the star insignia.

GREAT BRITAIN—Beginning early in WW I, British Empire forces used three-color circle insignia called "roundels," and three vertical rudder stripes with the blue forward. To avoid duplication of the similar French rudder stripes, the order was reversed in 1931. By 1937, however, when camouflage was adopted, rudder stripes were uncommon.

Roundels—The British roundels had standard proportions and were used in three basic arrangements during WW II. Figure 9 shows the standard proportions of the Type A roundel as it was used from 1916 through June 1942.

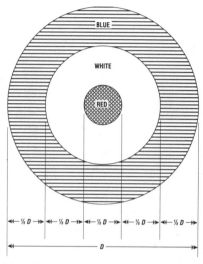

(Figure 9) A British Type A roundel, as used from WW I through June 1942. Note that the diameter of the roundel is divided into equal fifths by the three circles.

Note that the diameter of the insignia is divided into fifths. With the adoption of camouflage in 1937, the roundel was modified to Type A.1 (Figure 10) by the addition of a yellow ring around the blue, which divided the basic circle into sevenths. At first, type A.1 was used against all dark surfaces, but after 1940, it was used only on the fuselage sides of camouflaged planes. Type A was then used only on the undersides of wings, though it was used briefly on camouflaged sides in late 1939 and early 1940 in place of type A.1.

The Type B roundel originated in WW I as a reduced-visibility marking for night operations, and it remained in use on both day and night operations through WW II. Figure 11 shows that the red center was two-fifths (or 40 percent) the diameter of the overall marking. Type B was

WORLD WAR II COLOR AND MARKINGS

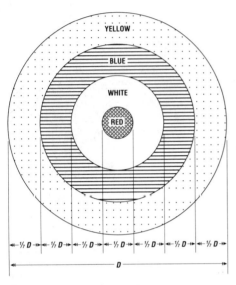

(Figure 10) The addition of a yellow outer ring to the Type A British roundel divided the diameter of the new Type A.1 marking into equal sevenths. It was used on camouflaged surfaces from 1937 through June 1942.

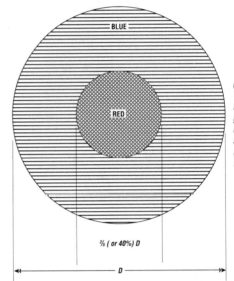

(Figure 11) This British Type B roundel was used for night operations, beginning in WW I, and was used on the upper wing surfaces of most other aircraft from 1940 until the end of WW II.

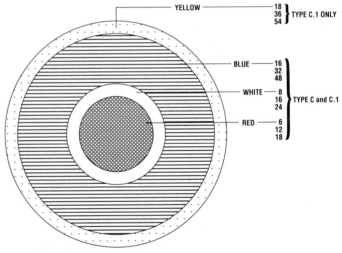

(Figure 12) British Type C and C.1 roundels were adopted in July 1942, and were laid out in the three sizes shown, rather than being divided into percentages of the overall diameter. They were used as direct replacements for Types A and A.1 roundels.

used mainly on upper wing surfaces through WW II, but it appeared on the fuselages and underwings of some special-purpose aircraft, such as blue-painted reconnaissance planes.

Type C and C.1 roundels were adopted in July 1942 as direct replacements for Types A and A.1. They were applied in only three sizes—small, medium and large—and were laid out to given dimensions rather than to fractions of the overall diameter. Figure 12

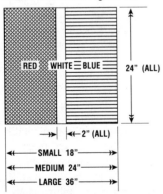

(Figure 14) The revised British Fin Flash of July 1942 was 24 inches high and used three widths (shown), all with a 2-inch-wide white center stripe.

gives the dimensions in inches for all three sizes in ascending order. Note that the yellow ring is used only on Type C.1. Some Type C roundels began to appear on upper wing surfaces just before the war ended.

Fin Flashes—During the Battle of France (May 1940), the Royal Air Force briefly used rudder stripes again. They were quickly abandoned, however, for what was called a "Fin Flash"; a smaller set of equal-width red, white and blue vertical stripes, with red forward, painted on the vertical fin. From late 1940 through June 1942, the flash was standardized at 24 inches wide and 27 inches high (Figure 13). After July 1942, the width of the white stripe was reduced to 2 inches. The standard flash then had a height of 24 inches, and it used red and blue stripes in three widths (Figure 14).

FRANCE—France origi-

nated the use of national airplane insignia before WW I, and it called its tricolor circles "cocardes." These were used only on wings until they were added to fuselages at the onset of WW II. Mainly, the proportions were as in Figure 15, with the radius divided into

thirds. Rudder stripes, with the blue forward, were used from WW I through WW II. France was one of the few nations to retain rudder stripes after most of the others had moved tail markings to the fin. The French marking situation was complicated after June 1940,

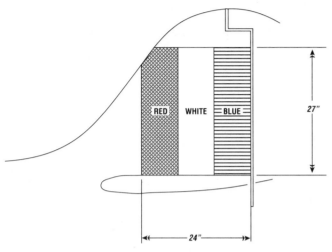

(Figure 13) The British Fin Flash was standardized late in 1940, and remained this size through June 1942. On airplanes with small fins (such as the Supermarine Spitfire), it was sometimes necessary to cut an upper corner of the flash.

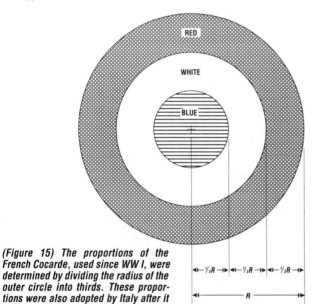

(Figure 15) The proportions of the French Cocarde, used since WW I, were determined by dividing the radius of the outer circle into thirds. These proportions were also adopted by Italy after it joined the Allies in 1943.

because "Vichy France" was subservient to Hitler, but "Free French" forces (who had escaped) joined the Allies, and both used the same basic national markings.

GERMANY—Germany was prohibited from having an air force by the Treaty of Versailles, which ended WW I. A secret Luftwaffe, however, was created in the early 1930s with airplanes that flew in civil markings. Proper military markings appeared when the new Luftwaffe was revealed to the world in 1935.

Crosses—White-bordered black crosses in various proportions were used from 1935 through 1939. These crosses were positioned midway between the trailing edge of the wing and the leading edge of the horizontal tail, and very close to the wing tips. After the Polish campaign that started the war, the proportions were standardized.

In the interest of reduced visibility, narrow-bordered crosses (Figure 16) were now used only on upper wing surfaces, and they were positioned 2 meters (6 feet, 6 inches) in from the wing tips.

Wide-bordered crosses (Figure 17) were used on the fuselage and on the underside of the wing, usually midway between the wing tip and the fuselage on single-engine types, and midway between the wing tip and the outer engine nacelle on multi-engine types.

Late in the war, the black part of the cross was sometimes omitted, leaving only a white border against the airplane's basic color. In other cases, the white outline was replaced by black (Figure 18).

Swastika—From 1935 through 1938, the German tail marking for all airplanes was a wide red band that covered the full chord of the fin and rudder. A white circle containing a black swastika standing on its corner was centered on the red band (Figure 19).

Before the war started, the red band and white circle were deleted from German Military

(Figure 16) The standard proportions of the narrow-bordered German cross, as used on upper wing surfaces from 1940 until the end of the war.

(Figure 17) Standard proportions of the wide-bordered German cross, as used on fuselage sides and wing under-surfaces from 1940 until the end of the war.

airplanes only. Some military prototypes were subsequently tested with civil markings, but camouflaged planes retained the band and circle.

The swastika was laid out to very rigid specifications

WORLD WAR II COLOR AND MARKINGS

(Figure 18) A German Focke-Wulf Fw.190A-3 carrying the black outlines of fuselage and wing crosses late in the war. Note the absence of a white border around the swastika on the fin.

(Figure 19) Panchromatic film and a filter lighten and emphasize the red band used on the vertical fins of German military airplanes from 1935 into 1938. The black swastika was moved to the fin after the red band and white circle were deleted. Civil-registered German airplanes retained the red band and white circle throughout the war.

(Figure 20), and on dark backgrounds, it had a narrow white border. For a short time after the red band had been removed, the swastika remained centered between the fin and the rudder. It was soon moved to the fin on most planes, but it was placed on the larger rudders of some aircraft with small fins.

It should be noted that very few WW II German aircraft models appear with swastikas today. Since the war's end, it has been against the law to display the swastika in Germany, and photos of wartime planes that appear in post-war issues of German magazines sometimes have the swastikas blanked out. Various anti-Nazi groups continue working to keep swastikas off all toys and representations of Nazi-era equipment, even in the United States.

JAPAN—Since WW I, Japan has used the "Rising Sun," or "Hinomaru," (the red disc of the Japanese flag), as its national aircraft marking. The Allies, particularly the Americans, derisively called it the "Meatball." When the Hinomaru was used against dark surfaces, it was usually outlined with a white border that was approximately 2 inches wide (Figure 21). The marking was standard for both the Japanese Army and its Navy. (The Hinomaru Red was much lighter and brighter than the dark American Insignia Red.)

At the war's end, a few Japanese military airplanes were allowed to fly during and beyond the surrender negotiations. These planes were painted white and were marked with dark green crosses (Figure 22). In a few cases, airplanes still in camouflage carried their new crosses on white squares that had been painted over the Hinomarus.

INVASION STRIPES

For the invasion of France in June 1944, participating U.S. and British airplanes carried hastily applied "Invasion Stripes" for quick, positive identification. These consisted of three white and two black equal-width stripes that completely encircled the rear fuselage and were applied full-chord to both upper and lower wing surfaces (Figure 23).

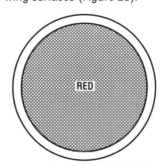

RED

(Figure 21) The Japanese red circle marking, officially called "Hinomaru," was usually outlined with a white border, approximately 2 inches wide, when it was used on dark surfaces.

Widths varied from 18 inches (on the P-51) to 20 inches (B-26 and P-47), and 24 inches (A-20). Four-engine bombers didn't use the stripes unless they had been diverted to glider-towing.

After the invasion of Normandy, the stripes were removed from the upper half of the fuselage and from the top of the wing. The stripes were retained on the lower surfaces for subsequent large-scale, airborne invasions, with some used on planes involved in the crossing of the Rhine in March 1945.

Invasion stripes are popular today for restored, camouflaged WW II airplanes, and they add variety to a collection of similarly camouflaged U.S. or British scale models.

Figure 22) A disarmed Japanese Mitsubishi G4M-1 Betty bomber painted white, with green crosses replacing the Hinomaru marking. It was used to transport Japanese surrender emissaries to Allied headquarters in August 1945.

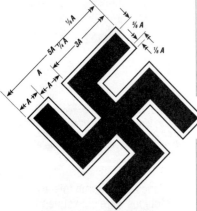

(Figure 20) The standard proportions of this white-bordered swastika were applied to the vertical fin of German airplanes from 1940 until the end of the war. The white border was eliminated on some light-colored airplanes.

Figure 23) An olive-drab Douglas A-20G with crudely applied black-and-white Invasion Stripes flies over the Allied Invasion Fleet on D-day, June 6, 1944.

The nations involved in WW II identified their military airplanes differently. France, Germany and Italy simply used the manufacturer's model designations (e.g., Messerschmitt 109, Fiat CR 42, etc.) France added the mission and seating to the designation painted on the rudder, as in "Douglas DB-7-B3." The "B3" indicated that it was a three-place bomber. A pursuit, like the Curtiss 75, was "75-C1," ("C1" indicated a one-place Chasse, or pursuit, type). The more involved British, U.S. and Japanese systems are described separately here.

GREAT BRITAIN—Great Britain used given names followed by progressive "Mark Numbers," such as the Westland Lysander Mk I, II, III, etc. Minor variants that didn't qualify for a new Mark number were given letters, such as "Lysander Mk IIIA." In some cases, the added letter identified a special feature, as with the Hawker Hurricane Mk IIC with cannon armament. Similar airplanes used for vastly different missions were sometimes given different names, such as the Douglas DB-7, which was called a "Boston" when it was used as a bomber, but a "Havoc" when it was used as a night fighter.

The practice of using different names or Mark Numbers for different missions was abandoned mid-war, in favor of adding prefix letters to identify the mission, such as "Spitfire F Mk IX" for a fighter, and "P.R. Mk XI" for photoreconnaissance. The letters "N.F." identified night fighters, and "T.T." identified target tugs.

UNITED STATES—The U.S. Army and Navy used two separate systems to identify the type, model, series and manufacturer of each airplane. The systems are too extensive to list here in their entirety, so only the basics will be presented.

U.S. Army—The Army used a Type-Model-Series system that was formalized in 1924 and is still used today by the U.S. Air Force. The type letter identified the basic mission of the airplane (e.g., "B" for bomber). The model number identified the number of the particular type contracted for, but not necessarily procured by, the Army, such as "B-17." The series letter identified the stage of model development, such as "B-17A." Starting in 1942, suffix letters were added to the Army designation to identify the actual builder of the airplane.

In early 1942, minor changes were often made that didn't justify a new series letter. Instead, the airplanes were identified with a block number, e.g., -1, -5, -10, and so on. The intervening numbers were reserved for changes made at modification centers (e.g., changes to a Republic P-47D-25 made it a P-47D-28).

U.S. Navy—The Navy tied in the airplane manufacturer with the airplane type and model designation, as with the "Grumman F4F-4." The first letter identified the type (e.g., "F" for fighter). The following number identified the number of different fighter designs ordered from that manufacturer, and the second letter identified the particular manufacturer. In this case the "F" identified "Grumman" because the logical letter "G" was in use by another manufacturer when Grumman became a Navy customer. The number "1" wasn't used for a manufacturer's first Navy model. Grumman's first Navy fighter was the FF-1, followed by the F2F-1, F3F-1, F3F-2, etc. The dash number that followed the last letter identified not the model number, but the sequential configuration of that model.

Multi-purpose Navy planes appeared in 1934 and were identified by two type letters, as in "PBY-5" for Consolidated's first Patrol Bomber. Specialized configurations were identified by suffix letters, as in "PBY-5A" for an amphibious version and "SB2C-4E" for a Scout bomber modified for electronics missions.

U.S. Popular Names—In October 1941, the U.S. Government adopted "popular" names for its military aircraft, such as "Mariner" for the Martin PBM and "Wildcat" for the Grumman F4F. Some names were already in use and were easy to adapt—Boeing had already been calling its B-17 the Flying Fortress—and other names were picked up from previous British use of American designs, such as "Catalina" for the PBY.

The purpose of catchall names was to conceal the actual development stage of a combat plane when it was discussed in the public press. A Flying Fortress was simply a B-17, not specifically a B17E, F, or G. These names were almost totally ignored by those associated with the airplanes (to whom accurate designations were important), and they didn't "take" well with the public, despite the efforts of the press.

JAPAN—The Japanese Army and Navy used a type identification system based on the named type and a one- or two-digit number identifying the Japanese Dynastic Year in which the airplane entered production, such as "Bomber Type 1" for the Mitsubishi G4M-1. The figure "1" in this case is the last digit of the year 2601 (equivalent to our calendar year 1941). The Japanese also gave names to many, but not all, of their military aircraft.

The Japanese Army also used a sequential "Kitai" numbering system that started in 1932, with the number for the Kawasaki Type 3 fighter appearing as "K1 61 Hein." The Japanese Navy system was based on the U.S. Navy system that identified the airplane by type and number of models procured from a particular manufacturer, such as "Mitsubishi A6M-2 Type 0" (1940) fighter Raiden.

The Allies stopped trying to use the various Japanese systems and gave all Japanese airplanes code names, such as "Tony" for the Ki 61 and "Zeke" for the A6M-2.

MULTIPLE MANUFACTURERS—In all of the warring nations, major combat planes were built in factories other than those of the original designers. In England and Germany, Spitfires and Me 109s were built by several manufacturers, with no indication in their designations as to who actually built them. Designations were different in the U.S.

U.S. Army—A B-17G was still a B-17G, no matter who built it, but the factories involved were included in the designation early in 1942. Boeing's Seattle plant built the B-17G-BO, Vega built the B-17G-VE and Douglas' Long Beach plant built the B-17G-DL. Different factories of the same manufacturer also got distinguishing letter designations, such as "BW" for Boeing's Wichita, KS, plant, and "BN" for its plant in Renton, WA.

U.S. Navy—When an established design, such as the Curtiss SB2C-4, was built by another firm, that firm used the same type designation but a different manufacturer's letter. The SB2C-4, built in Canada by Fairchild, became the SBF-4 because Canadian Fairchild had never built an SB type for the Navy. The same model built by Canadian Car & Foundry became the SBW-4 for the same reason.

DESIGNATIONS

AVRO LANCASTER

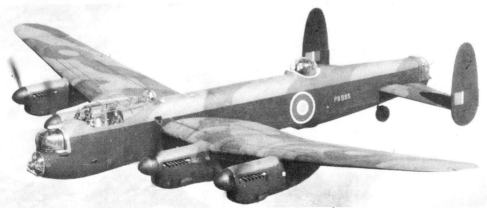

An Avro Lancaster I carrying standard British night-bomber camouflage. Note how far up the side of the fuselage the matte-black underside paint extends. Type B roundels are on top of the wing; Type C.1 roundels are on the fuselage. The fin flash is 24x36 inches.

THE Avro Lancaster was the most famous and widely used four-engine British bomber of WW II. Oddly, however, it didn't originate as a four-engine design. In 1937, the British Air Ministry issued a requirement for a heavy bomber to be powered with two new and still experimental 1,760hp Rolls-Royce Vulture engines.

A.V. Roe and Co., Ltd., of Newton Heath, Manchester, won the order with its Model 679—named "Manchester" by the Royal Air Force. The prototype was first flown in July 1939. The program was seriously delayed by a German air raid, and it was then ended by the shortcomings of the still-troublesome Vulture engine (priorities for the Merlin engine prevented Rolls-Royce from perfecting the Vulture). Only 200 Manchesters were built, some of which saw action over Germany (February 1941 to June 1942).

To save the Manchester program, Avro developed a four-engine modification of the basic airframe. It had a wider center section and longer wing panels for use with the 1,145hp Rolls-Royce Merlin engine (as used in the Hawker Hurricane and Supermarine Spitfire fighter). These changes increased the wingspan from 90 feet, 1 inch to 102 feet for the same 50,000-pound gross weight. The converted airframe, originally named "Manchester III," first flew on January 9, 1941. The Air Ministry was pleased with its performance and immediately ordered the revised design into production designated as the "Avro Model 683 Lancaster."

Demand was more than Avro could handle, so production of an eventual 7,374 Lancasters was distributed among two Avro plants and one Canadian and four other British manufacturers. The first production Lancaster I, powered by 1,260hp Merlin XX engines, flew on October 31, 1941. The short time it took to move the Lancaster from prototype to production can be attributed to its being essentially a modified Manchester, not a completely new design.

Both offensively and defensively, the Lancaster I was a formidable machine, with a gross weight of 65,000 pounds—greater than that of the American Boeing B-17. It could usually carry 7,000 pounds of bombs and was defended by four powered machine-gun turrets with 10 to 12 .303-caliber guns. Lancasters first went into action in March 1942 and were the backbone of the British heavy bomber fleet for the rest of the war.

As a precaution against a shortage of Merlin engines, a Lancaster II using the 1,650hp Bristol Hercules VI air-cooled radial engine was developed. A large production order was placed with one of the subcontractors, but the anticipated Merlin shortage didn't materialize, so the Lancaster II order was progressively reduced until only 300 were delivered. Lancasters that had Merlin engines built in the U.S. by Packard were designated "Lancaster III" (2,990 produced). The 430 built in Canada with Packard Merlins were identified as "Lancaster X."

Intermediate marks identified various improved versions: Marks IV and V were special long-range versions; Mark VI had improved 1,750hp Merlins; and Mark VII had 1,620hp Merlins but a gross weight of 68,000 pounds. Marks VIII and IX weren't used.

The Lancasters were used primarily as night bombers in the Allied program that bombed Germany "around the clock"—the Americans attacking by day, the British by night. Specially modified Lancasters were used on some spectacular missions, such as the breaching of the Möhne and Eder dams in May 1943 and the sinking of the battleship Tirpitz, hidden in a Norwegian fjord, with a single 12,000-pound bomb in November 1944. Special Lancasters modified to carry 22,000-pound Grand Slam bombs had gross weights of 72,000 pounds.

Lancasters remained in service with the Royal Air Force until February 1954 and with the Royal Canadian Air Force until April 1964. Only two flyable Lancasters remain today.

SPECIFICATIONS AND PERFORMANCE

Wingspan	102 ft.
High Speed	287mph
Length	69 ft., 4 in.
Cruising Speed	200mph
Wing Area	1,279 sq. ft.
Initial Climb	250 ft./min.
Empty Weight	36,457 lbs.
Ceiling	19,000 ft.
Gross Weight	68,000 lbs.
Range	2,530 miles

AVRO LANCASTER

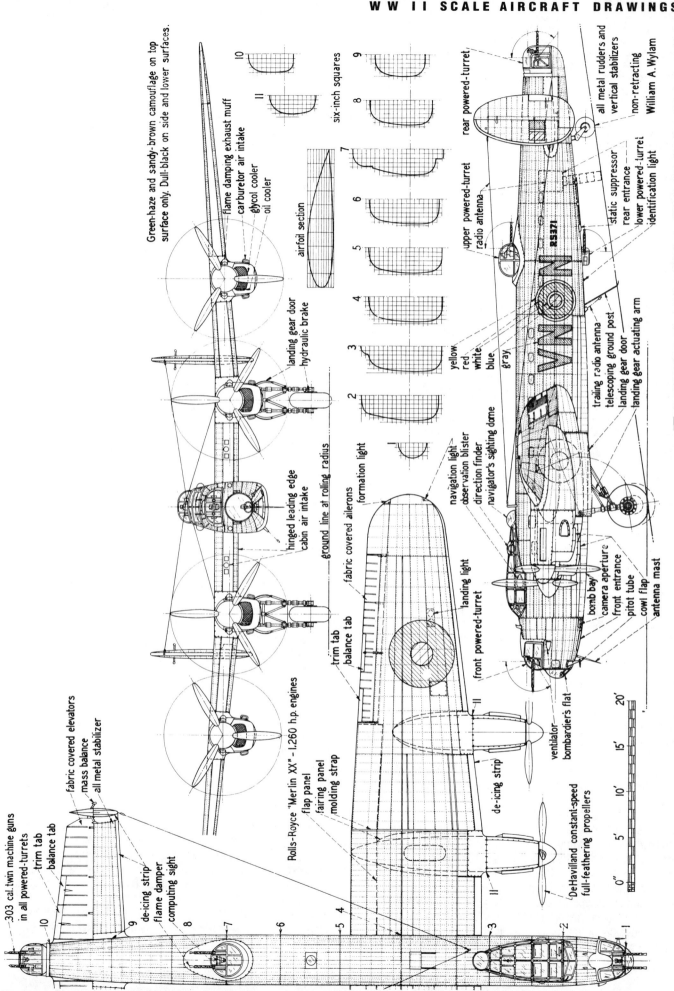

Green-haze and sandy-brown camouflage on top surface only. Dull-black on side and lower surfaces.

flame damping exhaust muff
carburetor air intake
glycol cooler
oil cooler

airfoil section

six-inch squares

landing gear door
hydraulic brake

hinged leading edge
cabin air intake

ground line at rolling radius

fabric covered ailerons
formation light

trim tab
balance tab

Rolls-Royce "Merlin XX"—1,260 h.p. engines

flap panel
fairing panel
molding strap

fabric covered elevators
mass balance
all metal stabilizer

.303 cal. twin machine guns
in all powered-turrets
trim tab
balance tab

de-icing strip
flame damper
computing sight

rear powered-turret

all metal rudders and
vertical stabilizers

non-retracting
William A. Wylam

upper powered-turret
radio antenna

static suppressor
rear entrance
lower powered-turret
identification light

trailing radio antenna
telescoping ground post
landing gear door
landing gear actuating arm

yellow
red
white
blue
gray

navigation light
observation blister
direction finder
navigator's sighting dome

landing light
front powered-turret

bomb bay
camera aperture
front entrance
pitot tube
cowl flap
antenna mast

ventilator
bombardier's flat

de-icing strip

DeHaviland constant-speed
full-feathering propellers

0"   5'   10'   15'   20'

BOEING B-17 FLYING FORTRESS

This B-17G-15-BO was delivered without the additional nose guns that were added to early B-17Gs at modification centers. Note that the exhausts for inboard engines are on the outer sides of nacelles; exhausts on the outboard engines are on the bottoms of nacelles. Also note the camouflage pattern on engine cowlings.

THE Boeing B-17 Flying Fortress was one of the few U.S. warplanes to have an accepted name as well as a standard military designation *before* being named by the British or included on the U.S. government's list of so-called "popular" planes late in 1941.

The B-17, a daring design at the time, was developed in response to a U.S. Army fly-off competition for multi-engine bombers announced in 1934. "Multi-engine" at that time was generally understood to mean "twin engine." Boeing realized that all the contestants, using the available engines and state-of-the-art airframes, would perform similarly, so it decided to take a gamble: use four engines to improve the performance of its entry while carrying the same bomb load as the competition. Previously, additional engines had been used to get larger airplanes with heavier loads into the air, rather than to improve the performance of smaller airplanes.

Built as the company-owned Model 299, the prototype of the 12,726 B-17s that were eventually built rolled out of the factory in July 1935. The name "Flying Fortress" (later copyrighted by Boeing) was bestowed on it by a Seattle newspaper reporter who was impressed by the five defensive machine-gun turrets of the new bomber. The aircraft's name was a natural, owing to its armament and the fact that it was intended to defend the U.S. coastline from invading surface fleets accompanied by carrier-based fighters.

Model 299 ran away with the contest. Performance was sensational—a top speed of 236mph at a gross weight of 38,059 pounds; a cruising speed of 140mph; and a range of 3,101 miles. On October 30, an army pilot took off with the control locks inadvertently engaged. The crash eliminated the Boeing from the competition, but the Army was sufficiently impressed with it to order 13 nearly identical planes for service testing as the YB-17. At the Army's request, the engines were changed from 750hp Pratt & Whitney R-1690 Hornets to 850hp Wright R-1820 Cyclones. Shortly before the first flight on December 2, 1936, the YB-17 designation was changed to Y1B-17.

The strength of an early Y1B-17 was proven in a violent storm, so the Army directed that a fourteenth airframe, ordered for a static test, be completed as the single Y1B-17A flight article. Boeing used this to develop turbo-supercharger installations used on all subsequent B-17s for improved altitude capability.

Orders for 39 production B-17Bs trickled in over nearly three years, owing mostly to cost problems—Boeing's cost of building the planes in small numbers and the Army's reluctance to pay the price. Many officials thought that the B-17 was too much airplane for pilots to handle, and they urged that the money instead be spent on smaller bombers.

Thirty-eight B-17Cs and 42 B-17Ds were delivered through April 1941, thanks to the increasing urgency of the war situation. They resembled the Y1B-17A, except for minor improvements and gradual upgrading of the armament installations, which had been designed according to out-of-date Army specifications. Armor was added, and fuel tanks were changed to the latest self-sealing type. The B-17D had 1,200hp R-1820-51 engines and a bomb load of 4,000 pounds at a gross weight of 47,242 pounds.

The combat inadequacies of the B-17 were revealed on 20

SPECIFICATIONS AND PERFORMANCE

Powerplant	Wright R-1820-97 1,200hp at 25,000 ft.
Wingspan	103 ft., 9 in.
Length	74 ft., 9 in.
Wing Area	1,420 sq. ft.
Empty Weight	36,135 lbs.
Gross Weight	65,500 lbs.
Top Speed	287mph at 25,000 ft.
Cruising Speed	182mph
Service Ceiling	35,600 ft.
Range	2,000 miles with 6,000-lb. bombs
Armament	13, .50-caliber machine guns

B-17Cs, which the U.S. Army transferred to the British as "Fortress I." Their first combat use was a raid on Wilhelmshaven, Germany, on July 8, 1941. The systems and armament of the B-17 had not been designed or modified for high-altitude operations under European combat conditions, so the Fortresses were quickly withdrawn.

In the Pacific, the few surviving B-17Cs and Ds did much better. Their perfor-

A B-17G-15-BO with representative 8th Air Force markings. Triangle A identifies the 91st Bomb Group, LG identifies the 322nd Bomb Squadron and R identifies the individual airplane in the group. Note the name "Chow Hound," and cartoon on the nose and the row of painted bombs indicating nine bombing missions.

mance and versatility so impressed the Japanese that they were described as "four-engine fighters used for all purposes."

The lessons of the European war came together in the first of 512 B-17Es, which left the factory in September 1941. The aircraft had a new rear fuselage structure that housed a tail "stinger" with

pounds by using external bomb racks under the wings.

With wartime demand exceeding Boeing's capability, Douglas and Vega (subsidiaries of Lockheed) were called on to build additional B-17Fs. The 2,300 built by Boeing were B-17F-BO; the 500 by Vega were -VE; and the 605 by Douglas were -DL. The B-17Fs were the first to use the block

straight-ahead fire.) Boeing developed a two-gun "chin" turret that was installed on the very last B-17F-VEs and -DLs and was to have been on the B-17F-135-BO. Boeing cancelled the F-135 and combined the new turret with other changes to produce the B-17G-1.

The B-17G looked identical to the late B-17Fs with chin

Vega.

The American bombing career of the B-17 ended on V-E Day, but the B-17s served the Army and, later, the U.S. Air Force (created September 18, 1947) in many utility roles until 1960. Its final role was as a live target for anti-aircraft missiles that were built, ironically, by Boeing.

Odd B-17F variants were

The first 112 B-17Es had small, remotely sighted belly turrets. The 113th B-17E and all later models used the manned Sperry Ball turret (shown).

Tail-gunner's station from the B-17E midway through B-17G production. Late Gs had a revised design that was developed at United Air Lines' modification center, site of earlier modifications.

two .50-caliber guns and top and bottom powered turrets, each with two .50s, and a single .50 in the waist stations and radio room (a total of nine .50s), plus the single .30 in the nose. The tail stinger was a big surprise to the Japanese, making them wary to approach all B-17s from the rear. Crews of older B-17s took advantage of this by putting dummy guns in their tail cones.

The most distinctive external feature of the B-17E was the larger vertical tail with a long dorsal fin. American B-17 operations over Europe began with a raid of 12 B-17Es over Rouen, France, on August 17, 1942, but it wasn't an all-American operation; the escorting fighters were British Spitfires.

The B-17F was outwardly similar to the E except for a slightly longer molded Plexiglas nose cone. Its bomb load increased to 8,000

number system, but there was no direct correlation between, say, a B-17F-5 built by Boeing, Vega, or Douglas.

Combat with B-17Es and early B-17Fs revealed the plane's vulnerability to fighter attack from straight ahead, so various additional nose-gun arrangements were tried on B-17Fs in combat. The best solution was to replace the .30-caliber nose gun with one or two .50s in the nose cone and to add a single .50 in a bulged blister on each side of the nose. (This permitted almost

turrets. Boeing built 4,035; Vega, 2,250; and Douglas, 2,395. The B-17G was the last production B-17. Designations as high as B-17P were postwar modifications.

Britain obtained additional Fortresses under Lend-Lease. The 19 Fortress IIs were B-17Fs. The 45 Fortress IIAs were B-17Es that carried later designations because existing airplanes were obtained while the Fortress IIs were being built. The 85 Fortress IIIs were B-17Gs; the first 30 built by Boeing and the remainder by

the B-40, the XB-40 modified by Vega and 20 service-test YB-40s converted by Douglas. They had two top turrets, twin, powered waist guns and extra armor, and they carried double the usual ammunition. They were intended as escorts for other B-17s before the long-range fighters were introduced. Their major shortcoming was that owing to the weight of their extra guns and armor, they couldn't keep up with the fast, light empty bombers on the run home.

At the end of the war, the U.S. Navy obtained 31 late B-17Gs for use as unarmed, radar-equipped PB-1Ws (Patrol, Boeing, Anti-Submarine Warfare). The U.S. Coast Guard also acquired 17 B-17Gs (designated "PB-1G"—"G" for Coast Guard) and used them for air-sea rescue work (sometimes with lifeboats under their bellies) and for routine patrol and mapping work. The last PB-1G mission was in October 1957.

A top-powered gun turret and forward navigator's astrodome were added to the B-17E and retained through subsequent models.

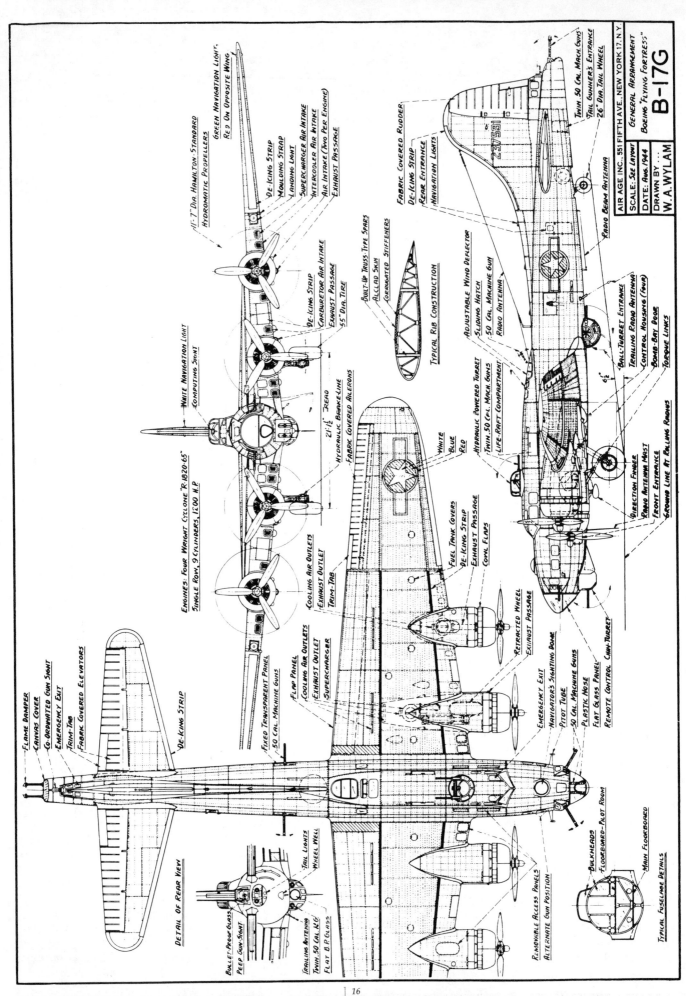

B-17G

Boeing "Flying Fortress"

GENERAL ARRANGEMENT

AIR AGE INC., 551 FIFTH AVE., NEW YORK 17, N.Y.

SCALE: See Layout
DATE: Aug. 1944
DRAWN BY ....
W. A. WYLAM

DETAIL OF REAR VIEW

TYPICAL RIB CONSTRUCTION

TYPICAL FUSELAGE DETAILS

BOEING B-17 FLYING FORTRESS

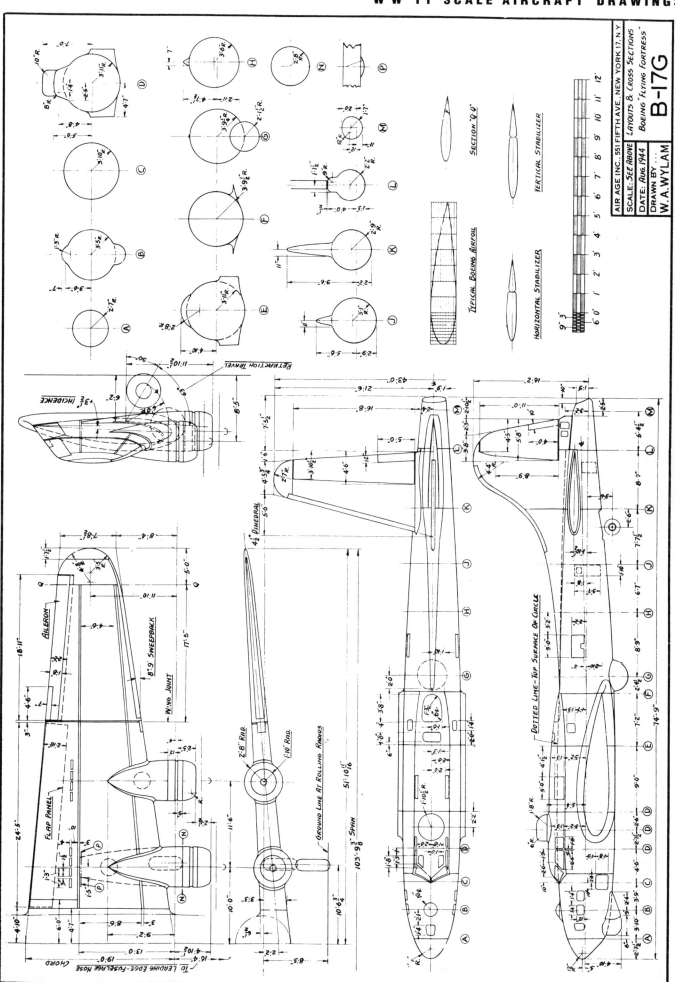

| AIR AGE INC., 551 FIFTH AVE., NEW YORK 17, N.Y. |
| SCALE: SEE ABOVE LAYOUTS & CROSS SECTIONS |
| DATE: Aug. 1944 BOEING "FLYING FORTRESS" |
| DRAWN BY W. A. WYLAM |

B-17G

BOEING B-29

A Boeing B-29A-5-BN in flight with both sets of bomb bay doors open Note the four powered, remote-control gun turrets above and below the fuselage, and the 20mm cannon supplementing two .50-caliber machine guns in the tail turret.

WHEN it entered service in June 1944, the Boeing B-29 was the largest, heaviest and most complex production airplane of its time—a masterpiece that pushed the state of the art to its limits. It had an 11-man crew, five powered gun turrets (each with two .50-caliber guns), a 20mm cannon in the tail turret, a pressurized fuselage and two bomb bays with a capacity of up to 20,000 pounds of bombs. Four 2,200hp Wright R-3350 engines, each fitted with two turbo-superchargers, plus slick aerodynamics, gave it the ability to bomb from over 30,000 feet and attain a top speed of 365mph at 25,000 feet and a range of 4,100 miles.

Development of the B-29 began in May 1939, after the U.S. had assessed its future airplane needs. It needed a bomber with a speed of 400mph, a range of 5,333 miles and the ability to deliver a 1-ton bomb load at the halfway point. The U.S. aircraft industry received the specification for such a bomber in February 1940, and Boeing responded with Model 341. The Army, however, kept changing its requirements for equipment, armor and armament, and self-sealing fuel cells, so Boeing had to develop a new Model 354 to

keep up. In June 1940, Boeing and Lockheed received Army contracts to build wooden mock-ups for evaluation. Lockheed dropped out, but Boeing was awarded a contract for two XB-29 prototypes in August, and Consolidated was to build a competing XB-32. Both received orders for a single additional XB in December.

The B-29 had an unprecedented procurement and development history. Army officials doubted Boeing's engineering and wind-tunnel test figures and insisted on a larger wing to reduce the then-fantastic wing loading of 69 pounds per square foot (much higher than that of contemporary fighters). Boeing argued that this would reduce speed and range, and that the B-29's huge Fowler flaps would keep landing speeds within reasonable limits. The Army was fi-

nally convinced and ordered 1,500 B-29s before the prototype flew.

With Boeing's Seattle factory choked with B-17s, the Army built a new factory for B-29 production alongside Boeing's existing plant in Wichita, KS, where the Kaydet trainers were being built. In February 1942, the Army started new plants for two other manufacturers—Bell Aircraft at Marietta, GA, and Glenn L. Martin Co. at Omaha, NE. The U.S. Navy had built a new factory at Renton, WA, near Seattle, for Boeing to build PBB-1 flying boats, but it cancelled the boats and turned the plant over to the Army for B-29 production.

Built in Seattle, the first of

SPECIFICATIONS AND PERFORMANCE

Powerplant	Wright R-3350-23 2200hp at 25,000 ft.
Wingspan	141 ft., 3 in.
Length	99 ft.
Wing Area	1,736 sq. ft.
Empty Weight	70,140 lbs.
Gross Weight	124,000 lbs.
Top Speed	358mph at 25,000 ft.
Cruising Speed	230mph
Service Ceiling	3,1850 ft.
Range	3,250 miles (B-29A, 4,100 miles)

the three XB-29s flew on September 21, 1942. The test program was seriously delayed by chronic troubles with the R-3350 engines, which had never been used in a production airplane. Fourteen service-

The Eddie Allen, named for the famous war correspondent, was paid for by Boeing-Wichita employees. Here it displays four camels on its nose, indicating four round-trip supply trips over the "Hump." This plane was so badly damaged over Tokyo in May 1945 that it had to be scrapped.

test YB-17s were built in Wichita, KS, but they, too (as well as early production models), were plagued with engine problems and difficulties with all the new equipment (from remotely sighted and controlled gun turrets to cabin pressurization), electrical trouble and radar installations.

Airplane deliveries were hampered by delays of material and equipment from the greatest network of sub-contractors and suppliers ever set up for an airplane production program. To prevent delays on the production lines, the planes were rushed through incomplete and sent to modification centers for final installations and necessary changes, particularly to the still-troublesome R-3350 engines.

Getting the first B-29s into combat was also an unprecedented operation. Japan was beyond the range of even the B-29 from U.S.-held bases in the Pacific, so several airfields were built by Chinese coolie labor in the vicinity of Chengtu, China, 1600 miles from the southern tip of Japan. The B-29s that used them were based in India but used the Chinese fields as points of departure for Japan. With no roads open for supply, all supplies (fuel, bombs, ammunition, spare engines, food, etc.) had to be air-lifted from India, 1,500 miles away, over the infamous "Hump" of the Himalaya Mountains. Each B-29 had to make several round trips to support one raid on Japan. Some B-29s were stripped of all military equipment and fitted with bomb-bay tanks, and they could ferry up to 4,000 gallons of fuel. These were facetiously called C-29s.

The first Asiatic B-29 raid was a 2,000-mile round trip from India to Bangkok, Thailand, on June 5, 1944. This was reported by Radio

Tokyo as having been flown by B-24s. The first raid against Japan was over the steel works at Yawata. Sixty-eight B-29s took off from Chengtu on June 15, but, hindered by bad weather, only 47 reached and bombed their target. Despite the B-29's capacious bomb bays, each plane carried only 1 ton of bombs in a necessary trade-off between bomb load and fuel for range. Seven B-29s were lost on that first raid; none to Japanese action.

As supplies increased, attacks on Japan from China increased, but they ended late in 1944 when the Japanese-held Marianas Islands in the Western Pacific were captured, and B-29 bases were built there. The distance from there to Japan was only slightly less, but supplies could be delivered by ship and the B-29s could fly westward from the U.S., instead of eastward via Africa and India. Bomb loads didn't increase significantly at first, because of the fuel required to reach the bombing altitude of 30,000 feet that was necessary to elude fighters and flak, and to battle the terrific head winds. The first strike against Tokyo since the Doolittle raid of April 1942, with B-25s launched from the aircraft carrier Hornet, was made of Saipan on November 24, 1944, with over 100 B-29s.

After capture, Iwo Jima, which is halfway between Saipan and Japan, served as a safe haven for damaged B-29s and for those low on fuel, and it also provided a base for P-51 fighters that could now accompany the B-29s to Japan. With Japanese fighter opposition virtually eliminated, the B-29s could go in at a lower altitude and with bigger bomb loads. This was the beginning of the

end. Incendiary bombs virtually wiped out whole cities until, on August 6 and 9, two atomic bombs were dropped on Hiroshima and Nagasaki to force a speedy end to the war.

During the war, some 118 B-29s were converted to long-range F-13 photo-reconnaissance planes and used to select targets in Japan and evaluate bomb damage after raids. Their photos also helped those who planned the U.S. invasion of the Philippines.

B-29 Production—Between them, the four factories turned out 3,960 B-29s, with the last one delivered from Renton in May 1946. Over 5,000 B-29s still on order were cancelled after V-J Day.

B-29—Most B-29s were designated simply "B-29." The

Major postwar use of the B-29 after Korea was as an aerial refueling tanker fitted with Boeing's "flying boom" refueling system. Here, a KB-29P refuels a Republic F-84F.

final models differed in detail from the early models, most notably in having four-gun upper forward turrets instead of two-gun turrets. Boeing built 1,634 B-29-BWs; Bell built 668 -BAs; and Martin built 536 -MOs.

B-29A—The B-29A had a new wing center section structure that added 1 foot to its wingspan. All 1,119 B-29A-BNs were built in Renton.

B-29B—A total of 311 Bell B-29s were modified in the factory and delivered as B-29Bs, stripped of all but tail guns. This cleaned-up version was as fast as Japanese fighters and could be attacked only from the rear. Also, the tail guns were aimed

and fired by a new AN/APG-15B radar fire-control system. The weight saved went to additional bomb load.

B-29C—This aircraft was to have been a B-29 with improved R-3350 engines, but it was never built.

B-29D—The B-29D was a major improvement of the B-29, with 3,500hp Pratt & Whitney R-4360 engines, a 75ST aluminum structure instead of 24ST, thermal anti-icing instead of rubber boots, and a taller tail. Two hundred were cancelled after V-J Day, but the Army got 60 reinstated by saying that they were 75-percent-new airplanes designated "B-50." A total of 371 B-50s through TB-50H were built through March 1953.

B-29s Postwar—The B-29 remained the standby of the Strategic Air Command in the early, post-WW II years and served in the Korean War of 1950-53, with many of its logical targets declared off limits by political considerations. Its range was increased for global operations in 1948 by converting 92 B-29s to KB-29M hose tankers and another 74, supplemented by B-50As, to hose receiver B-29MRs. Later, 116 were converted to KB-29P boom tankers.

After Korea, a few B-29s continued to serve the Air Force in utility and training roles until 1960. One flyable B-29 survives today, and several are on view in museums.

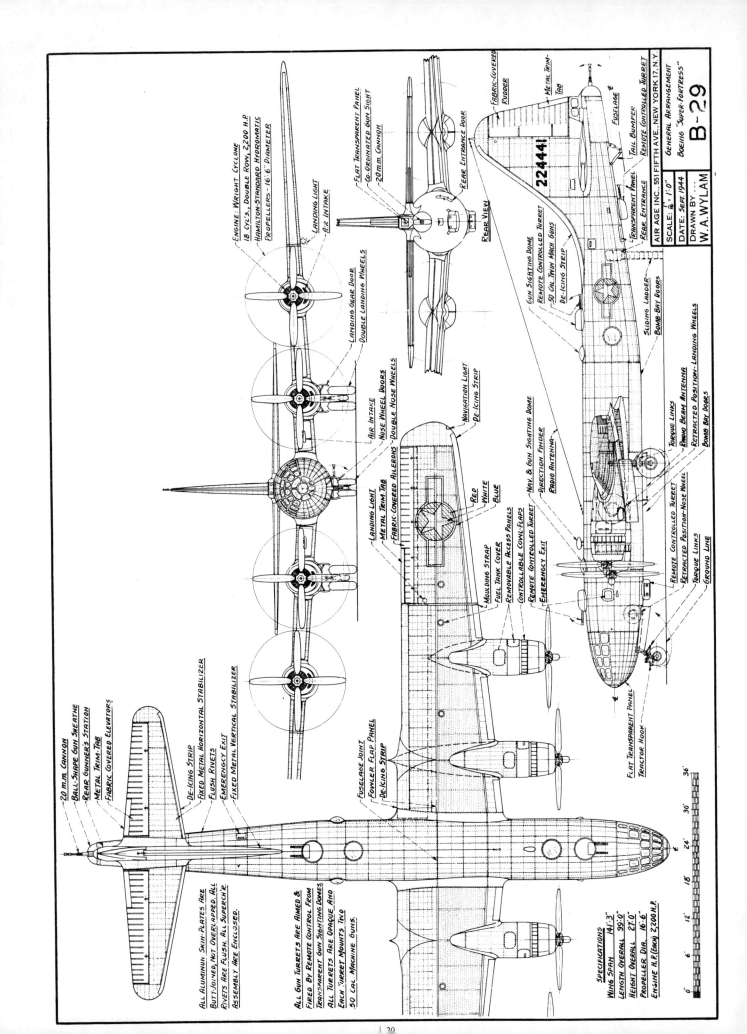

B-29

GENERAL ARRANGEMENT
BOEING "SUPER-FORTRESS"

AIR AGE INC., 551 FIFTH AVE., NEW YORK 17, N.Y.

SCALE: 1/16" = 1'-0"
DATE: SEPT. 1944
DRAWN BY...
W. A. WYLAM

ENGINE: WRIGHT CYCLONE
18 CYLS., DOUBLE ROW, 2,200 H.P.
HAMILTON-STANDARD HYDROMATIC
PROPELLERS - 16'-6" DIAMETER

LANDING LIGHT
AIR INTAKE

LANDING GEAR DOOR
DOUBLE LANDING WHEELS

AIR INTAKE
NOSE WHEEL DOORS
DOUBLE NOSE WHEELS

NAVIGATION LIGHT
DE-ICING STRIP

LANDING LIGHT
METAL TRIM-TAB
FABRIC-COVERED AILERONS

RED
WHITE
BLUE

MOULDING STRAP
FUEL TANK COVER
REMOVABLE ACCESS PANELS
CONTROLLABLE COWL-FLAPS
REMOTE CONTROLLED TURRET
EMERGENCY EXIT

FLAT TRANSPARENT PANEL
CO-ORDINATED GUN SIGHT
20 M.M. CANNON

REAR ENTRANCE DOOR

REAR VIEW

FABRIC-COVERED
RUDDER
METAL TRIM-
TAB

22444

FUSELAGE

TAIL BUMPER
REMOTE CONTROLLED TURRET

TRANSPARENT PANEL
REAR ENTRANCE

GUN SIGHTING DOME
REMOTE CONTROLLED TURRET
50 CAL. TWIN MACH GUNS
DE-ICING STRIP

SLIDING LADDER
BOMB BAY DOORS

NAV. & GUN SIGHTING DOME
DIRECTION FINDER
RADIO ANTENNA

TORQUE LINKS
RADIO BEAM ANTENNA
RETRACTED POSITION - NOSE WHEEL
BOMB BAY DOORS

REMOTE CONTROLLED TURRET
RETRACTED POSITION - LANDING WHEELS
TORQUE LINKS
GROUND LINE

FLAT TRANSPARENT PANEL
TRACTOR HOOK

20 M.M. CANNON
BALL-SHAPE GUN SHEATHE
REAR GUNNER'S STATION
METAL TRIM-TAB
FABRIC COVERED ELEVATORS

DE-ICING STRIP
FIXED METAL HORIZONTAL STABILIZER
FLUSH RIVETS
EMERGENCY EXIT
FIXED METAL VERTICAL STABILIZER

FUSELAGE JOINT
FOWLER FLAP PANEL
DE-ICING STRIP

ALL ALUMINUM SKIN-PLATES ARE
BUTT-JOINED, NOT OVERLAPPED. ALL
RIVETS ARE FLUSH. ALL SUPERCHR.
ASSEMBLY ARE ENCLOSED.

ALL GUN TURRETS ARE AIMED &
FIRED BY REMOTE CONTROL FROM
TRANSPARENT GUN SIGHTING DOMES.
ALL TURRETS ARE OPAQUE AND
EACH TURRET MOUNTS TWO
50 CAL. MACHINE GUNS.

SPECIFICATIONS
WING SPAN   141'-3"
LENGTH OVERALL   99'-0"
HEIGHT OVERALL   27'-0"
PROPELLER DIA.   16'-6"
ENGINE H.P.(EACH)   2,200 H.P.

0' 6' 12' 18' 24' 30' 36'

1 20

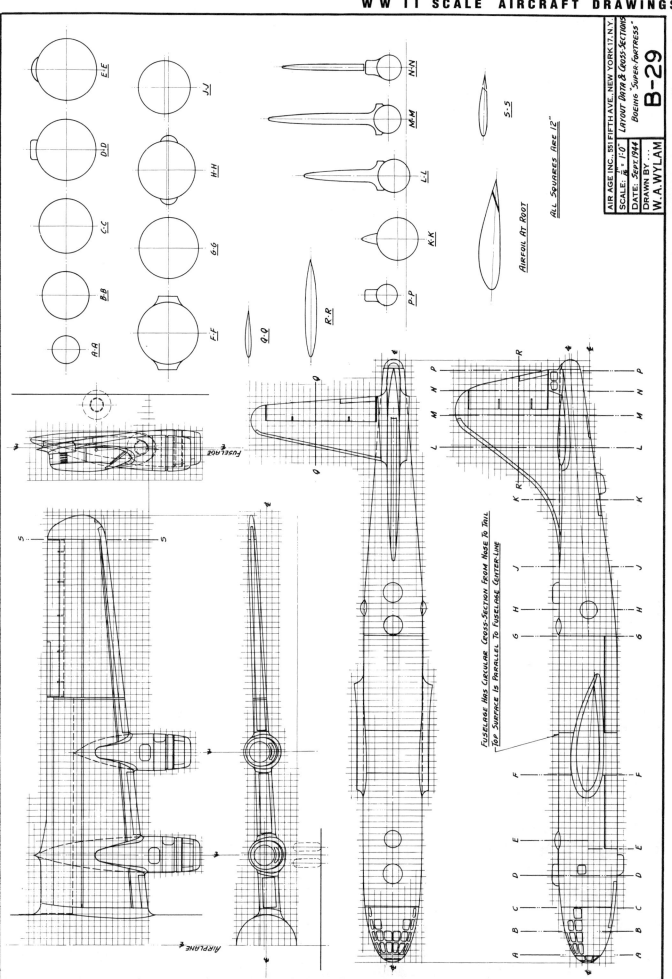

BOEING B-29

B-29

AIR AGE INC., 551 FIFTH AVE., NEW YORK 17, N.Y.

SCALE: $\frac{1}{16}'' = 1'-0''$

LAYOUT DATA & CROSS-SECTIONS

DATE: *Sept. 1944*

BOEING "SUPER-FORTRESS"

DRAWN BY.... W.A. WYLAM

ALL SQUARES ARE 12"

AIRFOIL AT ROOT

FUSELAGE HAS CIRCULAR CROSS-SECTION FROM NOSE TO TAIL
TOP SURFACE IS PARALLEL TO FUSELAGE CENTER-LINE

FUSELAGE

AIRPLANE ₡

CONSOLIDATED PBY-5A CATALINA

A Consolidated PBY-5A ashore. Note the ram air scoops on the tops of the engines (not shown on drawing) and the hook-on access ladder at the side blister. Sea-blue camouflage on top of the wing is carried around to the bottom of the retracted wing-tip float.

THE Consolidated PBY flying boat, named "Catalina" by the British, was one of the oddities of the war. A 1933 design, it was widely used by the U.S. Navy, but was nearly obsolete by 1940. With no immediate replacement in sight, it was kept in production by the U.S. Naval Aircraft Factory (N.A.F.) at two Consolidated factories and in two Canadian plants. Eventually, it distinguished itself by becoming the most prevalent flying boat of all time: 3,276 were built in the U.S. and Canada, plus an estimated 150 under license in Russia.

In competition against the Douglas XP3D-1 patrol plane, Consolidated's XP3Y-1 was the winner and went into production as the dual-purpose PBY-1 patrol bomber—the first monoplane ordered by the Navy for service with the fleet.

The prototype's powerplant was the 825hp Pratt & Whitney R-1830-58 twin-row engine, but this grew to the 1,200hp R-1830-92 in the final PBY-5A and PBY-6A models. The most notable outward changes were the large, transparent blisters over the side gun ports (first shown on the PBY-4) and the retractable tri-cycle landing gear introduced on the PBY-5A ("A" for amphibian), which greatly increased its usefulness and production life. A taller tail appeared on the N.A.F. PBN-1 and the later PBY-6A.

A Consolidated plant was built in New Orleans to supplement PBY-5 production at San Diego. The N.A.F. made minor changes to the 156 versions of the PBY-5, which was originally built as the "PBN-1" and later renamed "Nomad."

The Vickers plant in Cartierville, Canada, built 369 PBY-5s as "PBV-1As," with 230 going to the U.S. Army as "OA-10A" Observation Amphibians and 139 to the R.C.A.F., which named them "Cansos."

Boeing's Canadian plant in Vancouver built 317 PBY-5s on U.S. Navy contracts as "PB2B." The slight difference in designation was owing to Boeing's having already built a PBB-1 design of its own. Boeing built 250 PB2B-1s, some of which were assembled from parts provided by Consolidated. Sixty-seven more PB2B-2s duplicated the high-tailed PBN-1 flying boat. Boeing also built 17 Catalina boats for the R.C.A.F. and 55 Canso amphibians. Consolidated built one PBY-5, 782 PBY-5As and 237 PBY-6As at New Orleans, with 75 of those 237 going to the U.S. Army as "OA-10Bs."

The PBYs saw service in all theaters of the war. An R.A.F. Catalina spotted the elusive German battleship Bismark, and this lead to its destruction. U.S. Navy PBY-5s and 5As were used for the additional duty of air-sea rescue, particularly in the Pacific, where

A PBY-5A afloat with its landing gear retracted.

some carried lifeboats under their wings. Other PBYs, painted dull, matte black, were used for night intruder operations against the Japanese. Rescue PBYs were nicknamed "Dumbo," while the intruders were referred to as "Black Cats."

The U.S. Navy operated PBYs until the late 1940s, but the Coast Guard and the Naval Reserves retained them until 1954 and '57, respectively.

SPECIFICATIONS AND PERFORMANCE

Wingspan	104 ft.
Length	63 ft., 10 in.
Wing Area	1,400 sq. ft.
Empty Weight	20,190 lbs.
Gross Weight	35,420 lbs.
High Speed	175mph at 7,000 ft.
Cruising Speed	1,13mph
Armament	3x.30-caliber MG; 2x.50-caliber MG; 4x1,000-lb. bombs or depth charges.

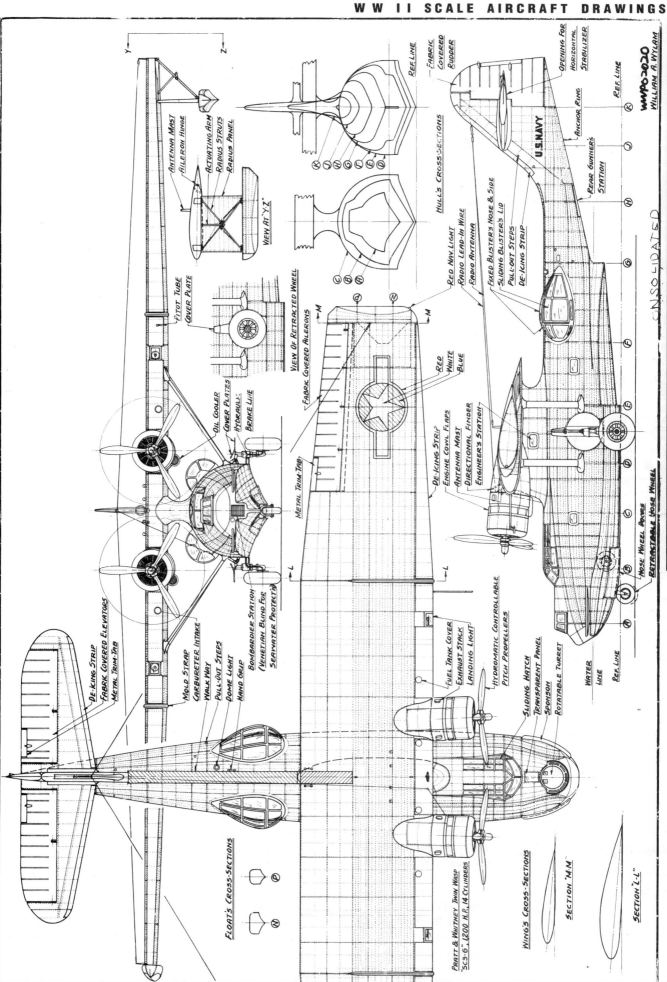

CONSOLIDATED PBY-5A CATALINA

WWPD2020 — William A. Wylam

CONSOLIDATED

U.S. NAVY

Antenna Mast
Aileron Hinge
Actuating Arm
Radius Struts
Radius Panel

View at "Y-Z"

Pitot Tube Cover Plate

Hulls Cross-Sections

Ref. Line
Fabric Covered Rudder

Opening for Horizontal Stabilizer
Ref. Line
Anchor Ring
Rear Gunner's Station

Fixed Blister's Nose & Side
Sliding Blister's Lid
Pull-out Steps
De-Icing Strip

Red Nav. Light
Radio Lead-In Wire
Radio Antenna

View of Retracted Wheel
Fabric Covered Ailerons

Oil Cooler
Cover Plates
Hydraulic
Brake Line

De-Icing Strip
Engine Cowl Flaps
Antenna Mast
Directional Finder
Engineer's Station

Red
White
Blue

Metal Trim-Tab

Mold Strap
Carbureter Intake
Walk Way
Pull-out Steps
Dome Light
Hand Grip

Bombardier Station
(Venetian Blind For
Seawater Protection)

Nose Wheel Doors
Retractable Nose Wheel

Water Line
Ref. Line

De-Icing Strip
Fabric Covered Elevators
Metal Trim-Tab

Fuel Tank Cover
Exhaust Stack
Landing Light

Hydromatic Controllable Pitch Propellers

Sliding Hatch
Transparent Panel
Sponson
Rotatable Turret

Pratt & Whitney Twin Wasp
S.C.3-G, 1200 H.P. 14 Cylinders

Floats Cross-Sections

Wing's Cross-Sections

Section "N-N"

Section "L-L"

CONSOLIDATED B-24 LIBERATOR

The B-24H-5-FO was built by the Ford Motor Co. with late-type waist gunners' windows. Camouflage was deleted from most U.S. Army combat planes in production early in 1944.

BESIDES being one of the major U.S. heavy bombers of the war, the Consolidated B-24, named the "Liberator," has a distinction held by no other American military airplane: more B-24s were built (18,482) than any other mass-produced fighters, including the Curtiss P-40 (13,738) and the Republic P-47 (15,683).

The design of the B-24, Consolidated Model 32, originated in January 1939, as a counter-proposal to a U.S. Army request that Consolidated build Boeing B-17s under license. The proposal was accepted, and the XB-24 flew on December 29, 1939. Such rapid development of a new model resulted from fitting a new bomber fuselage to the wing and tail of the existing Model 31 flying boat and adding two engines.

The Liberator was continually improved throughout the war. The early B-24A had 1,200hp Pratt & Whitney R-1830-33 engines without turbo-superchargers, but no armor or self-sealing fuel tanks, and it was defended by six .30-caliber, hand-swung machine guns. A powered top turret with two .50-caliber guns was added to the B-24C, as was a similar tail turret. Turbo-superchargers were added to the R-1830-41 engines of the B-24C to maintain takeoff power to 25,000 feet. The first significant production version, and the first to be combat-worthy, was the B-24D. A few of the final B-24Ds had retractable two-gun belly turrets, but that feature did not become standard until the B-24G, which also introduced a powered nose turret midway through production. Final defensive armament was 10, .50-caliber machine guns. Maximum bomb load was 8,000 pounds, usually reduced by the trade-off between bomb load and fuel for range.

Consolidated was allowed to build export versions for France, designated the "LB-30," and at the same time, the earliest B-24s were being built for the Army. This order was taken over by Britain. The R.A.F. also took some of the earliest B-24s, including six of the seven service-test YB-24s, but it released 26 of them, following the LB-30s to the U.S. Army. The Army used them initially as unarmed, long-range transports, but it used some as bombers in the Southwest Pacific after Pearl Harbor. Later, the Army requisitioned 75 undelivered LB-30s, but it eventually returned 23 to the R.A.F.

The B-24 was superior to the B-17 only in range, thanks to its high-aspect-ratio wing and new Davis airfoil section, so B-24s took over the long-range bombing in the Pacific until the B-29 came along. In Europe and North Africa, B-24s competed intensely against the B-17. The U.S. Navy acquired 977 B-24s from D through J. Despite their significant differences, all were designated "PB4Y-1 Patrol Bombers."

To meet its need for long-range transports, the Army had consolidated complete 287 B-24 airframes as unarmed C-87s, with elongated, streamlined noses and an airliner-type cabin, complete with passenger windows.

Britain ordered 159 LB-30s on cash contracts as "Liberator I" and "II," then received 2,040 B-24s from "D" through "L" under Lend-Lease. The British Liberator Mark numbers did not correspond directly to equivalent U.S. Army models. The 222 British B-24Ds were either Liberator Mark III bombers or Mark V patrol and reconnaissance planes, depending on how they were equipped. A mix of mostly B-24Js and a few Ls became 1,618 Liberator VIs and VIIIs. The 24 Mark VIIs were C-87s, not B-24s.

A few B-24s were converted and redesignated for other purposes—C-109 fuel transporters used in Africa and China, F-7 long-range photo-planes and AT-22 navigation trainers.

The demand for B-24s far exceeded the capacity of Consolidated's San Diego plant to produce them (it was also building PBY and PB2Y flying boats), so a Consolidated plant was built in Ft. Worth, TX. Three other manufacturers were also called on to supplement B-24 production. The output of B-24s at all five factories is listed below:

Consolidated, San Diego, CA (-CO)—1 XB-24 (converted to XB-24B); 159 LB-30; 7 YB-24; 9 B-24A; 9 B-24C. Mass-production of 2,452 D; 1,780 H; 2,792 J; 417 L; 916 M.

Consolidated, Ft. Worth, TX (-CF)—303 D; 244 F; 738 H; 1,558 J.

Douglas, Tulsa, OK (-DT)—10 D; 167 E; 582 H; 205 J.

Ford Motor Co., Ypsilanti, MI (-FO, built specifically for B-24 production)—480 E; 1,780 H; 1,587 J; 1,250 K; 1,677 M; 1 XB-24N; 7YB-24N.

North American, Dallas, TX (-NT)—430 G (-NT only); 536 J.

SPECIFICATIONS AND PERFORMANCE

Powerplant	P&W R-1830-65 1,200hp at 25,000 ft.
Wingspan	110 ft.
Length	67 ft., 2 in.
Wing Area	1,048 sq. ft.
Empty Weight	36,500 lbs.
Gross Weight	64,500 lbs.
High Speed	300mph at 30,000 ft.
Range	2,100 miles at 215mph at 25,000 ft.

CONSOLIDATED B-24 LIBERATOR

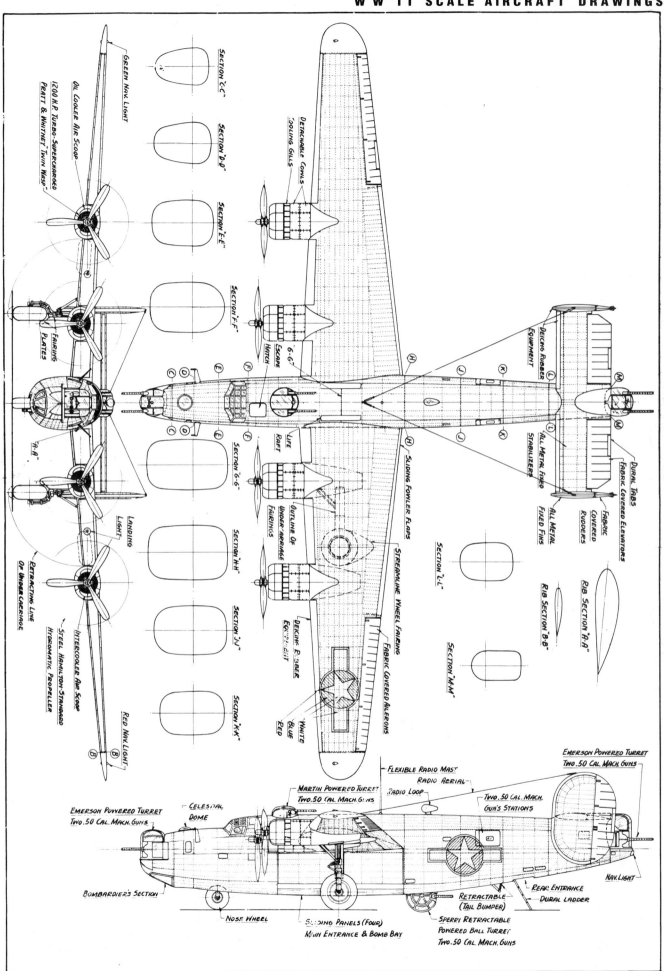

CURTISS P-40 D-E-F KITTYHAWK

★ ★ ★

The British Curtiss Model 87A-2 Kittyhawk is similar to the U.S. Army P-40D. It has the standard coloring of the 1941-early 1942 period, with sand-and-spinach camouflage on the top and side surfaces, light-blue underneath, Type A roundels under the wing, Type B on top of the wing and Type A.1 on the side of the fuselage.

THE P-40 was already obsolete when it first appeared in 1939, because it was a variant of the Curtiss Model 75, which was a prototype of the radial-engined U.S. Army P-36A that flew early in 1935. Export sales of the 81 and 87 models with liquid-cooled Allison V-1710 engines were good because of the desperate need for fighters of any kind. The P-40 was kept in production long past its prime.

U.S. Army Models—The Curtiss Model 87, used by the Army as the P-40D, E and F (plus later P-40s not listed here), differed notably from the earlier P-40 through P-40C (Curtiss Model 81) because the 1,040hp planetary-geared Allison V-1710-33 engine was replaced with the 1,150hp -39 model that used spur gears, which raised the thrust line and notably changed the

nose contours. In the 22 P-40Ds, the two .50-caliber machine guns were omitted from the nose, and two .50s were put in each wing panel to replace the two .30s there. Cockpit rear-view windows were also enlarged. Empty weight of the P-40D was 5,790 pounds; gross weight was 8,670 pounds; top speed was 354mph at 15,000 feet. Wing area was the same as earlier models—236 square feet.

P-40E—These models were improved P-40Ds, with -39 engines, six wing guns and a gross weight of 8,840 pounds. The Army bought 2,320. Early versions saw action in the Pacific and China, but most were used as fighter-trainers in the U.S.

P-40E-1—With passage of the famous Lend-Lease Act of March 1941, the U.S. provided the Allies with military aircraft.

Because these were procured and paid for through the appropriate military channels, they were required to have standard U.S. designations and serial numbers and to conform more closely to U.S. specifications. The Kittyhawk IA that was on order by Britain was almost a duplicate of the Army's P-40E, differing mainly in its use of British equipment and civil Allison V-1710-F3R engines. One year before adoption of the block number system, it was given the U.S. Army designation of P-40E-1 to accommodate its differences in the U.S. system. Some P-40E-1s were used by the U.S. Army and flew with U.S. markings over their British camouflage.

P-40F—A serious attempt was made to improve the performance of the obsolete P-40 when the Allison engine was replaced with the Ameri-

canized 1,300hp British Rolls-Royce Merlin engine (built by Packard as the V-1650-1). Unfortunately, the P-40 was too old, structurally and aerodynamically, to benefit as much from this change as did the North American P-51. The only outward difference from the P-40E was the elimination of the carburetor air scoop on top of the nose. Its gross weight increased to 9,870 pounds, and the only improvement was the speed at altitude — 364mph at 20,000 feet.

Despite this, the Army bought 1,311 P-40Fs (calling it Warhawk instead of Kittyhawk) as well as later models through P-40N. The first 699 P-40Fs were delivered before adoption of the block number system. The P-40F-5s and on had the rear fuselage lengthened 20 inches to improve directional stability. The Army took over 150 P-40Fs built for Britain as Kittyhawk II for use in North Africa in 1942 and '43.

British Designations—The Royal Air Force called its early Model 81 P-40s "Tomahawk,"

but the improved Model 87 was called "Kittyhawk," and retained its identification with Curtiss's "Hawk" for its export fighters.

The export Model 87 was originally ordered by France, but Britain took over the order. Major British use of Tomahawks and Kittyhawks was in North Africa starting in mid-1940.

Kittyhawk I—Britain bought 560 equivalents of the four-gun P-40D on cash contracts, with deliveries beginning in August 1941.

Kittyhawk IA—The 1,500 Kittyhawk IAs were equivalent to the P-40E and were delivered under Lend-Lease as P-40E-1 because of their differences in detail.

Kittyhawk II—The R.A.F. did not adopt the American

name of Warhawk when it acquired 330 P-40Fs and P-40Ls, but simply called them Kittyhawk II and Kittyhawk IIA. Eighty-one already delivered to the R.A.F.

were transferred to the U.S. Army for use in North Africa, and others, with U.S. insignia over British camouflage, were delivered to the Army straight from the Curtiss factory.

Several P-40Es and ex-R.C.A.F. Kittyhawks can be seen flying today in the Warbird movement.

★ ★ ★

P-40E-1 was the U.S. Army designation given to Kittyhawk IAs that were delivered to Britain. This one has Army markings over British camouflage. Note the 52-gallon auxiliary fuel tank on the belly bomb rack.

This P-40F was repossessed from a British Kittyhawk II order and used by the U.S. Army in North Africa in 1943. Note the British-type unit markings, camouflage and fin flash.

> *Note: To match the Wylam drawings, this description will cover only the "Short Fuselage" Curtiss Model 87s; the U.S. Army P-40D through P-40F; and the British "Kittyhawk" series.*

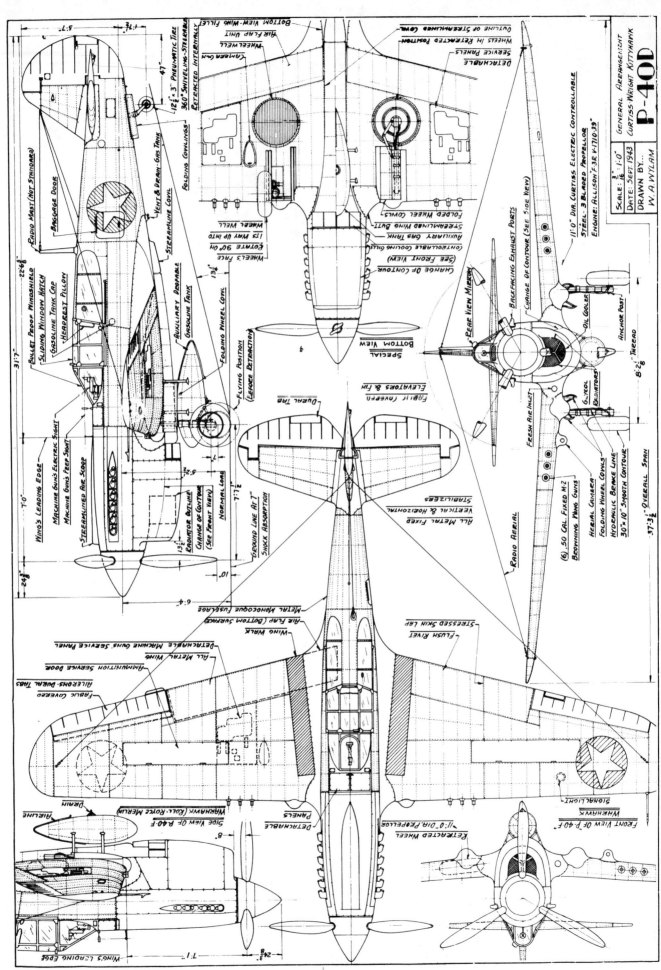

GENERAL ARRANGEMENT
CURTISS-WRIGHT KITTYHAWK

P-40D

SCALE: $\frac{3}{16}'' = 1'-0''$
DATE: 16 SEPT. 1943
DRAWN BY...
W. A. WYLAM

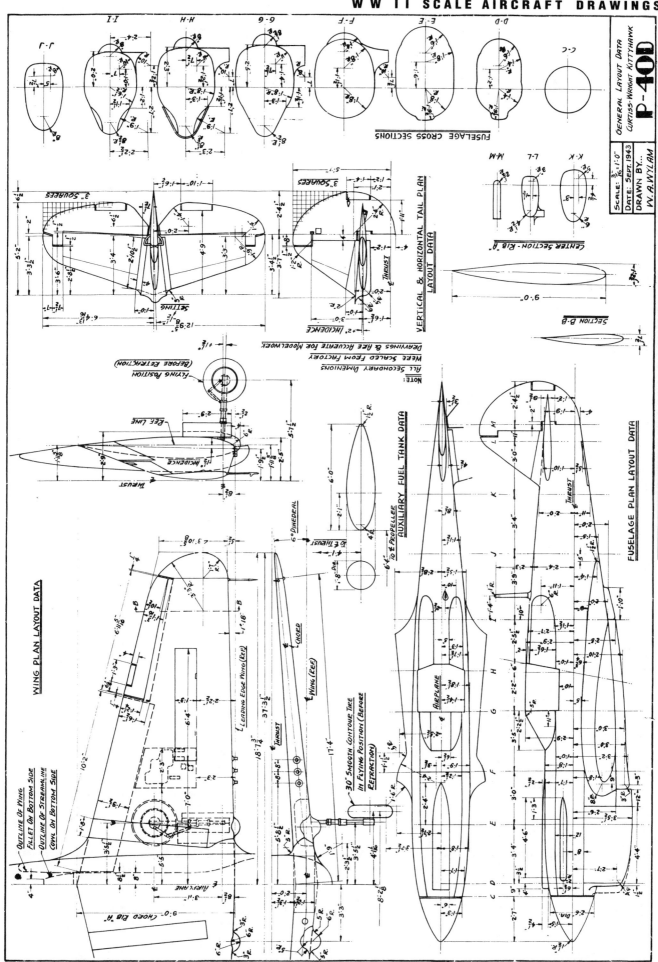

CURTISS P-40 D-E-F KITTYHAWK

P-40D

General Layout Data
Curtiss-Wright Kittyhawk

Scale: 3/16":1'-0"
Date: Sept. 1943
Drawn by:... W. A. Wylam

CURTISS SB2C HELLDIVER

An SB2C-1C with its retractable, leading-edge wing-slats open. Note the short-lived red border around the insignia as used in July/August 1942, and the use of topside camouflage on the outer (folding) panels of the wing. The plane in the background has folded wings and open bomb-bay doors.

THE SB2C Helldiver, which was the third Curtiss dive bomber to carry the name, became an effective attack plane late in the war, after a long development and debugging period. The XSB2C-1 flew in December 1940, but the production version didn't appear until June 1942. The design was seriously handicapped by contradictory Navy requirements, with dimensions limited by aircraft carrier space requirements and performance handicapped by the required military payload and equipment. Helldiver operations began in the Pacific in November 1943.

The final Curtiss Helldiver model—the SB2C-5. Note the four-blade propeller, the 100-gallon drop tanks on wing bomb racks, the mounts for 5-inch rockets and the overall midnight-blue finish adopted for carrier-based airplanes early in 1944.

Helldivers were built in great variety. The 200 SB2C-1S ("SB" for Scout Bomber) were armed with four .50-caliber machine guns in the wings, two power-driven .50s in the rear cockpit, a 1,000-pound bomb in an internal bomb bay and an additional 1,000 pounds of bombs under the wings. Wing area was 422 square feet and gross weight was 16,607 pounds. Top speed was 273mph at 13,000 feet, but diving speed was limited by perforated and split trailing-edge flaps that served as dive brakes.

An oddity of the SB2Cs with 1942 to '43-style camouflage was that the undersides of the outer wing panels carried dark topside camouflage because the undersurfaces were visible from above when the wings were folded.

The U.S. Army ordered 900 SB2C-1s under the designation of A-25A. These were built in Curtiss' existing St. Louis plant instead of the Columbus, OH, plant that had been built for SB2C production. Ten A-25As were sent to the Royal Australian Air Force, but they were rejected.

The 410 SB2C-1As were A-25As that were transferred to the U.S. Marines for use as trainers. The 778 SB2C-1Cs ("C" for Cannon) were successors to the SB2C-1, with two 20mm cannon substituting for the four .50-caliber machine guns in the wings. This was the standard armament for subsequent Helldivers. The single XSB2C-2 was a twin-float seaplane that wasn't successful.

The 1,112 SB2C-3s were improved structurally and aerodynamically and used four-blade propellers on 1,900hp R-2600-20 engines. These were followed by 1,985 SB2C-4s, which had wing racks added for eight 5-inch rockets. Some SB2C-4s were fitted with a radar pod on the right-wing bomb rack for night operations and were designated SB2C-4E ("E" for Electronics). Curtiss' final production models were 970 SB2C-5s with increased fuel capacity.

Other manufacturers were called on to increase Helldiver production. The Canadian branch of Fairchild built 50 SB2C-1s as SBF-1 and 150 SB2C-3s as SBF-3. These were followed by 100 SB2C-4Es as SBF-4E.

Canadian Car and Foundry Company (Can-Car) built 40 SB2C-1s as SBW-1. A further 26 out of 200 ordered by Britain were delivered as SBW-1B ("B" for Britain). Can-Car then built 413 SB2C-3s as SBW-3, followed by 96 SB2C-4Es as SBW-4E. The 86 SBW-5s were completed from the cancelled SBW-1B order.

CURTISS SB2C HELLDIVER

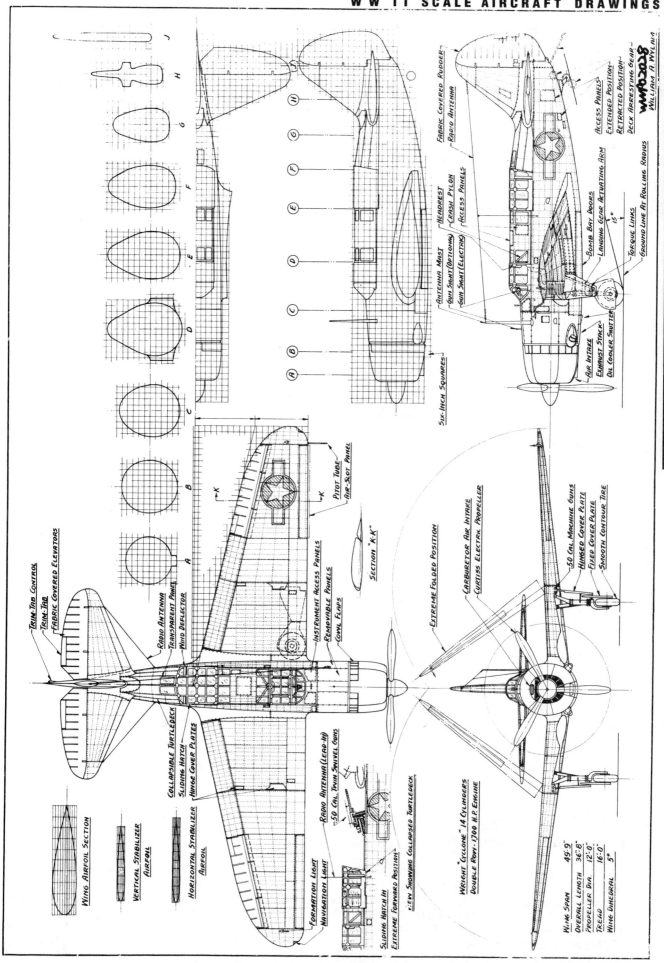

WILLIAM A WYLAM

Six-Inch Squares

Fabric Covered Rudder
Radio Antenna
Access Panels
Extended Position
Retracted Position
Deck Arresting Gear
Ground Line At Rolling Radius
Torque Links
Landing Gear Actuating Arm
Bomb Bay Doors
Oil Cooler Shutter
Exhaust Stack
Air Intake
Access Panels
Crash Pylon
Gun Sight (Electric)
Gun Sight (Optional)
Headrest
Antenna Mast

Section "K-K"

Pitot Tube
Air-Slot Panel

Trim-Tab Control
Trim-Tab
Fabric Covered Elevators
Radio Antenna
Transparent Panel
Wind Deflector
Instrument Access Panels
Removable Panels
Cowl Flaps
Collapsible Turtledeck
Sliding Hatch
Hinge Cover Plates
Radio Antenna (Lead-In)
.50 Cal. Twin Swivel Guns
Formation Light
Navigation Light
Sliding Hatch In
Extreme Forward Position
View Showing Collapsed Turtledeck

Extreme Folded Position
Carburetor Air Intake
Curtiss Electric Propeller
.50 Cal. Machine Guns
Hinged Cover Plate
Fixed Cover Plate
Smooth Contour Tire

Wright "Cyclone" 14 Cylinders
Double Row - 1700 H.P. Engine

Wing Airfoil Section
Vertical Stabilizer Airfoil
Horizontal Stabilizer Airfoil

Wing Span	49'.9"
Overall Length	36'.8"
Propeller Dia.	12'-0"
Tread	16'-0"
Wing Dihedral	5°

DOUGLAS BOSTON/ HAVOC/A-20

Sixty of the U.S. Army Douglas A-20s were completed as radar-equipped night fighters armed with four 20mm cannon in a belly pack. Note the overall matte-black finish and undersize national insignia.

DB-7s—This designation stood for Douglas Bomber, Model 7. The first production version was ordered by France in February 1939 as a three-seat bomber powered with 1,000hp Pratt & Whitney R-1830-SC3-G Twin Wasp engines. It had a transparent bomber nose, four fixed forward-firing French machine guns, one flexible gun in the rear cockpit and a 2,000-bomb load.

DB-7A—Improved DB-7s with 1,600hp Wright R-2600-A5B Twin Cyclone engines and higher vertical tails. All DB-7As ordered by France were delivered to Britain.

DB-7B—Further improved models ordered by Britain.

DB-7C—Improved DB-7B; 48 were ordered for the Netherlands East Indies with interchangeable noses; one for a bomber and one containing four 20mm cannon. Only half of the order could be delivered, and it was in U.S. Army A-20C form.

DB-73—Similar to the DB-7B, 480 were ordered by France in May 1940. They were redesignated by Douglas to distinguish them from the differently equipped DB-7Bs for Britain.

British Designations—Britain's Royal Air Force identified its airplanes by given names rather than model numbers, so the diverted French DB-7s and the new American models were named "Havoc" and "Boston".

Havoc I—Former French DB-7s modified to British standards. Four different missions were performed by Havoc Is, with the following special configurations:

1. Intruder—Essentially French DB-7s with British armament and instruments replacing the French originals.

2. Night Fighter—These had solid noses containing British AI Mk.IV radar, eight .303-caliber machine guns and a crew capacity reduced to two.

3. Pandora—Twenty DB-7s with bomb bays modified to carry a large aerial mine and 2,000 feet of cable. The object was to trail the mine ahead of enemy bomber formations and hope that it would hit one.

4. Turbinlite—Twenty unarmed ex-night fighters fitted in the nose with 2,700 million candlepower searchlights for finding and illuminating enemy aircraft for the night fighters.

Havoc II— One hundred ex-French DB-7As converted to night fighters with 12 .303 guns in a solid nose.

Boston I—Twenty of the earliest French DB-7s used as trainers by the R.A.F.

Boston II—Original designation for later French DB-7s; later redesignated Havoc I.

Boston III—The initial British order for 300 DB-7Bs was followed by the transfer of 240 French-ordered DB-73s built by Douglas, and 240 that Douglas sub-contracted to Boeing. Tankage increased from the DB-7A's 240 U.S. gallons to

At left: an early Douglas A-20A. Note the DB-7B-type nose, external pack for nose machine guns and use of rudder stripes and two wing stars before the marking change of February 1941. At right: an A-20G-40 with four .50-caliber nose machine guns and a long-range ferry tank under the belly.

DOUGLAS BOSTON/HAVOC/A-20

394 gallons to allow bomber operations over occupied Europe from England. Starting in mid-1941, many Boston IIIs were drafted into the U.S. Army Air Forces.

Boston IIIA—Later DB-7Bs procured for Britain via Lend-Lease were identified by the U.S. Army as A-20C and by Britain as Boston IIIA because of their differences from the all-British Boston III.

Boston IV—U.S. Army A-20Js, complete with American armament and coloring; 169 delivered to the R.A.F.

Boston V—Ninety U.S. Army A-20Ks delivered to the R.A.F.

U.S. Designations—There were several experimental and one-off variants of the U.S. Army A-20 and P-70 models, but only significant production versions will be detailed here. When the U.S. gave "popular" names to military aircraft for public discussion in October 1941, the A-20s and P-70s were given the existing British name of Havoc.

A-20—An improved DB-7A with side-mounted turbo-superchargers on 1,700hp military R-2600-7 engines (as distinguished from the civil-designated engines of the export models). Original armament was four .30-caliber machine guns in the nose, two flexible .30s in the rear cockpit, a flexible .30 in a ventral tunnel and a fixed .30 in each engine nacelle firing rearward. Normal bomb load was 16 100-pound bombs or four 250-pounders. Self-sealing, 394-gallon fuel tanks were an innovation for an American warplane.

The turbo proved to be troublesome, so it was removed (since a plane intended for low-altitude work didn't need the high-altitude benefits of such an installation). The first A-20 was converted to the XP-70 night-fighter prototype, and three others became XF and YF-3 photoplanes. The remaining 59 A-20s were converted to P-70s.

A-20A—A further 123 improved models ordered on the same June 30, 1939, contract as the A-20s, but all were delivered with R-2600-11 engines without turbos.

A-20B—Improved A-20A with DB-7 nose, which was its principal recognition feature.

A-20C—Production models similar to the DB-7B except for their U.S. equipment; 375 were built by Douglas as A-20C-DO and 140 by Boeing as A-20C-BO.

A-20G—Major production A-20; 2,850 were built with solid noses and R-2600-23 engines. Early versions had four 20mm cannon in the nose, but these were replaced by four to six .50-caliber machine guns starting at A-20G-5. From A-20G-20 and on, the single .50-caliber gun in the rear cockpit was replaced by a pair of .50s in a Martin-powered turret, and a single .50 replaced the .30 in the ventral tunnel. Internal bomb load was 2,000 pounds, but an additional 2,000 pounds could be carried on four wing racks. Gross weight increased to 25,700 pounds.

A-20H—Similar to late A-20Gs but used 1,700hp R-2600-29 engines; 412 built.

A-20J—The 450 A-20Js featured a lengthened Plexiglas bomber nose that contained two fixed .50-caliber guns and the famous Norden bomb sight. These were "Lead Bombers" that sighted the target for other A-20s that released their bombs when signaled by the leader.

A-20K—This was the final model of the A-20 series, with the last of the 413 built delivered September 20, 1944. The airframe was similar to the A-20H, but it was equipped as the A-20J.

F-3 Series—The seventh A-20 was converted to the XF-3 photographic plane, still with turbos. The bomb racks were removed and a T-3A camera was installed in the bomb bay, but the defensive armament was retained. Two other A-20s became YF-3s without the turbos. In 1944, 46 A-20Js and A-20Ks were converted to F-3As and saw action in Europe.

P-70 Series—Sixty A-20s were re-equipped as matte-black night fighters and redesignated P-70. These had radar in a solid nose and four 20mm cannon in a pack under the bomb bay. Engines were non-turbo R-2600-11s. The 39 P-70A-1s were A-20Cs with improved radar and six to eight .50-caliber guns in a belly pack. The A-20C defensive armament was retained. The 65 P-70A-2s were A-20Gs that were equipped as the P-70A-1s except for the deletion of flexible guns and the change to a glossy black finish. The P-70B-2s were modifications of 105 A 20Gs and A-20Js. The single P-70B-1 was an experimental model.

U.S. Navy BD Series—After testing of a former A-20 as the XF-3, the same airplane was stripped of armament and turbos, refitted with R-2600-3 engines and delivered to the U.S. Navy as the BD-1 (Bomber, first model from Douglas, initial configuration) for utility work, such as target towing. It was followed by eight A-20Bs that were designated BD-2.

The British Havoc IV is a U.S. Army A-20J with the original Army serial number on the fin painted out. Note the lengthened Plexiglas nose, power turret and 500-pound bomb on the wing rack.

☆ ☆ ☆

NOTE: Since the Nye drawings contain production figures, dimensions and performance data, the text concentrates on model designations and the differences between them.

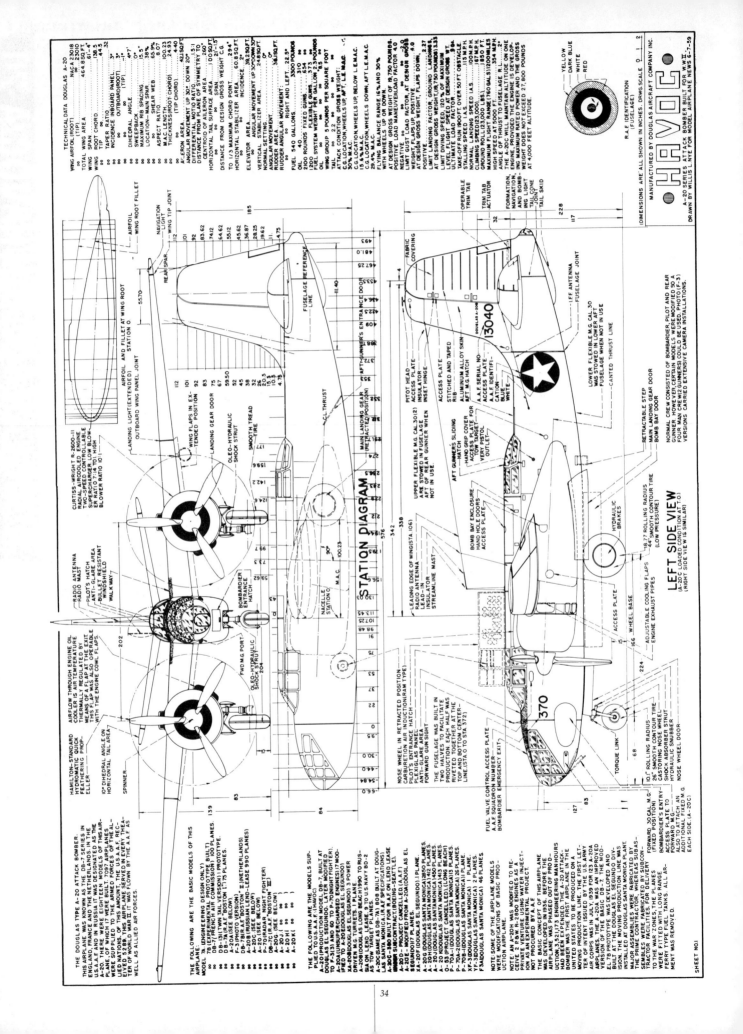

HAVOC

A-20 SERIES ATTACK BOMBER BUILT FOR W.W.II

MANUFACTURED BY DOUGLAS AIRCRAFT COMPANY INC.
DRAWN BY WILLIS L. NYE FOR MODEL AIRPLANE NEWS 6-7-59

DIMENSIONS ARE ALL SHOWN IN INCHES. DRWG SCALE

STATION DIAGRAM

LEFT SIDE VIEW

SHEET NO. 1

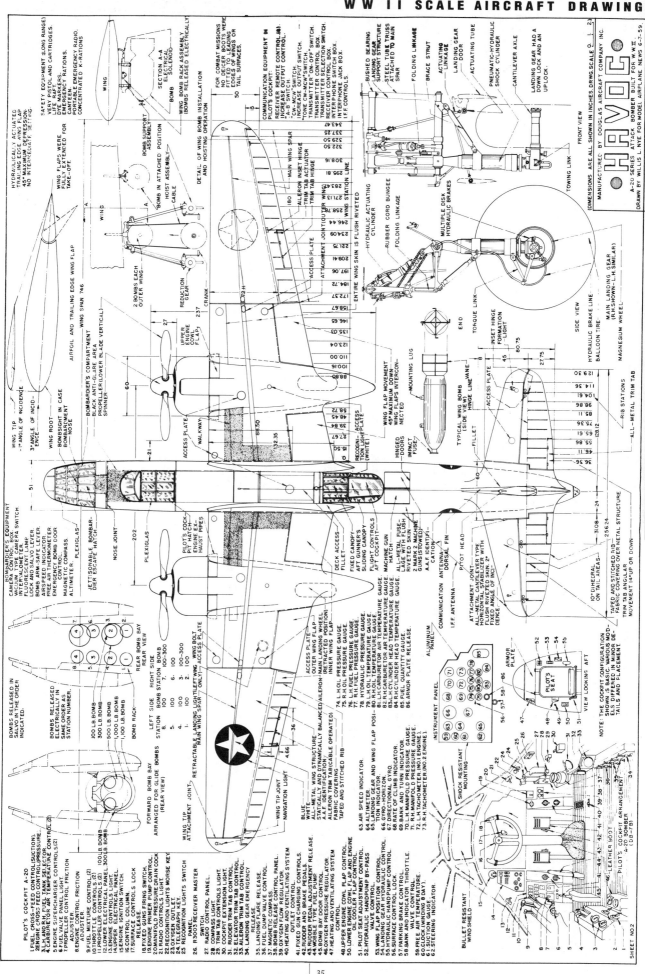

DOUGLAS BOSTON/HAVOC/A-20

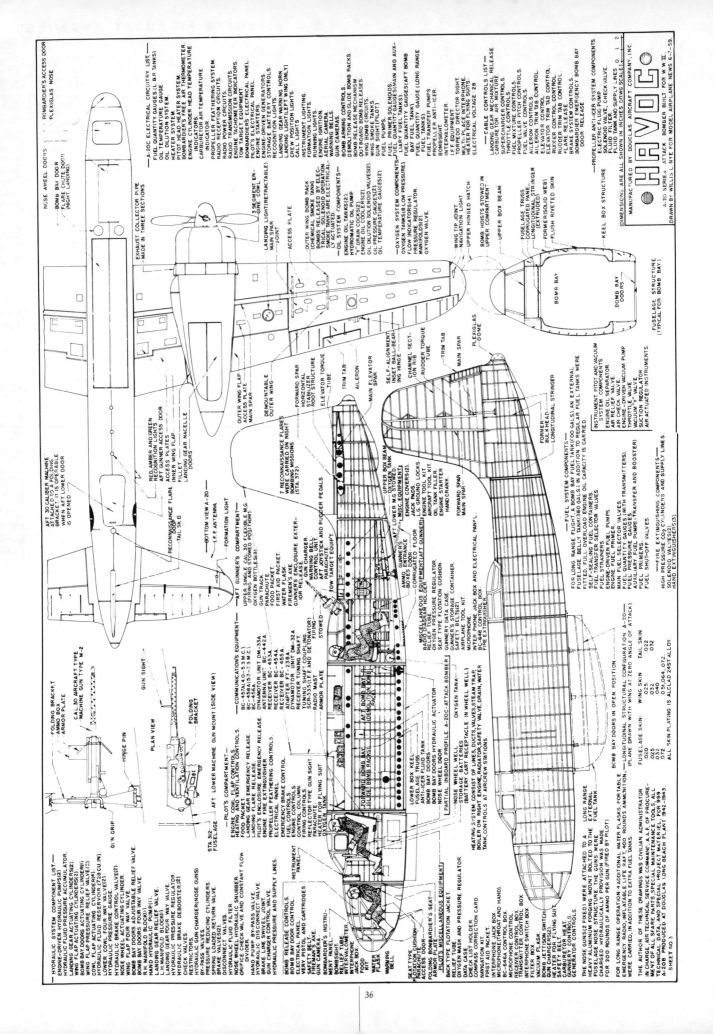

HAVOC

A-20 SERIES ATTACK BOMBER BUILT FOR W.W.II.
DRAWN BY WILLIS L. NYE FOR MODEL AIRPLANE NEWS 6-7-59.

(DIMENSIONS ARE ALL SHOWN IN INCHES. DRWG SCALE)

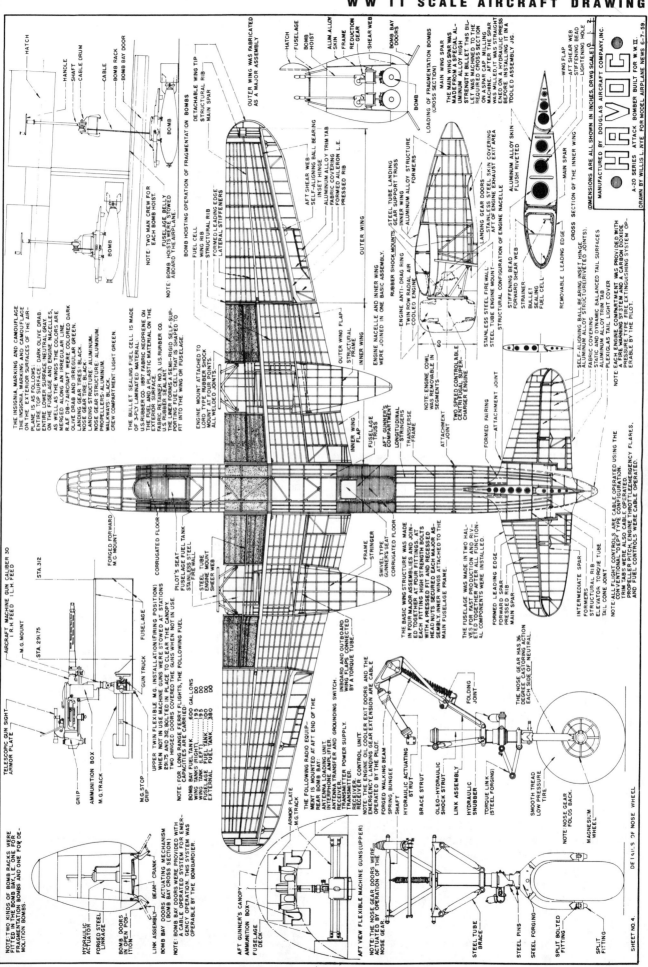

HAVOC

DOUGLAS BOSTON/HAVOC/A-20

A-20 SERIES ATTACK BOMBER BUILT FOR W.W.II.

DRAWN BY WILLIS L. NYE FOR MODEL AIRPLANE NEWS 6-7-59

MANUFACTURED BY DOUGLAS AIRCRAFT COMPANY, INC.

DIMENSIONS ARE ALL SHOWN IN INCHES. DRWG SCALE 0.

SHEET NO. 4.

DOUGLAS A-26 INVADER

THE Douglas A-26 Invader was a logical successor to the A-20 Havoc that took advantage of combat experience, updated technology and improved mass-production methods. The design was proposed to the Army in January 1941, and a contract for three prototypes was received soon after. The first, designated XA-26, was a three-seat bomber similar to the A-20A; the second, XA-26A, was a two-seat night fighter. The XA-26B used the same airframe, but mounted a 75mm cannon in the right side of the nose.

The principal differences from the A-20 were a wider fuselage with side-by-side seating for the pilot and co-pilot/bombardier, two remotely-sighted turrets, each with two .50-caliber guns, and 2,000hp Pratt & Whitney R-2800 Double Wasp engines.

The night-fighter concept was dropped, and production concentrated on two basic versions. The three-seat A-26B attack plane had a solid nose and a variety of fixed, forward-firing, .50-caliber guns. Six to eight were in the nose, and, in some cases, an additional four were carried in paired pods on each side of the nose. Some late versions even had three guns in each outer wing panel, plus wing racks for bombs or 5-inch rockets. With external bombs, the total bomb load was 6,000 pounds. As a result of early A-26 combat experience, the pilots' canopy was bulged slightly upward, which increased head room and greatly improved all-around visibility.

The A-26C was the light bomber variant, still with the turrets but normally carrying only two .50-caliber guns in a lengthened Plexiglas bomber nose. Late A-26Cs also carried six wing guns.

The XA-26 first flew on July 10, 1942, and production models were in combat in the Pacific by the spring of 1944, but were not notably successful until improvements were

Close-up of a black-painted A-26C shows the molded Plexiglas bomber nose and the bulged pilots' canopy adopted after early A-26 combat experience.

SPECIFICATIONS AND PERFORMANCE A-26B

Wingspan	70 ft., 0 in.
Length	50 ft., 0 in.
Wing Area	540 sq. ft.
Empty Weight	22,370 lbs.
Gross Weight	27,600 lbs.
High Speed	355mph at 15,000 ft.
Normal Range	1,400 miles

made. Operations in Europe, starting in September, were more successful.

The Long Beach plant built 1,150 A-26B-DLs and five A-26C-DLs. A new plant in Tulsa, OK, built 205 A-26B-DTs and 1,086 A-26C-DTs.

The A-26s were redesignated B-26 in 1948 and saw extensive service in the Korean War, and some service in the Vietnam war until 1969. The R.A.F. had ordered 140 A-26Bs but received only two before V-J day. The U.S. Navy received 152 surplus A-26Cs

after the war and used them as JD-1 utility planes. They were redesignated UB-26J in 1962. The Air Force retained B-26s as trainers and utility types until 1972.

★   ★   ★

The XA-26B below shows the large propeller spinners used only on the prototypes and the 75mm cannon that was fitted to some production A-26Bs.

Bottom: A Douglas A-26B-30-DL with four .50-caliber machine guns in the right side of the nose and two in the left. The standard turrets for all A-26s are not shown on the drawing.

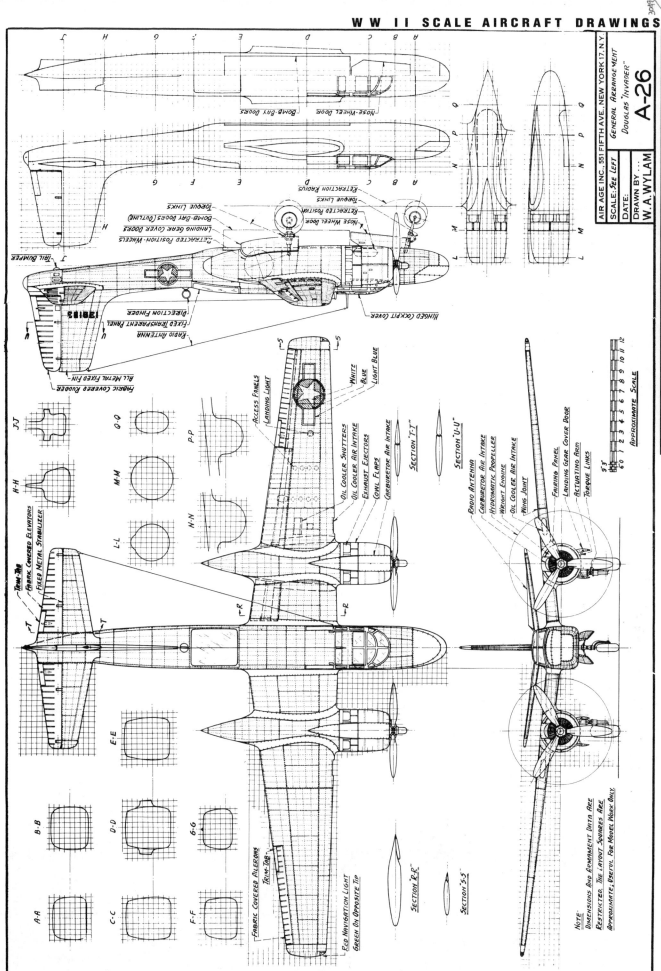

DOUGLAS A-26 INVADER

AIR AGE INC., 551 FIFTH AVE., NEW YORK 17, N.Y.
GENERAL ARRANGEMENT
SCALE: See Left
DATE:
DRAWN BY...
W. A. WYLAM
DOUGLAS "INVADER"
A-26

NOTE:
DIMENSIONS AND PERMANENT DATA ARE
RESTRICTED. THE LAYOUT SQUARES ARE
APPROXIMATE, USEFUL FOR MODEL WORK ONLY.

APPROXIMATE SCALE

39

DOUGLAS C-54 SKYMASTER

The third Douglas DC-4 was built as an airliner but was delivered to the U.S. Army in war paint as a C-54.

THE Douglas DC-4 Skymaster, which was produced for the U.S. Army as the C-54, was the most widely used four-engine transport and cargo plane of World War II, with 953 planes built in seven Army versions. Surprisingly, though, the plane didn't originate as a military airplane.

Early in 1936, five U.S. airlines put up $100,000 each to help Douglas develop a new, long-range airliner, the DC-4, that would meet their antici-

pated requirements. Two airlines soon backed out, but the DC-4 was completed and flown in June 1938. Its powerplants were new 1,450hp Pratt & Whitney R-2180-S1A1-Gs; its wingspan was 138 feet, 3 inches; and its gross weight was 65,000 pounds. It proved to be too difficult to maintain, however, and with a passenger capacity of only 52, it wasn't cost-effective. After the DC-4 was tested on the three

airlines' routes, the airlines and Douglas decided to develop a smaller, more efficient model, still called DC-4. The original was then redesignated DC-4E (" E " for Experimental) and was sold to Japan.

In mid-1939, Douglas began work on a new design to meet the airlines' revised requirements. This airplane had a wingspan of only 117 feet and a wing area of 1,460 square feet (compared to the 2,155-square-foot wingspan

of the DC-4Es). Gross weight was 62,000 pounds, and passenger seating was 40, with a four-man cockpit crew. The engines were 1,350hp Pratt & Whitney R-2000-2SD1-Gs, and the production DC-4 and its military successors were the only airplanes to use them. About the only significant detail retained from the DC-4E was the tricycle landing gear, which was an innovation that proved to be well-suited to large airplanes. Top speed was 265mph; cruising speed was 192mph at 10,000 feet.

Douglas started a production line at Santa Monica for 61 DC-4s that were ordered by the airlines, but military demands precluded their delivery. Even before the first DC-4 flew in February 1942, the entire production was requisitioned by the U.S. Army. The first 24, which were well along in construction as airliners, were designated C-54. Later airframes, which could be modified to meet military requirements, were designated C-54A.

This U.S. Navy R5D-2 was originally a C-54B built for the Army. Note the large, single-wing, trailing-edge flaps and the application of a U.S. Navy serial number and Naval Air Transport Service insignia to the nose.

This view of a C-54D shows the large, two-section cargo doors fitted to all C-54s from the C-54A on. Note the Army Air Transport Command insignia on the rear fuselage.

The demand for C-54s was so great that Douglas established a new plant in Chicago for additional production. The C-54s built in Santa Monica were designated C-54-DO; those built in Chicago were designated C-54-DC. The U.S. Navy also used C-54s under the designation of R5D, but they weren't ordered directly from Douglas. All the Navy models were transferred from the Army, as were 23 Skymasters for Britain.

Only the first few C-54s, and none of the R5Ds, were camouflaged, as they weren't expected to fly into combat zones. Army C-54s were procured in the following versions:

C-54—The initial 24 started as airliners and were delivered to the Army with minimal modification. Four fuel tanks were installed in the cabin for extra range, and an extra compartment was built ahead of a shorter cabin for additional military crew. Passenger capacity was reduced to 14. The civil engines were redesignated R-2000-3.

C-54A—The remainder of the original airline orders and later Army production totaled 252: 97 C-54A-DOs and 155 C-54-DCs. Major changes were a large 67x94-inch, two-section cargo door on the left side of the fuselage and a reinforced floor to accommodate heavy cargo. Gross weight increased to 73,000 pounds with the addition of R-2000-7 engines.

C-54B—These were improved C-54As with additional wing fuel tanks replacing two of the cabin tanks. There were 100 C-54B-DOs and 120 C-54B-DCs produced.

C-54C—One C-54A-DO was modified for President Franklin D. Roosevelt, and included a cargo elevator (for bringing him aboard in his wheelchair), luxurious cabin furnishings and amenities suited to a VIP. The airplane was given such special attention that it was irreverently nicknamed "The Sacred Cow."

C-54D—Built only in Chicago, the 380 C-54D-DCs were improved C-54Bs with R-2000-11 engines.

C-54E—The 125 C-54E DOs were built in Santa Monica and were similar to C-54Bs except for their increased fuel capacity. The cabin was rearranged to permit a quick change from all-cargo to 50 troops in canvas seats.

XC-54F—One C-54B-DC had jump doors on each side of the fuselage for testing as a paratroop deployment aircraft. No production was undertaken on this model.

C-54G—The final production model was the C-54G, with 162 built at Santa Monica as personnel transports. A further 235 were cancelled at the war's end, but Douglas completed them, and built others, as civil transports.

Below: this photo of the original DC-4E shows the many differences between it and the production-model DC-4. The plane's main contribution to later models was the tricycle landing gear.

U.S. Navy Skymasters—The C-54s transferred to the U.S. Navy were designated as follows: R5D-1: 56 C-54A, R5D-2: 30 C-54B, R5D-3: 86 C-54D, R5D-4: 20 C-54E and R5D-5: 13 C-54G.

Postwar Use—Civil DC-4s and converted C-54s went into airline service soon after the war. Although they outnumbered the newer Lockheed Constellation, they were at a competitive disadvantage because they weren't pressurized. The most notable postwar uses of the C-54 RHD were the Berlin Airlift of 1948-49, with 336 Skymasters involved, and a major airlift operation during the Korean War.

Postwar modifications and redesignations of C-54s and R5Ds resulted in designations as high as C-54S. The last Air Force and Navy C-54s weren't retired until the early 1970s.

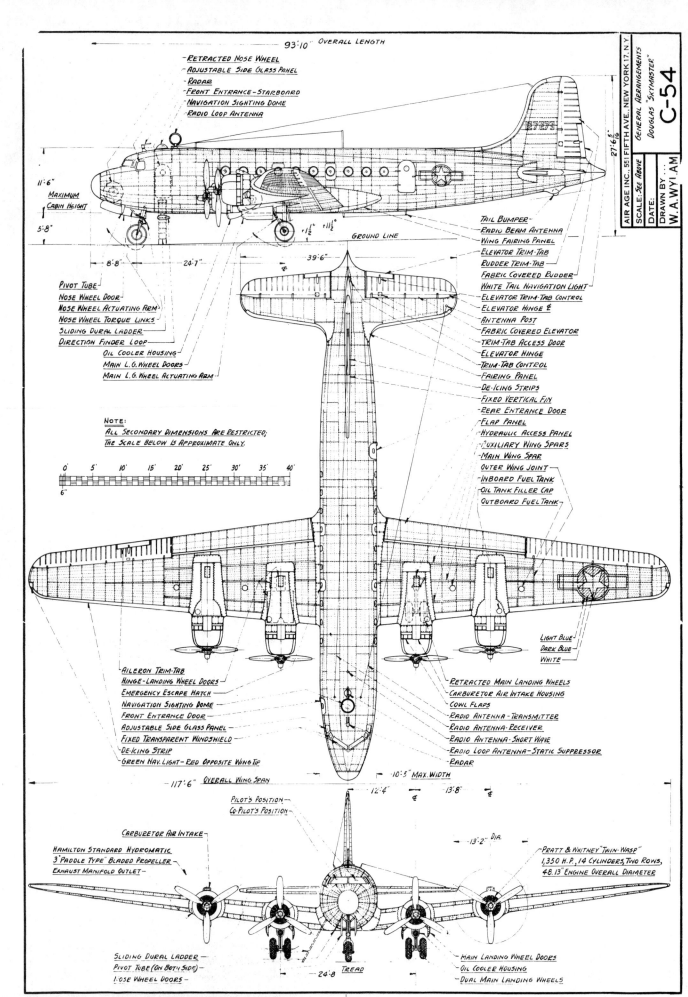

93'10" OVERALL LENGTH

- RETRACTED NOSE WHEEL
- ADJUSTABLE SIDE GLASS PANEL
- RADAR
- FRONT ENTRANCE - STARBOARD
- NAVIGATION SIGHTING DOME
- RADIO LOOP ANTENNA

AIR AGE INC., 551 FIFTH AVE., NEW YORK 17, N.Y.
SCALE: SEE ABOVE
DATE:
DRAWN BY
W. A. WYLAM
GENERAL ARRANGEMENTS
DOUGLAS "SKYMASTER"
C-54

127273

27'6⁵⁄₁₆"

11'6"
MAXIMUM
CABIN HEIGHT

5'8"

+½° +1½°

GROUND LINE

8'8"   24'7"   39'6"

PIVOT TUBE
NOSE WHEEL DOOR
NOSE WHEEL ACTUATING ARM
NOSE WHEEL TORQUE LINKS
SLIDING DURAL LADDER
DIRECTION FINDER LOOP
OIL COOLER HOUSING
MAIN L.G. WHEEL DOORS
MAIN L.G. WHEEL ACTUATING ARM

NOTE:
ALL SECONDARY DIMENSIONS ARE RESTRICTED;
THE SCALE BELOW IS APPROXIMATE ONLY.

0   5'   10'   15'   20'   25'   30'   35'   40'
6"

TAIL BUMPER
RADIO BEAM ANTENNA
WING FAIRING PANEL
ELEVATOR TRIM-TAB
RUDDER TRIM-TAB
FABRIC COVERED RUDDER
WHITE TAIL NAVIGATION LIGHT
ELEVATOR TRIM-TAB CONTROL
ELEVATOR HINGE &
ANTENNA POST
FABRIC COVERED ELEVATOR
TRIM-TAB ACCESS DOOR
ELEVATOR HINGE
TRIM-TAB CONTROL
FAIRING PANEL
DE-ICING STRIPS
FIXED VERTICAL FIN
REAR ENTRANCE DOOR
FLAP PANEL
HYDRAULIC ACCESS PANEL
AUXILIARY WING SPARS
MAIN WING SPAR
OUTER WING JOINT
INBOARD FUEL TANK
OIL TANK FILLER CAP
OUTBOARD FUEL TANK

LIGHT BLUE
DARK BLUE
WHITE

AILERON TRIM-TAB
HINGE-LANDING WHEEL DOORS
EMERGENCY ESCAPE HATCH
NAVIGATION SIGHTING DOME
FRONT ENTRANCE DOOR
ADJUSTABLE SIDE GLASS PANEL
FIXED TRANSPARENT WINDSHIELD
DE-ICING STRIP
GREEN NAV. LIGHT - RED OPPOSITE WING TIP

RETRACTED MAIN LANDING WHEELS
CARBURETOR AIR INTAKE HOUSING
COWL FLAPS
RADIO ANTENNA - TRANSMITTER
RADIO ANTENNA - RECEIVER
RADIO ANTENNA - SHORT WAVE
RADIO LOOP ANTENNA - STATIC SUPPRESSOR
RADAR

117'6"   OVERALL WING SPAN

10'5" MAX. WIDTH

12'4"   13'8"

PILOT'S POSITION
CO-PILOT'S POSITION

CARBURETOR AIR INTAKE

HAMILTON STANDARD HYDROMATIC
3 "PADDLE TYPE" BLADED PROPELLER
EXHAUST MANIFOLD OUTLET

13'2" DIA.

PRATT & WHITNEY "TWIN-WASP"
1,350 H.P., 14 CYLINDERS, TWO ROWS,
48.13" ENGINE OVERALL DIAMETER

SLIDING DURAL LADDER
PIVOT TUBE (ON BOTH SIDE)
NOSE WHEEL DOORS
24'8"   TREAD

MAIN LANDING WHEEL DOORS
OIL COOLER HOUSING
DUAL MAIN LANDING WHEELS

DOUGLAS C-54 SKYMASTER

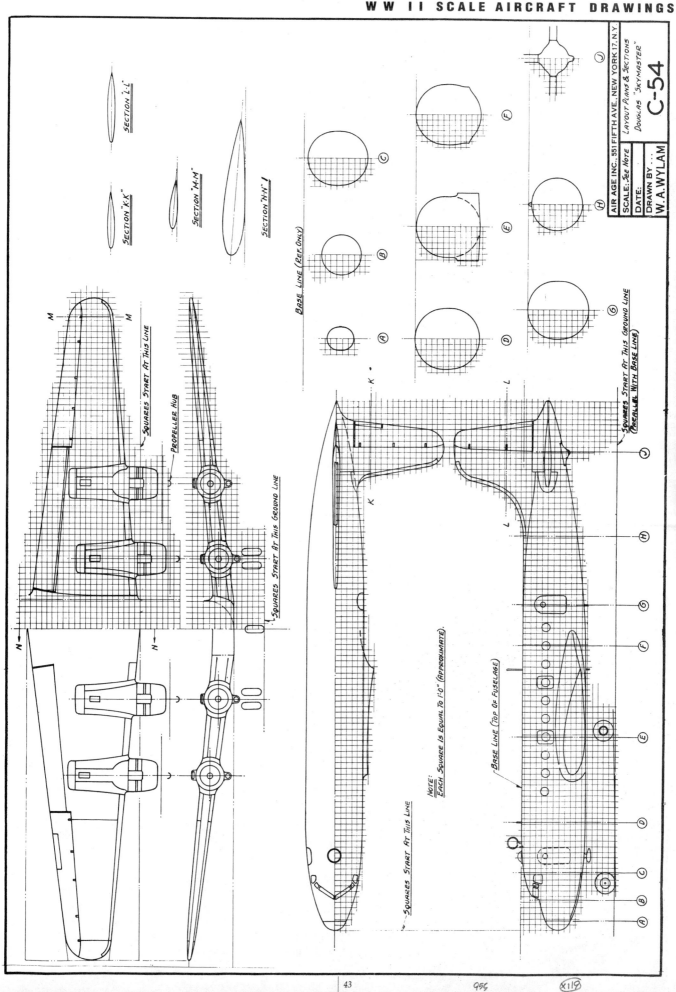

SECTION "L-L"

SECTION "K-K"

SECTION "M-M"

SECTION "N-N"

BASE LINE (REF. ONLY)

Squares Start At This Line

PROPELLER HUB

Squares Start At This Ground Line

Squares Start At This Ground Line

NOTE:
Each Square Is Equal To 1'0" (Approximate).

Squares Start At This Line

Squares Start At This Ground Line (Parallel With Base Line)

BASE LINE (TOP OF FUSELAGE)

Squares Start At This Line

AIR AGE INC., 551 FIFTH AVE., NEW YORK 17, N.Y.
LAYOUT PLANS & SECTIONS
DOUGLAS "SKYMASTER"
C-54
SCALE: See Note
DATE:
DRAWN BY ....
W. A. WYLAM

FAIRCHILD PT-19, PT-23, PT-26

A silver Fairchild-built PT-23 with 220hp Continental Radial engine and 1942-43 star markings.

THE Fairchild M-62, which was the U.S. Army PT-19, was one of several successful entrants in a 1939 competition for new Army primary trainers and, with another winner, the Ryan ST-A (PT-16), it introduced monoplane primary trainers to the Army.

The PT-19 had a welded steel-tube fuselage with plywood-covered wooden wing and fixed tail surfaces, and fabric covering for fuselage and control surfaces. Its initial powerplant was the 175hp inverted, six-cylinder, air-cooled Ranger L-440-1 engine. Because of the low-wing configuration, a stout steel turnover pylon was built between the two open cockpits.

The initial 1939 order for 270 PT-19s was soon supplemented by orders for 3,702 PT-19As with 200hp L-440-3 engines and 917 PT-19Bs equipped for instrument training. The demand for PT-19As was more than Fairchild could handle, so the work was split up. Fairchild built 3,181 PT-19A-FAs, Aeronca (-AE) built 477 and St. Louis (-SL) built 44. Aeronca also built 143 PT-19Bs; Fairchild built 774.

As a hedge against a shortage of Ranger engines, the 220hp Continental R-670-4 radial engine was substituted in two PT-23s that were built by Fairchild, 375 by Aeronca, 199 by Howard (-HO), 200 by St. Louis and 93 by Fleet Aircraft in Canada (-FE).

Under the Lend-Lease Program of March 1941, the U.S. Army provided British Empire forces with a winterized version of the PT-19A, which was designated PT-26. Fairchild built 670 as Cornell I;

Fleet built 807 as Cornell II. Fleet built a further 250 PT-26Bs as Cornell III. Most of these carried R.A.F. or R.C.A.F. markings and serial numbers and were painted yellow, and because they were being paid for with U.S. Army funds, they also carried the appropriate U.S. Army designation and serial numbers. The U.S. Army received 517 Canadian-built PT-26As with U.S. markings.

The drawing shows an R.C.A.F. Cornell II built by Fleet. Although it was delivered in 1943, it carried the wide, late-1940-style fin flash and the Type-A roundels that were discontinued in June 1942. Canada was noted for using older markings on new-production aircraft until the end of the war.

The plane illustrated here carried three military serial numbers—U.S. Army 42-65690; FV215, originally assigned by the R.A.F.; and 15116, adopted after it was transferred to the R.C.A.F. Most PT-26s were yellow, but some were finished in silver. U.S. Army PT-19s were prewar blue and yellow through the spring of 1942; after that, they were silver.

The low cost and simplicity of the various Fairchild PTs made them popular on the surplus market after the war, and many are still used by private owners.

SPECIFICATIONS AND PERFORMANCE PT-26A

Wingspan	35 ft., 11 in.
Length	27 ft., 8 in.
Wing Area	200 sq. ft.
Empty Weight	2,020 lbs.
Gross Weight	2,630 lbs.
High Speed	128mph

Above: The first Fairchild-built PT-26 was a winterized PT-19A with enclosed cockpits. This airplane carried Royal Air Force serial number FH651 and U.S. Army serial number 42-12499. The R.A.F. designation was Cornell I. Roundels and fin flash are correct for the 1940 to mid-1941 period.

Below: A blue and yellow U.S. Army Fairchild PT-19 over Randolph Field, TX, in 1941.

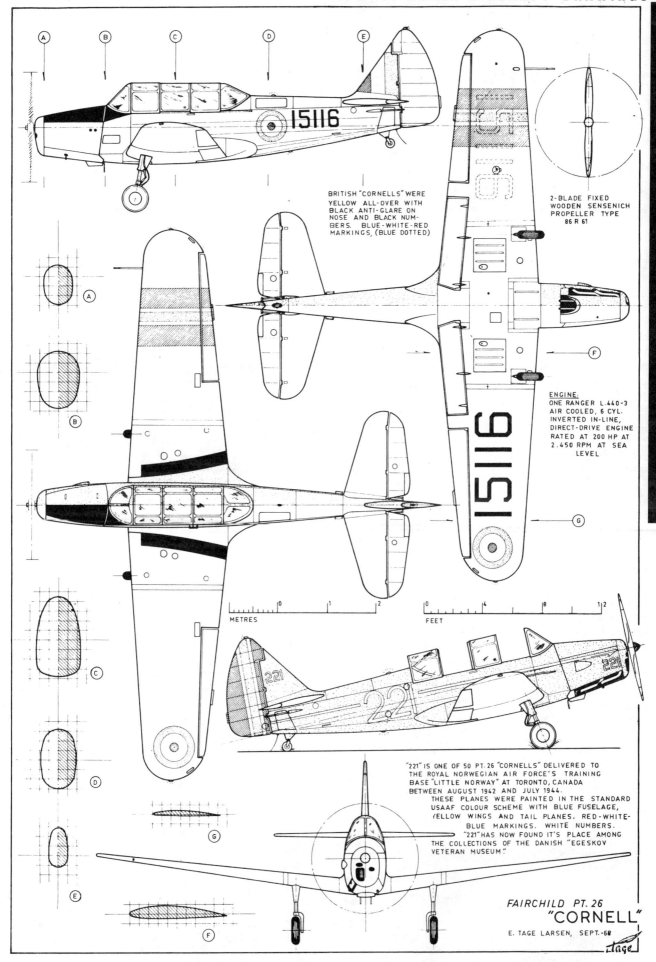

FAIRCHILD PT-19, PT-23, PT-26

BRITISH "CORNELLS" WERE YELLOW ALL-OVER WITH BLACK ANTI-GLARE ON NOSE AND BLACK NUMBERS. BLUE-WHITE-RED MARKINGS, (BLUE DOTTED)

2-BLADE FIXED WOODEN SENSENICH PROPELLER TYPE 86 R 61

ENGINE:
ONE RANGER L.440-3 AIR COOLED, 6 CYL. INVERTED IN-LINE, DIRECT-DRIVE ENGINE RATED AT 200 HP AT 2.450 RPM AT SEA LEVEL

15116

METRES

FEET

"221" IS ONE OF 50 PT.26 "CORNELLS" DELIVERED TO THE ROYAL NORWEGIAN AIR FORCE'S TRAINING BASE "LITTLE NORWAY" AT TORONTO, CANADA BETWEEN AUGUST 1942 AND JULY 1944.
THESE PLANES WERE PAINTED IN THE STANDARD USAAF COLOUR SCHEME WITH BLUE FUSELAGE, YELLOW WINGS AND TAIL PLANES. RED-WHITE-BLUE MARKINGS. WHITE NUMBERS.
"221" HAS NOW FOUND IT'S PLACE AMONG THE COLLECTIONS OF THE DANISH "EGESKOV VETERAN MUSEUM."

FAIRCHILD PT. 26
"CORNELL"
E. TAGE LARSEN, SEPT.-68

FIAT CR 42 FALCON

The CR 42 that was captured during the Battle of Britain is shown here, with its original 1940 Italian camouflage and markings restored. The number BT474 on the fuselage isn't Italian; it's the R.A.F. serial number assigned to the plane when it was test-flown in England.

THE Italian Fiat CR 42 Falco (Falcon) has the distinction of being the last biplane fighter to be produced and put into first-line service by a major warring power. The prototype of this thoroughly anachronistic, open-cockpit, fabric-covered biplane with fixed landing gear flew early in 1939. Production continued into 1942, and 1,781 were built.

The initials "CR" in the designation identify Celestino Rosatelli, a famous designer of long standing. His CR 42 evolved from a long line of CR fighters, starting with the CR 20 of 1923. All shared the unique feature of the Warren-Truss arrangement of the wing struts. All models through the CR 33 featured liquid-cooled engines, while subsequent models used air-cooled radial engines.

Its powerplant was the 840hp Fiat A.74 R.C.38 twin-row radial engine, and the initial armament was one 7.7mm and one 12.7mm machine gun in the nose. The later CR 42*ter* (third version) had four 12.7mm guns, two of which were in blisters in the lower wing. The CR 42 A.S. ("A.S." for "Africa Settentrionale," or North Africa) was a ground-attack version with two 220-pound bombs, and the CR 42 C.N. ("CN" for "Caccia Notturna," or Night Fighter) was used as a defensive night fighter in Northern Italy. There was also a twin-float seaplane version, the ICR 42 ("I" for "Idrovolante," or Seaplane).

One CR 42 was fitted with a 1,020hp German Daimler-Benz DB-601 liquid-cooled engine, (used in the Me.109 as CR 42B), and turned in the almost unbelievable speed (for a biplane) of 323mph.

Italy entered the war on June 10, 1940, with 300 CR 42s. These planes fought everywhere the Italian Air Force was engaged, and were involved in some of the last significant biplane vs. biplane battles when CR 42s fought British Gloster Gladiators over Greece, North Africa and Malta.

Some CR 42s took part in Italy's token raids on England during the Battle of Britain in the fall of 1940. One was forced down intact and can be seen today in the Battle of Britain Museum near London. At least 113 CR 42s were still in service when Italy surrendered to the Allies on September 8, 1943. Italy joined the Allies and declared war on Germany on October 13, but the CR 42s were all in the hands of the part of Italy that remained loyal to Hitler. Four "escaped," however, to join the anti-Fascist Co-Belligerent Air Force.

The performance and price of the CR 42 made it popular on the export market. Sweden bought 72 CR 42*bis* (second version) models, each with two 12.7mm guns, and kept them in first-line service until 1945. Belgium bought 34 in September 1939, but most of these were destroyed on the ground by the Luftwaffe in the 1940 Blitz. Hungary also bought export models.

SPECIFICATIONS AND PERFORMANCE
CR-42

Wingspan	31 ft., 9 3/4 in.
Length	27 ft., 2 3/4 in.
Wing Area	240.5 sq. ft.
Gross Weight	5,042 lbs.
High Speed	244mph at 6,560 ft.

Prewar Italian rudder markings were red, white and green stripes, with the crest of the ruling House of Savoy at the top of the white stripe.

FIAT CR 42 FALCON

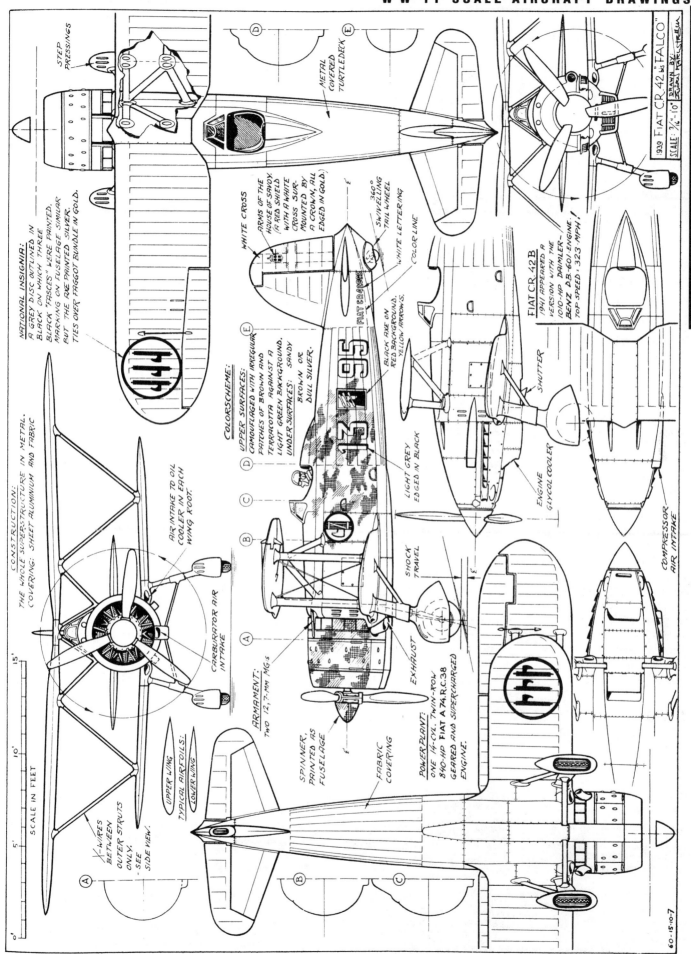

939 FIAT CR 42 bis "FALCO"
DRAWN BY: Björn Karlström
SCALE: 3/16" = 1'-0"

STEP PRESSINGS

METAL COVERED TURTLEDECK

NATIONAL INSIGNIA:
A GREY DISC OUTLINED IN BLACK ON WHICH THREE BLACK "FASCES" WERE PAINTED. MARKING ON FUSELAGE SIMILAR BUT THE AXE PAINTED SILVER. TIES OVER FAGGOT BUNDLE IN GOLD.

WHITE CROSS

ARMS OF THE HOUSE OF SAVOY. (A RED SHIELD WITH A WHITE CROSS SURMOUNTED BY A CROWN, ALL EDGED IN GOLD.

COLORSCHEME:
UPPER SURFACES:
CAMOUFLAGED WITH IRREGULAR PATCHES OF BROWN AND TERRACOTTA AGAINST A LIGHT GREEN BACKGROUND.
UNDER SURFACES: SANDY BROWN OR DULL SILVER.

360° SWIVELLING TAIL WHEEL

WHITE LETTERING

COLOR LINE

BLACK AXE ON RED BACKGROUND. YELLOW ARROWS.

FIAT CR 42 B
1941 APPEARED A VERSION WITH THE 1010-HP DAIMLER-BENZ D.B.601 ENGINE.
TOP SPEED: 323 MPH.!

SHUTTER

ENGINE GLYCOL COOLER

COMPRESSOR AIR INTAKE

CONSTRUCTION:
THE WHOLE SUPERSTRUCTURE IN METAL.
COVERING: SHEET ALUMINIUM AND FABRIC

AIR INTAKE TO OIL COOLER IN EACH WING ROOT.

CARBURATOR AIR INTAKE

LIGHT GREY EDGED IN BLACK

SHOCK TRAVEL

SCALE IN FEET

WIRES BETWEEN OUTER STRUTS ONLY. SEE SIDE VIEW.

UPPER WING
TYPICAL AIRFOILS:
LOWER WING

SPINNER, PRINTED AS FUSELAGE

FABRIC COVERING

EXHAUST

ARMAMENT:
TWO 12,7-MM MG's

POWER PLANT:
ONE 14-CYL. TWIN-ROW 840-HP FIAT A74.R.C.38 GEARED AND SUPERCHARGED ENGINE.

60-15-10-7

FOCKE-WULF 190A

THE design of the Focke-Wulf 190 began in 1937 as a back-up to the Messerschmitt 109 that had been selected as the standard German fighter. The design concept was entirely different, featuring an air-cooled BMW radial engine and a wide-track, inward-retracting landing gear. The first flight of the FW-190V-1 prototype was on June 1, 1939, but production models weren't in combat until September 1941.

As a fighter, the FW-190A outperformed the older British Spitfire Vs that were surpassing the contemporary Me-109s. The Spitfire didn't catch up to the FW-190A until the appearance of the Spitfire IX in July 1942. Although it was designed as a fighter, the FW-190 was readily adaptable to many other missions. The FW-190A reached the -10 variant, with many sub-

A "factory-fresh" FW-190A-1. Note the distinctive rear-sliding canopy and the wide-track landing gear. The unit markings on the fuselage are black.

variants carrying special equipment for specialized missions. These included aerial cameras for reconnaissance, batteries of up to six 30mm cannon for use against tanks and naval torpedoes for attacks against ships. There were even two-seat trainer versions.

Twin-engine German bombers had difficulty reaching targets in England in 1942 and 1943, so some FW-190A-5s were fitted with bomb racks and auxiliary fuel tanks. Normal bomb load was one 500kg (1,100-pound) bomb under

the fuselage and two 250kg (550-pound) bombs under the wings, but some could carry a single 1,000kg (2,200-pound) bomb. This was so close to the ground that the lower fin of the bomb had to be clipped for the plane to take off. These long-range fighter-bombers were very successful in penetrating British defenses and completing effective raids.

The armament differed greatly in fighter versions, from the initial four 7.9mm machine guns (two in the nose and two in the wings), to a standard of two nose guns

and a variety of up to four wing guns or four 20mm wing cannon. For attacks on Allied bomber formations, some FW-190A-5/R6s were fitted with underwing pods for 210mm rockets.

Improved versions of the FW-190 were tested with features such as cabin pressurization and a water-methanol injection that increased the normal 1,600hp of the engine to 2,100hp for brief periods. Other engines were tried: the Me-109's 1,750hp Daimler-Benz DB-603, used in the experimental FW-190C, and the 1,776hp Junkers Jumo 213A, used in the production FW-190D. Later FW-190D variants were so extensively altered from the short-nose, radial-engined FW-190A series that they were redesignated "Ta-152" (for designer Kurt Tank).

Altogether, some 20,000 FW-190s were built in six Focke-Wulf plants, two Arado plants, one Ago plant and one Fieseler plant.

SPECIFICATIONS AND PERFORMANCE FW-190A-8

Wingspan .... 34 ft., 5½ in.

Length .... 20 ft.

Wing Area .... 196.9 sq. ft.

Empty Weight .... 7,000 lbs.

Gross Weight .... 9,750 lbs.

Overload Weight . 10,805 lbs.

High Speed .... 408mph at 19,680 ft.; 355mph at sea level.

Normal Range .... 500 miles

This elevated view of an FW-190A-0 corrects the erroneous crosses on the drawing. Note the narrow borders and the locations of the upper wing crosses. The crosses on the underside of the wing are in the same position, but they're the wide-border type used on the fuselage.

FOCKE-WULF 190A

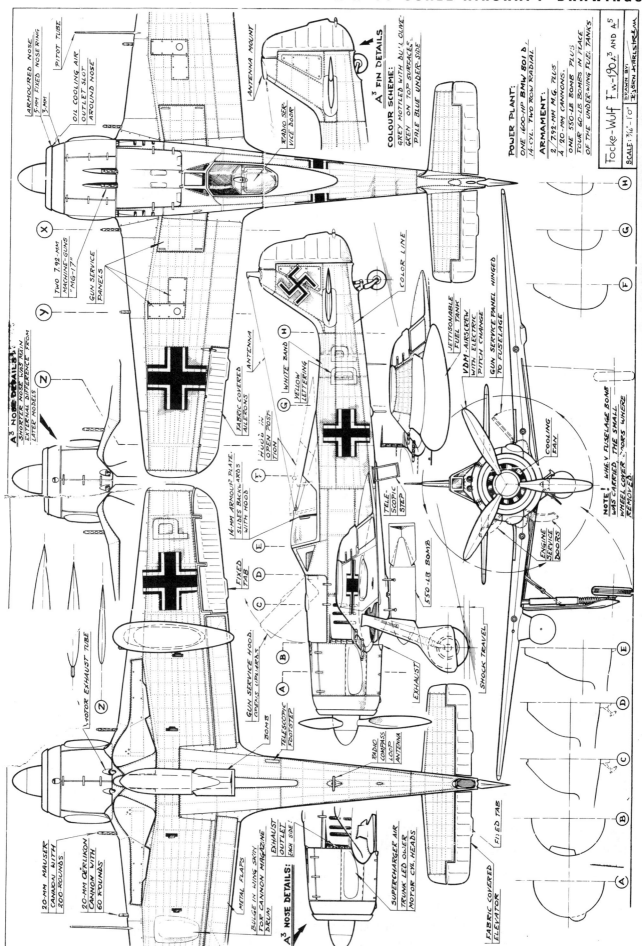

ARMOURED NOSE
5-MM FIXED NOSE RING
3-MM

PITOT TUBE

OIL COOLING AIR
OUTLET SLOT
AROUND NOSE

ANTENNA MOUNT

RADIO SERVICE DOOR

A³ FIN DETAILS

COLOUR SCHEME:
GREY MOTTLED WITH DU'L OLIVE
GREEN ON TOP SURFACES,
PALE BLUE UNDER-SIDE

POWER PLANT:
ONE 1600-HP BMW 801 D,
14-CYL. TWO ROW RADIAL

ARMAMENT:
2/7.92-MM M.G. PLUS
4/20-MM CANNONS.
ONE 550-LB BOMB PLUS
FOUR 60-LB BOMBS IN PLACE
OF THE UNDER-WING FUEL TANKS

Focke-Wulf Fw-190A³ AND A⁵
DRAWN BY: BJÖRN KARLSTRÖM
SCALE: 3/16=1'0"

Two 7.92-MM
MACHINE-GUNS
"MG-17"

GUN SERVICE
PANELS

A³ NOSE DETAILS:
SHORTER NOSE WAS MAIN
EXTERNAL DIFFERENCE FROM
LATER MODELS

FABRIC COVERED
AILERONS

ANTENNA

COLOR LINE

JETTISONABLE
FUEL TANK

VDM AIRSCREW
WITH ELECTRIC
PITCH CHANGE

GUN SERVICE PANEL
HINGED TO FUSELAGE

WHITE BAND H

YELLOW
LETTERING

HOOD IN OPEN POSITION

14-MM ARMOUR PLATE
SLIDES BACKWARDS
WITH HOOD

TELESCOPIC
STEP

550-LB BOMB

COOLING
FAN

ENGINE
SERVICE
DOORS

NOTE! WHEN FUSELAGE BOMB
WAS CARRIED, THE SMALL
WHEEL COVER DOORS WHERE
REMOVED.

FIXED
TAB

GUN SERVICE HOOD.
OPENS UPWARDS.

SHOCK TRAVEL

MOTOR EXHAUST TUBE

BOMB

TELESCOPIC
FOOTSTEP

RADIO
COMPASS
LOOP
ANTENNA

EXHAUST

20-MM MAUSER
CANNON WITH
200 ROUNDS

20-MM OERLIKON
CANNON WITH
60 ROUNDS

METAL FLAPS

BULGE IN WING SKIN
FOR CANNON MAGAZINE
DRUM

SUPERCHARGER AIR
TRUNK LED OVER
MOTOR CYL. HEADS

EXHAUST
OUTLET
(EACH SIDE)

A³ NOSE DETAILS:

FABRIC COVERED
ELEVATOR

FIXED TAB

GLOSTER GLADIATOR

THE evolution of the Gloster Gladiator, England's last biplane fighter, can be traced back to WW I. It was designed by H.P. Folland, who also designed the famous SE-5 used in that war, and the particular chord-gap-stagger relationships of the Gladiator's wings are strongly reminiscent of the SE-5. The Gladiator represented the final stage in England's development of the classic biplane fighter. It featured such latter-day refinements as single-leg landing gear and enclosed cockpit, and it reflected the trend toward increased armament.

The company-owned prototype, then designated S.S.17, flew in September 1934. Orders for 23 and then 186 were placed in July 1935. The Gladiator I's powerplant was the 840hp Bristol Mercury I, which drove a two-blade, fixed-pitch, wooden propeller. Its armament was four .303-caliber machine guns (two in troughs in the fuselage sides and two in the lower wing). Later, a fixed-pitch, three-

This restored Gladiator I has the postwar British civil registration G-AMRK. The prewar R.A.F. serial number was L8032. Note the absence of guns from fuselage troughs and underwing pods.

SPECIFICATIONS AND PERFORMANCE GLADIATOR I

Wingspan .... 32 ft., 3 in.

Length .... 27 ft., 5 in.

Wing Area .... 323 sq. ft.

Gross Weight .... 4,750 lbs.

High Speed .... 253mph at 14,500 ft.

blade metal propeller was adopted.

By the time war started in September 1939, 13 R.A.F. squadrons were equipped with Gladiators, and several squadrons of "navalized" Sea Gladiators were in service aboard aircraft carriers. Extensive export sales started in 1937 and continued after the war began. Twenty-six went to Latvia, 14 to Lithuania and 36 to China. Sweden ordered 55, but 30 of these were later passed to Finland, where they fought Russian Polikarpov L-153 biplanes in the Russo-Finnish war of 1940. Some of these operated on skis.

Belgium received 22 Gladiators; Norway received 12. Most of these, however, were destroyed on the ground by the Luftwaffe in April and

May of 1940. Almost all of the 15 Gladiators sold to Iraq were destroyed by the R.A.F. when they suppressed a revolt there in May 1941.

Two R.A.F. Gladiator squadrons were sent to France as soon as the war started. In April 1940, one squadron was flown to Norway to assist in its defense and was soon joined by several squadrons of Sea Gladiators. In the absence of suitable airfields, these fighters operated from the surfaces of frozen lakes. One squadron of Gladiators fought over England during the Battle of Britain.

Sea Gladiators saw extensive action in the Mediterranean Theater and engaged Italian Fiat CR 42 biplanes over Greece, North Africa and particularly Malta, where four won great fame during their lone defense of the island in

Line-up of nine Gladiator Is in prewar, all-silver finish. Note the large, fixed-pitch wooden propellers, (later replaced with three-blade metal models), and the hinge-down door for cockpit access.

April 1940. The last Gladiators were retired from the R.A.F. late in 1941, but some of the exported and passed-on models continued to fight on.

GLOSTER GLADIATOR

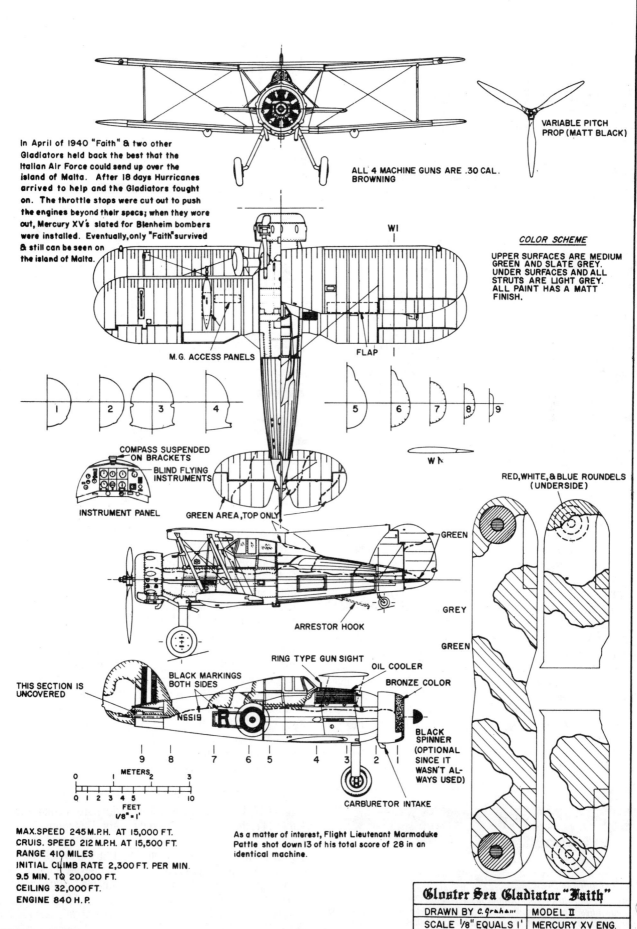

VARIABLE PITCH PROP (MATT BLACK)

In April of 1940 "Faith" & two other Gladiators held back the best that the Italian Air Force could send up over the island of Malta. After 18 days Hurricanes arrived to help and the Gladiators fought on. The throttle stops were cut out to push the engines beyond their specs; when they wore out, Mercury XV's slated for Blenheim bombers were installed. Eventually, only "Faith" survived & still can be seen on the island of Malta.

ALL 4 MACHINE GUNS ARE .30 CAL. BROWNING

W1

COLOR SCHEME

UPPER SURFACES ARE MEDIUM GREEN AND SLATE GREY. UNDER SURFACES AND ALL STRUTS ARE LIGHT GREY. ALL PAINT HAS A MATT FINISH.

M.G. ACCESS PANELS

FLAP

COMPASS SUSPENDED ON BRACKETS

BLIND FLYING INSTRUMENTS

INSTRUMENT PANEL

GREEN AREA, TOP ONLY

W1

RED, WHITE, & BLUE ROUNDELS (UNDERSIDE)

GREEN

ARRESTOR HOOK

GREY

GREEN

RING TYPE GUN SIGHT

OIL COOLER

BRONZE COLOR

BLACK MARKINGS BOTH SIDES

THIS SECTION IS UNCOVERED

N5519

BLACK SPINNER (OPTIONAL SINCE IT WASN'T ALWAYS USED)

CARBURETOR INTAKE

METERS

FEET
1/8" = 1'

MAX. SPEED 245 M.P.H. AT 15,000 FT.
CRUIS. SPEED 212 M.P.H. AT 15,500 FT.
RANGE 410 MILES
INITIAL CLIMB RATE 2,300 FT. PER MIN.
9.5 MIN. TO 20,000 FT.
CEILING 32,000 FT.
ENGINE 840 H.P.

As a matter of interest, Flight Lieutenant Marmaduke Pattle shot down 13 of his total score of 28 in an identical machine.

Gloster Sea Gladiator "Faith"

DRAWN BY C. Graham	MODEL II
SCALE 1/8" EQUALS 1'	MERCURY XV ENG.

(192)

3048/3175 → 96

GRUMMAN F4F WILDCAT

FROM 1934, when Boeing delivered its last F4B-4, until 1939, the Grumman Aircraft Company of Bethpage, Long Island, NY, was the sole supplier of single-seat fighters to the U.S. Navy. In 1936, Grumman designed its Model 16, a biplane fighter that was designated "XF4F-1." Before it was built, however, the Navy ordered a new monoplane fighter, the XF2A-1, from Brewster. Realizing that the era of the biplane fighter was ending, Grumman got Navy authorization to discontinue the XF4F-1 and redesign it as a monoplane, designated "XF4F-2," Grumman Model 18. It flew on September 2, 1937.

The XF4F-2 was powered with a 1,050hp Pratt & Whitney R-1830-66 engine and had two .50-caliber guns mounted in the nose. It lost to the XF2A-1 in the initial Navy fly-off competition, returned to the factory and was extensively rebuilt as the XF3F-3, Grumman Model 36. Grumman won an order for an eventual 285 F4F-3s and 95

A Grumman F4F-3 ready for delivery to Squadron VF-41 aboard the carrier U.S.S. Ranger in December 1940. It was silver, with chrome-yellow wing tops and the green tail that was on all Ranger aircraft. The star insignia on the nose identifies the plane as one that was used in the U.S. Navy's Atlantic Neutrality Patrol in 1940-41.

F4F-3As named "Wildcat," which started the famous line of Grumman Navy fighters with various "Cat" names that continues today.

PRODUCTION GRUMMAN WILDCATS—The production F4F-3s differed from the prototype in that they had a 1,200hp R-1830-76 or -86 engine and four .50-caliber guns in the fixed wings instead of two in the nose. One plane was tested as the

F4F-3S seaplane on twin floats, but it wasn't produced. The F4F-3As had a 1,200hp R-1830-90 engine with single-stage superchargers instead of the two-stage models of the F4F-3. Deliveries of the F4F-3 began in August 1940 and didn't end until May 1943, five months after the last F4F-4 was delivered.

Grumman's major production model was the F4F-4, which differed from the -3 in that it had manually folded wings and six wing guns. Grumman built 1,168 F4F-4s and 220 F4F-4Bs that went to the R.A.F. as "Wildcat IV." The first F4F-4 flew on November 7, 1941; the last was delivered on December 31, 1942.

Grumman built experimental variants of the Wildcat through XF8F-8, but they didn't build any production versions.

GENERAL MOTORS WILDCATS—When Grumman couldn't keep up with the demand for Wildcats, the Navy asked General Motors to become a second source. Parts were built in three GM plants in New Jersey and were brought together for final assembly at GM's Eastern Aircraft Division in Linden, NJ. The 1,060 FM-1s differed from the F4F-4 mainly in that they had only four wing guns but carried more ammunition. The 4,777 FM-2s were production versions of Grumman's XF4F-8, a lighter version of the Wildcat intended for operations from small escort carriers. This model had only four guns and was powered by the 1,350hp Wright R-1820-56 single-row engine. The most notable feature of the XF4F-8 and the FM-2 was the higher vertical tail. Late FM-2s could

An F4F-3 Wildcat with the oversize star insignia and the rudder stripes that were used early in 1942 for positive identification. The fuselage legend 41-F-8 identifies Airplane No. 8 of the first (of two) fighter squadrons aboard Ranger (CV-4), identified by the figure "4." At that time, carrier-based squadrons used the hull number of their parent carrier.

The British Martlet I was one of the 91 Grumman G-36As built for France that couldn't be delivered. This model had two nose guns and two to four wing guns, and Wright Cyclone engines instead of the Pratt & Whitney Twin Wasp of the equivalent F4F-3.

carry up to six 5-inch rockets under the wings. Production of the FM-2 continued until August 1945.

EXPORTED WILDCATS AND MARTLETS—Late in 1939, the Navy authorized the sale of the Grumman Model G-36A (export equivalents of the F4F-3) to France. These differed from the Navy models in that they used the 1,200hp commercial Wright Cyclone G-205A (R-1820) engine, French instrumentation, and the unique French reverse-throttle system in which the throttle was pulled back (rather than pushed forward)

for "open." Its armament was a pair of French Darne 7.5mm guns in the nose and two to four others in the wings. The first of 91 G-36As flew on May 10, 1940, the day Hitler invaded France, so the planes were taken over by Britain. Early in 1941, the Navy released 30 F4F-3As to Greece.

These were sent by ship in March, but Greece fell to Hitler while they were at sea, and they were diverted to England.

BRITISH MARTLETS AND WILDCATS—In addition to the aircraft that it ordered from the U.S., Britain acquired many planes that had been ordered by other countries but couldn't be delivered. The 91 Martlet Is, so named before the Navy named the Wildcat, were French G-36As modified to use British equipment. The 100 Martlet IIs were ordered by the R.A.F. as equivalents to the F4F-3A, but with civil Pratt & Whitney S3C-4G Twin Wasp

engines. The first 10 had fixed wings and four guns; the rest had folding wings and six guns.

Britain decided to go along with the Navy name for the Lend-Lease Wildcats that they received. The 30 F4F-3As destined for Greece were therefore designated "Wildcat III,"

using the Navy name, but continuing to use the Martlet numbers. The 220 Wildcat IVs were Lend-Lease F4B-4Bs ("B" for Britain), the 312 Wildcat Vs were FM-1s and the 370 Wildcat VIs were FM-2s.

WILDCATS IN ACTION—The first combat by Wildcats (actually Martlets) was in October 1940. One of the ex-French G-36As of the Fleet Air Arm based in the Orkney Islands shot down a Junkers Ju 88 for the first victory by an American fighter in British service. Martlets and Wildcats saw extensive service from British carriers throughout the

war, including the invasions of North Africa, Sicily and Italy. Their main service was in the North Atlantic, operating from small escort carriers, where they were highly successful in destroying German aircraft that were shadowing and attacking the Allied convoys.

Initial U.S. Navy and Marine

Corps wartime experience with Wildcats was disastrous. Many were destroyed on the ground during the attacks on Wake Island and Hawaii, and the surviving F4F-3s on Wake Island were soon overwhelmed by superior Japanese forces. The Wildcat was no match for the Japanese Zero, but it could absorb punishment better. By the time the U.S. went on the offensive in August 1942, the Navy had developed Wildcat tactics specifically for use against the Zero, and the victory record became impressive. Of 11 Marine Corps pilots who won the Medal of Honor during the war, six flew Wildcats.

As the Wildcats were replaced on the large carriers by Hellcats, they were reassigned to the smaller escort carriers and saw extensive service in support of the U.S. invasions

Below: General Motors Wildcats. At left, an FM-1, similar to Grumman's F4F-4. At right, an FM-2 in British markings as "Wildcat VI." Note the increased height of the vertical tail on this Cyclone-powered plane.

of Japanese-held islands in the Pacific. Carrier-based Wildcats supported the U.S. invasion of North Africa in November 1942, and, accompanied by British Martlets, shot down many defending Vichy French aircraft, including American-built Curtiss 75 fighters.

★　　　★　　　★

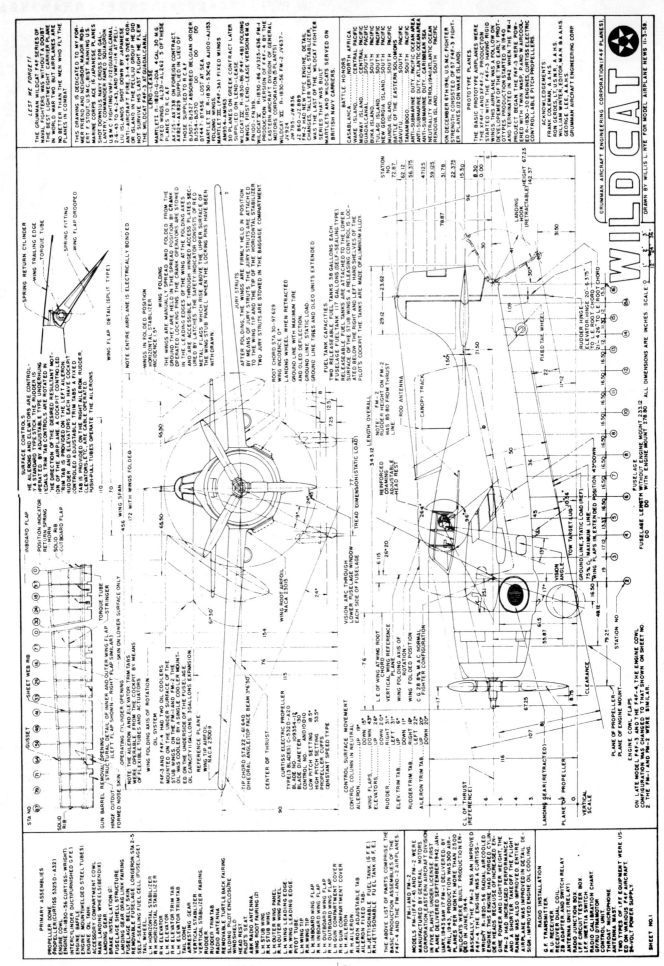

WILDCAT

Grumman Aircraft Engineering Corporation (F4F Planes)

DRAWN BY WILLIS L. NYE for MODEL AIRPLANE NEWS 11-3-59.

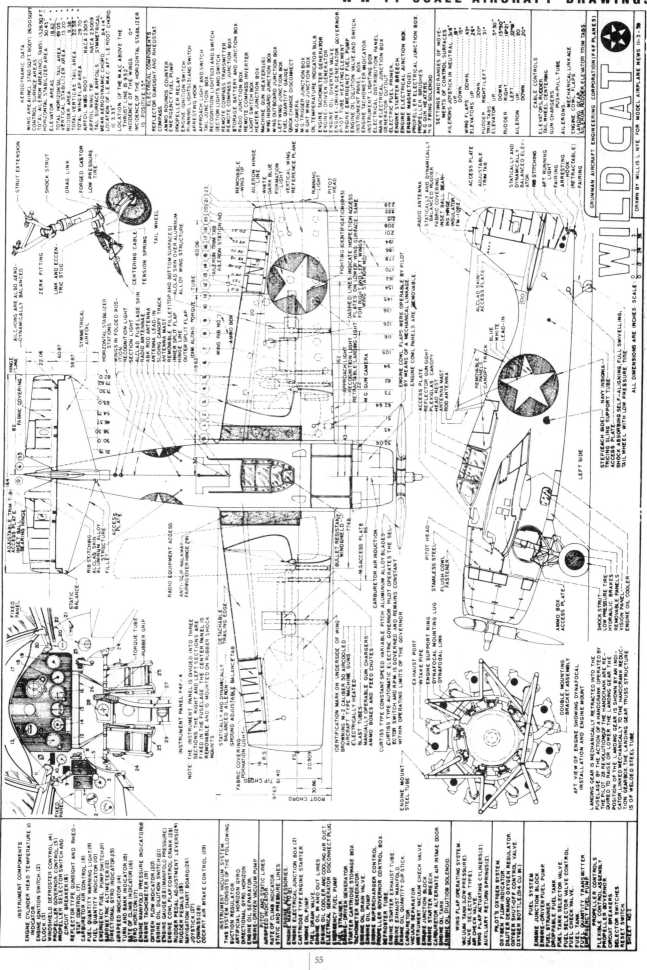

GRUMMAN F4F WILDCAT

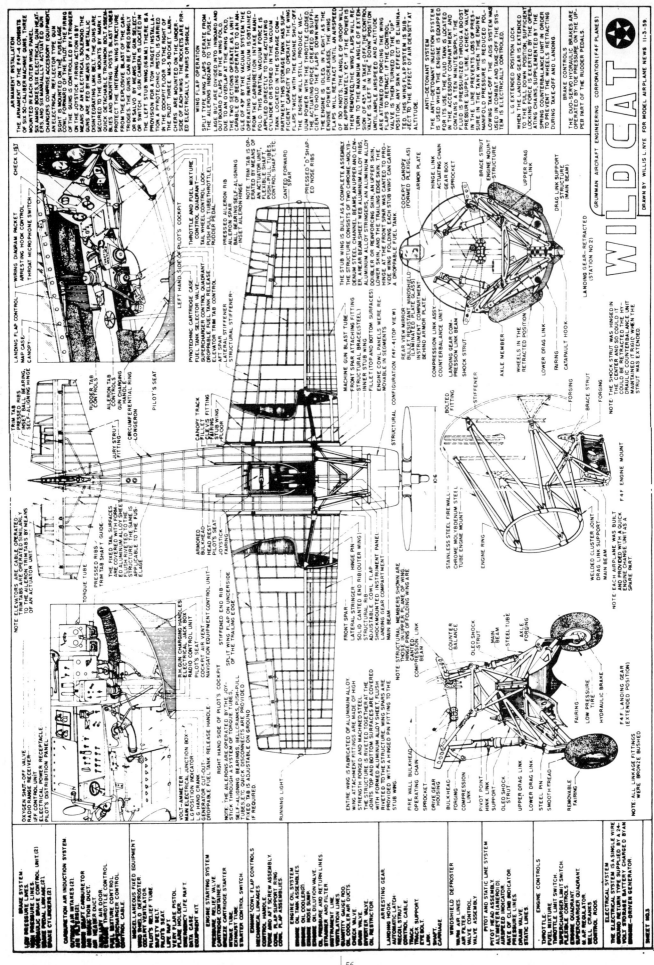

GRUMMAN F4F WILDCAT

WILDCAT

DRAWN BY WILLIS L. NYE FOR MODEL AIRPLANE NEWS 11-3-59.

Grumman Aircraft Engineering Corporation (F4F PLANES)

PERFORMANCE DATA

GROSS WEIGHT	7,340 LBS.
"TAKE-OFF DISTANCE(21 MPH. HEAD WIND)	794 FEET.
BEST CLIMBING SPEED AT SEA LEVEL	144 M.P.H.
LANDING RUN AT SEA LEVEL	794 FEET.
LANDING SPEED (I.A.S.)	84 MPH.
ENGINE MILITARY POWER	96.5 H.G
ENGINE MANIFOLD PRESSURE	
STICK SETTING	LOW
MIXTURE SETTING	AUTO LEAN
FUEL CONSUMPTION(MAXIMUM)	.147 G.P.H.
CRUISING SPEED(23,000 FT.)	252 M.P.H.
FUEL CONSUMPTION(CRUISE)	56 G.P.H.
MAXIMUM SPEED(20,000 FT.)	330 M.P.H.
TAKE-OFF POWER(1200 R.P.M.)	1200 H.P.
NORMAL RATED POWER	1200 H.P.
FUEL GRADE	100/130
SERVICE CEILING	28,000 FT.
MAXIMUM RATE OF CLIMB	

COLOR SYSTEM

THE EXTERIOR SURFACES WERE PAINTED NON-SPECULAR WHITE, INTERMEDIATE BLUE, SEA BLUE AND SEA BLUE SEMI-GLOSS. MARKED COLORS ARE BLENDED TO AVOID HARD EDGES. THIS IS A-VOIDED BY APPLYING THE COLORS IN AN IRREGULAR WAVY LINE AND THEN FEATHERING.

COCKPIT INTERIOR	BLACK
INSTRUMENT PANEL	DARK GREEN
LANDING GEAR FAIRING	BLACK
PITOT TUBE	NON-SPECULAR BLACK
LANDING GEAR	NON-SPECULAR BLACK
WHEELS TO MATCH FUSELAGE AREA	
WALKWAYS	BLACK
ENGINE	BLACK
PROPELLER HUB	BLACK
PROPELLER CUFF	BLACK
PROPELLER BLADE (REAR)	BLACK
PROPELLER BLADE (FRONT)	ALUMINUM
TIRES	BLACK
DROP TANKS	WHITE

NAVY F4F-3P WAS A MODIFIED VERSION INTENDED FOR LONG RANGE PHOTO RECONNAISSANCE. IT WAS EQUIPPED WITH A MULTIPLE AERIAL CAMERA INSTALLATION. ONLY A FEW PLANES WERE SO MODIFIED.

GRUMMAN G-36

THIS AIRPLANE WAS BUILT FOR EXPORT AND VARIOUS FOREIGN COUNTRIES. THE MODEL F4F-3 WITH RIGID WINGS. THE FIRST AIRPLANE CONTRACT FOR F4F-3 WILDCATS WAS DELIVERED TO THE U.S. NAVY IN 1940.

FIRST PRODUCTION

THE FIRST FIGHTERS COMPLYING WITH NAVAL CARRIER QUALIFICATIONS WERE THE MODEL F4F-3 WITH RIGID WINGS.

MACHINE GUN HEATERS

GUN HEATERS ARE LOCATED OVER THE GUN BREECH AND RETRACTING SLIDE. THE CIRCUIT IS CONNECTED DIRECTLY TO THE ELECTRIC GENERATOR.

ELECTRICAL SWITCHES

SECTION LIGHTS
FORMATION LIGHTS
FLASH SWITCH
WING NAV. LIGHTS
TAIL RUNNING LIGHT
GUN MASTER SWITCH
PITOT TUBE HEATER
FUEL PRIMER
GUN SELECTOR (2)
STORAGE BATTERY
RECOGNITION LIGHTS
GENERATOR FIELD
EMERGENCY IGNITION
MASTER RADIO SWITCH
RADIO DESTRUCTOR
MACHINE GUN HEATER
ENGINE IGNITION

RHEOSTATS
ELECTRIC PANEL LIGHTS
COCKPIT LIGHTS
COMPASS LIGHT
INSTRUMENT PANEL
CHART BOARD LIGHT

SCALE FOR FUSELAGE CUTAWAY

FRONT VIEW
(TAKE-OFF ATTITUDE)

HYDRAULIC
BRAKE LINE

FUSELAGE OVERTURN STRUCTURE

NOTE: THE FUSELAGE IS A SEMI-MONOCOQUE STRUCTURE COMPOSED OF CIRCUMFERENTIAL RINGS AND TRANSVERSE BULKHEADS WHICH ARE JOINED BY LONGERONS AND STRINGERS THE STRESSED SKIN COVERING CONSISTS OF ALCLAD FORMED CONE SHAPED SECTIONS OVERLAPPING AT THE JOINTS WHICH ARE SEALED AND FLUSH RIVETED.

NOTE: THE CABLES ARE SCHEMATICALLY SHOWN ACTUAL COURSE OF CABLES VARIES ON THE FULL SIZE PLANE.

NOTE: THE PILOT'S CANOPY SLIDES BACK TO PERMIT ENTRANCE, AND THE CANOPY CAN BE LOCKED AT FOUR POSITIONS. FOR EMERGENCY EXIT, THE CANOPY LOCK IS MANUALLY OPERATED BY AN EXTERIOR RELEASE LEASE/OUTSIDE. THE SIDE LIGHTS ARE CLEAR PLEXIGLAS.

NOTE: THE FUEL TANK CAN BE REMOVED BY REMOVAL OF THE ACCESS PANELS BETWEEN STATIONS 2 AND 5 ON THE BELLY OF THE FUSELAGE.

NOTE: A PILOT'S BAGGAGE COMPARTMENT IS ACCESSIBLE THROUGH A HINGED ACCESS DOOR AT STATION 9 RIGHT SIDE OF FUSELAGE.

LATERAL STIFFENER
WING SKIN
TRUSS MEMBER
FT. SPAR

LATERAL STIFFENER
CRIMPED NOSE

TYPICAL OUTER WING RIB
BUILT IN 3 SECTIONS STA.136.
ALL RIVETED CONSTRUCTION.

CANTED FORWARD SPAR
SOLID WEB

SOLID WEB

NACA 23015
AIRFOIL

0 15 20 25 30 40 50 60 70 80 85 90 95 100

NOTE:
THE F4F-4 COULD NOT OUTPERFORM THE JAPANESE ZERO FIGHTER, BUT BEING A STURDY BUILT AIRPLANE, IT COULD WITHSTAND AERIAL COMBAT DAMAGE TO A GREATER DEGREE AND PROVIDE SAFETY FOR THE PILOT. LATE IN THE WAR, THE WILDCAT AND A JAPANESE ACE, SAKAI FOUGHT AGAINST THE WILDCAT.

NOTE:
FOR FIGHTER BOMBER GROUND SUPPORT OPERATIONS A 100 LB FRAGMENTATION BOMB CAN BE CARRIED ON EACH OUTER RACK. 100 LB FRAGMENTATION BOMBS OR BOMB ET LAUNCHER (2 PER PLANE)

INSIGNIA

NOTE: ROCKET INSTALLATION

EARLY MODEL F4F-4 WERE EQUIPPED WITH SINGLE ROCKET LAUNCHERS ON EACH WING. LATE MODEL F4F-4 AND FM-1 AND -2 WERE FITTED WITH THREE MK-3 ROCKET LAUNCHERS THE ELECTRIC FIRING IS CONTROLLED BY A STATION DISTRIBUTOR AND TWO STREAMLINE STEEL TUBE POSTS THE TWIN LAUNCHER CONSISTS OF A FUSE ARMING CONTROL. THE AFT POST CONTAINS A RECEPTACLE FOR THE ROCKET FIRING LEAD AND A LATCH TO RESTRAIN THE ROCKET UNTIL THE INSTANT OF FIRING. ROCKETRY FIRE ON GROUND TARGETS WAS CONTROLLED BY AIMING THE AIRPLANE. ROCKETS WERE NOT CARRIED ON COMBAT SORTIES AGAINST HOSTILE AIRCRAFT.

NOTE: PERMISSIBLE ACCELERATIONS

GROSS WT. LBS.	POSITIVE ACCELERATION
7400	7.5
8000	7.4
8200	7.0
WITH FILLED DROP TANKS	4.0

ANTI-DETONANT TANK
ANTI-DETONANT REGULATOR UNIT
DOWN DRAFT RAM AIR DUCT
ENGINE BAFFLE RING
CARBURETOR AIR DUCT
PRESSURE BAFFLE
CUFF

REFLECTOR GUN SIGHT
COCKPIT AIR INDUCTION
JURY STRUT FITTING
HINGE PIN FAIRING
WING LOCK
M.G. PORT

SLIDING PLEXIGLAS CANOPY
PILOT'S HEAD REST(ADJUSTABLE)
REFLECTOR TYPE GUNSIGHT
JOYSTICK
PILOT'S SEAT(ADJUSTABLE)
BULLET RESISTING WINDSHIELD
INSTRUMENT PANEL
ARMOR PLATE
FIREWALL(STAINLESS STEEL)
OIL TANK
ENGINE MOUNT

CURTISS 3-BLADE PROPELLER
PROPELLER CONTROL BY THE PILOT'S HEAD REST(ADJUSTABLE)
CONTROL CABLE RUNNING FROM THE GOVERNOR BY MEANS OF AN ELECTRICAL PITCH CHANGE AND A GOVERNOR CONTROL.

BENDIX AIR-OIL
SHOCK STRUT
AIR PRESSURE
200-800PS.I.

REAR VIEW PANORAMIC MIRROR
BULLET RESISTANT PANEL
RADIO ANTENNA
APPROACH LIGHT
HINGE PIN FAIRING
JURY STRUT FITTING
MACHINE GUN PORT

WING FLAP(EXTENDED)
LANDING LIGHT(EXTENDED)
ENGINE OIL COOLER
BENDIX
26 X 6, 8 PLY TIRE
BENDIX DUO-SERVO HYDRAULIC BRAKES

SIDE VIEW DROPPABLE TANK
(PLAN VIEW- SIMILAR)
58 GALLON CAPACITY

NOTE: TIRES ARE INFLATED TO 85 P.S.I. FOR A TAKE OFF AT MAXIMUM GROSS WEIGHT OF 8500 POUNDS. THE DROPPABLE FUEL TANKS ARE USED ONLY FOR LONG RANGE MISSIONS AND RELEASED WHEN THE AIRPLANE ENGAGES IN COMBAT.

JOINT
MK-5 ROCKET
AFT SWAY BRACE
FORE SWAY BRACE
PITCH LIGHT
RUNNING LIGHT

PRESSED ALUMINUM
ALLOY SHELL
WELDED FLANGE

WING FITTINGS

THE WING FITTINGS FOR THE STUB WINGS ARE ATTACHED TO THE FIRING STUB, STRUCTURAL BULKHEAD AND ARE OF THE PIN TYPE.

1 2 3 4 5 6
SCALE

GUN CAMERA
A 16 M.M. ELECTRICALLY OPERATED AND HEATED GUN CAMERA IS LOCATED IN THE LEFT WING STUB WHEN THE GUN TRIGGER IS OPERATED THE CAMERA TAKES A MOVING PICTURE AUTOMATICALLY TO CHECK GUNNERY RESULTS. THE CAMERA TEMPERATURE IS THERMOSTATICALLY CONTROLLED.

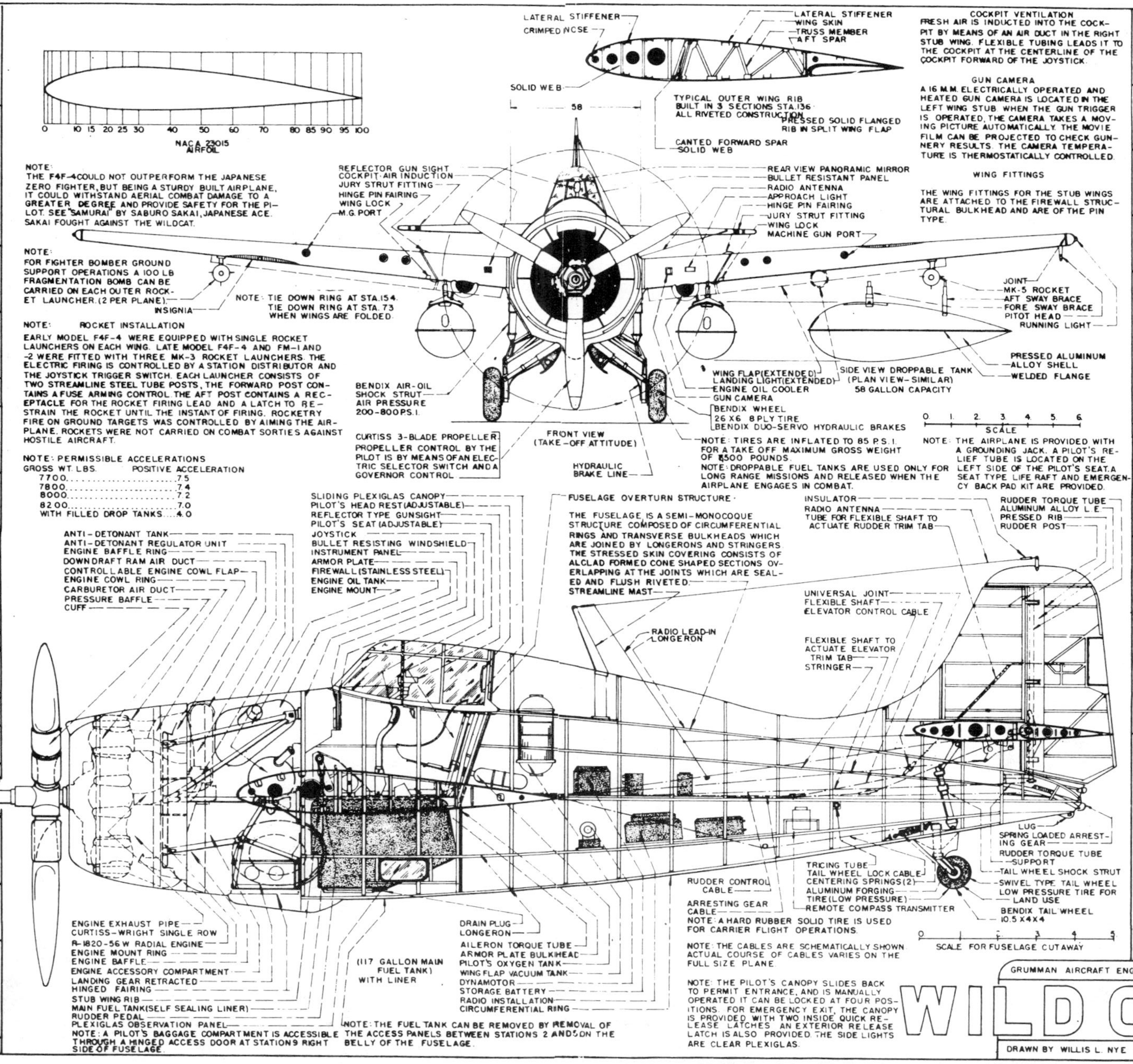

COCKPIT VENTILATION

FRESH AIR IS INDUCTED INTO THE COCKPIT BY MEANS OF AN AIR DUCT IN THE RIGHT STUB WING. A FLEXIBLE TUBE LEADS IT TO THE COCKPIT LEFT SIDE CARRYING ONE OF THE COCKPIT FORWARD OF THE JOYSTICK.

INSULATOR
RADIO ANTENNA
TUBE FOR FLEXIBLE SHAFT TO
ACTUATE RUDDER TRIM TAB

RUDDER TORQUE TUBE
ALUMINUM ALLOY L.E.
PRESSED RIB
RUDDER POST

TRICING TUBE
TAIL WHEEL LOCK CABLE
CENTERING SPRINGS(2)
TIRE(LOW PRESSURE)
REMOTE COMPASS TRANSMITTER

TAIL WHEEL SHOCK STRUT
SWIVEL TYPE TAIL WHEEL
LOW PRESSURE TIRE FOR
CARRIER FLIGHT OPERATIONS
NOTE: A HARD RUBBER SOLID TIRE IS USED FOR CARRIER FLIGHT OPERATIONS.

SPRING LOADED ARRESTING GEAR
RUDDER TORQUE TUBE
SUPPORT
BENDIX TAIL WHEEL
10.5 X 4 X 4

UNIVERSAL JOINT
FLEXIBLE SHAFT
ELEVATOR CONTROL CABLE

FLEXIBLE SHAFT TO
ACTUATE ELEVATOR
TRIM TAB
STRINGER

RUDDER CONTROL
CABLE

ARRESTING GEAR
CABLE

RADIO LEAD-IN
LONGERON

DRAIN PLUG
LONGERON
AILERON TORQUE TUBE
ARMOR PLATE BULKHEAD
PILOT'S OXYGEN TANK
ENGINE DRIVEN VACUUM TANK
GENERATOR
STORAGE BATTERY
RADIO INSTALLATION
CIRCUMFERENTIAL RING

(117 GALLON MAIN
FUEL TANK)
WITH LINER

ENGINE EXHAUST PIPE
ENGINE MOUNT RING
ENGINE ACCESSORY COMPARTMENT
LANDING GEAR RETRACTED
HINGED FAIRING
P-1820-56 W RADIAL ENGINE
STUB WING RIB
MAIN FUEL TANK(SELF SEALING LINER)
PLEXIGLAS OBSERVATION PANEL

Left column technical notes

WINDSHIELD DEFROSTING
THE WINDSHIELD IS DEFROSTED BY THE INTRODUCTION OF HEATED AIR INTO THE SPACE BETWEEN THE FORWARD GLASS AND THE BULLET RESISTANT GLASS. THE HEATED AIR IS DRAINED FROM A SHROUD AND RAM AIR RANGE PROM THE PILOT. IT IS NORMALLY OPERABLE BY THE PILOT. A VALVE OPERABLE BY THE PILOT IS INSTALLED AS WELL AS AN AIR FILTER.

ARRESTING GEAR OPERATION
THE ARRESTING GEAR CONSISTS OF A CARRIER ARRESTING HOOK OPERATED BY THE PILOT. A HOOK OPERATING IN A TRACK INSTALLED AT FUSELAGE STATION 13. THE OPERATION OF THE HOOK IS CONTROLLED BY CABLE THE PILOT. BY MEANS OF A CABLE THE HOOK LOADS ON THE CABLE BY MEANS OF A LATCH REACHING HOOK LOADS ARE TRANSMITTED FROM THE ARRESTING HOOK TO THE FUSELAGE STRUCTURE. SPRING AND SHOCK STRUT MAINTAINS FORCE ON THE HOOK WHEN IT IS EXTENDED.

CATAPULTING
THE AIRPLANE CAN BE CATAPULTED FROM THE DECK OF AN AIRCRAFT CARRIER. FITTINGS ARE PROVIDED ON THE LANDING GEAR SUPPORT STRUCTURE AND THE EMPENNAGE.

ENGINE OIL DILUTION
SOLENOID VALVE.
DIVERTER VALVE.
RESTRICTED OIL DILUTION FITTING.
MANUALLY OPERATED SHUT-OFF VALVE.

PROPELLER GOVERNOR OPERATION
THE ENTIRE PROPELLER IS ELECTRICALLY CONTROLLED PROPELLER RPM. IS CONTROLLABLE BY THE PILOT WITHIN THE RANGE OF THE GOVERNOR. ONCE THE RPM IS SET, THE GOVERNOR CONTROLS THE RPM BY LOW OR HIGH BLOWER, DEPENDING UPON THE OPERATING RANGE OF THE GOVERNOR. THE GOVERNOR IS NOT EFFECTIVE OVER 2700 R.P.M.

ENGINE STARTER OPERATION
THE ENGINE STARTER BREECH IS LOCATED ON THE RIGHT SIDE OF THE ENGINE COMPARTMENT. A CARTRIDGE IS INSERTED INTO THE BREECH. PILOT FIRES THE CARTRIDGE ELECTRICALLY. THE EXPANDING GASES ENERGIZE THE ENGINE GEAR MECHANISM. 8 CARTRIDGES ARE CARRIED IN A CONTAINER.

ENGINE EXHAUST SYSTEM
THE EXHAUST PIPES ARE ATTACHED TO THE ENGINE EXHAUST PORTS. FOUR PIPES ON THE LEFT SIDE AND FIVE ON THE RIGHT SIDE. THE ENGINE COWLING IS CONCAVE AND IS MADE OF STAINLESS STEEL.

ENGINE QUICK CHANGE UNIT
THE ENGINE QUICK CHANGE UNIT IS SUPPLIED AS A SPARE TO FACILITATE ENGINE CHANGE. AND REPAIR UNDER COMBAT MAINTENANCE CONDITIONS. THE UNIT CONSISTS OF ALL COMPONENTS WHICH ARE ATTACHED TO THE ENGINE ON THE ENGINE MOUNT. INCLUDED IN THE UNIT ARE THE COWLING AND THE ENGINE MOUNT.

CARBURETOR AIR FILTER
AIR FILTERS ARE INSTALLED IN THE CARBURETOR AIR HEADER.

MACHINE GUN CHARGERS
THE MACHINE GUN CHARGERS ARE CABLE OPERATED. THE HANDLES FOR MANUAL OPERATION ARE LOCATED ON EACH SIDE OF THE PILOT'S SEAT.

MACHINE GUN FIRING
THE GUNS ARE FIRED ELECTRICALLY BY SOLENOIDS MOUNTED ON EACH GUN. THEY CAN BE FIRED AS A BATTERY OR IN UNITS SELECTED BY A SELECTOR SWITCH. THE SELECTOR SWITCH MAKES THIS POSSIBLE. STICK TYPES. GUNS ARE MANUALLY AND OPTICALLY BORESIGHTED.

SHEET NO. 4

GRUMMAN TBF AVENGER

WHEN the obsolete Douglas TBD-1 Devastator was retired after the Battle of Midway in June 1942, the Grumman-designed Avenger became the only designated Torpedo-Bomber to serve with the U.S. Navy. Other types could and did carry and launch torpedoes, but that wasn't their primary duty.

In April 1940, the Navy awarded Grumman a contract to design and build two XTBF-1s (Grumman Model G-40). These followed the Navy tradition of a using a large, three-seat, single-engine airplane as its dedicated torpedo plane. The configuration of the TBF, later named "Avenger," drew heavily on Grumman's F4F fighter. It featured the same kind of wing folding, but had the landing gear installed on a fixed stub center section, with the wheels retracting outward into the outer wing panels. A naval torpedo or up to 2,000

A General Motors-built TBM-1 Avenger. The blue-gray and light-gray color scheme was used into early 1943; the centerless, unbordered star was used from May 15, 1942, through June 29, 1943.

pounds of bombs could be carried in a completely enclosed bomb bay—the first on a Navy torpedo plane. The initial armament was a single .50-caliber machine gun in the nose, a single .50-caliber in a dorsal turret and a single .30-caliber firing rearward from the belly.

The first XTBF-1 flew on August 1, 1941; the first production model, ordered in December 1940, flew in January 1942. Because Grumman's plant was heavily involved in fighter production, the Eastern Aircraft plant of General Motors was asked to build Avengers (in addition to the Wildcats already being built there), and designate them "TBMs." The two plants produced 9,836 Avengers: 2,990 by Grumman and 7,546 by General Motors. Grumman's production ended early in 1944, but General Motors carried on until the postwar cancellations.

While both firms developed several experimental variants of the Avenger, the principal production versions were -1s from Grumman and -1s and -3s from GM. Grumman built 1,525 TBF-1s and 764 TBF-1Cs (the latter had two .50-caliber guns in the wings). General Motors built 550 TBM-1s, 2,730 TBM-1Cs and 4,657 TBM-3s.

Special-purpose variants of the Avenger were plentiful. The TBF-1D had special radar, and the TBF-1CP had reconnaissance cameras. The TBF-1E had search radar for anti-submarine patrol, the TBF-1J was equipped for all-weather flying, and the TBF-1L carried a searchlight in the bomb bay for night attack missions.

Similar suffix letters (plus others) applied to the TBM-3s. The TBM-3H had special search radar, and the TBM-3W, widely used after the war, had APS-20 search radar in a large belly radome, which required additional vertical fins for longitudinal stability. The similar TBM-3W2 had the dorsal turret removed and faired over. These planes teamed with TBM-3S Strike variants to form anti-submarine Hunter-Killer pairs. Other postwar TMB-3 variants were the TBM-3U target tug, the TBM-3N night fighter, the

A Grumman TBF-1 with two-tone camouflage and the Navy rudder stripes used only from January 4, 1942, through May 15, 1942.

A TBM-3 with the white and gray camouflage adopted in June 1944 for anti-submarine patrol missions. Note the underwing posts for rockets and the camera outboard of the rocket mounts.

TBM-3Q (for radar counter-measures) and the seven-seat TBM-3R transport.

Britain's Royal Navy received 957 Avengers (which they originally named "Tarpon") as follows: Avenger I, 401 TBF-1Bs ("B" for Britain) and TBF-1Cs; Avenger II, 334 TBM-1s; Avenger III, 222 TBM-3.

The combat debut of the Avenger at the Battle of Midway on June 6, 1942, was a complete disaster. Crews from Torpedo Squadron 8 on the carrier U.S.S. Hornet flew six new TBF-1s from the East Coast all the way to Hawaii. There they found that their ship, with the squadron's old TBDs, had already left for Midway Island, so the Avengers had to fly there.

The battle, although a major victory for the U.S., was a disaster for Torpedo 8. It proved that big, slow, low-level torpedo planes couldn't penetrate the defenses of a complete fleet on the open sea that was defended by surface guns and carrier-based fighters. All of Torpedo 8's TBDs and five of its six TBFs were wiped out, and the survivor was severely crippled. The major damage to the Japanese ships was done by Douglas SBD Dauntless dive bombers.

Loss of the torpedo planes in this first attack on a complete high-seas fleet didn't diminish the Navy's interest in the type (as shown by the production figures), but it did change their tactics. TBMs remained in first-line fleet service until June 1954, and others served in the reserve training squadrons for several more years. Surplus Avengers were widely used as aerial tankers (to fight forest fires), and some are still in use in 1990—50 years after the Avenger was designed.

☆　　☆　　☆

In a typical WW II publicity photo, Navy crewmen load a torpedo into the bomb bay of a TBM-1.

A General Motors TBM-3 Guppy with a belly radome and faired-over dorsal gun turret. Note the added fin area. It had the overall glossy sea-blue camouflage adopted for ship-based fighters in March 1944. Other carrier types adopted it in October.

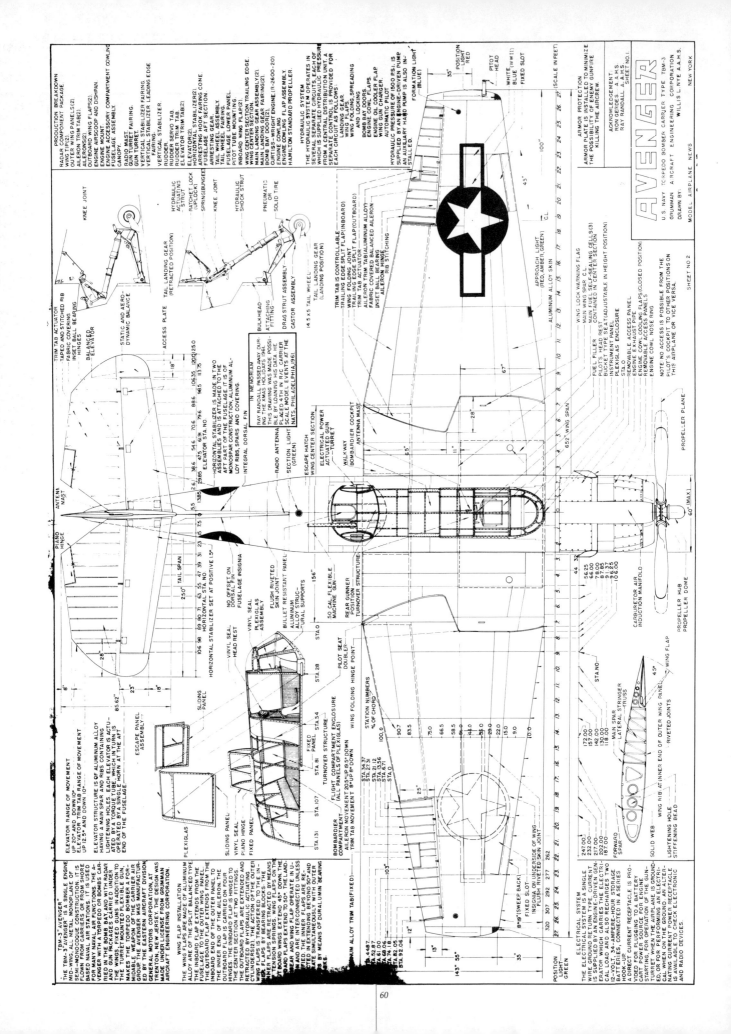

AVENGER

U.S. NAVY TORPEDO BOMBER CARRIER TYPE TBM-3

GRUMMAN AIRCRAFT ENGINEERING CORPORATION

DRAWN BY
WILLIS L. NYE A.A.H.S.

MODEL AIRPLANE NEWS   SHEET NO.1

ACKNOWLEDGED
RON GERIDES A.A.H.S.
RAY RANDALL A.A.H.S.
NEW YORK

60

GRUMMAN TBF AVENGER

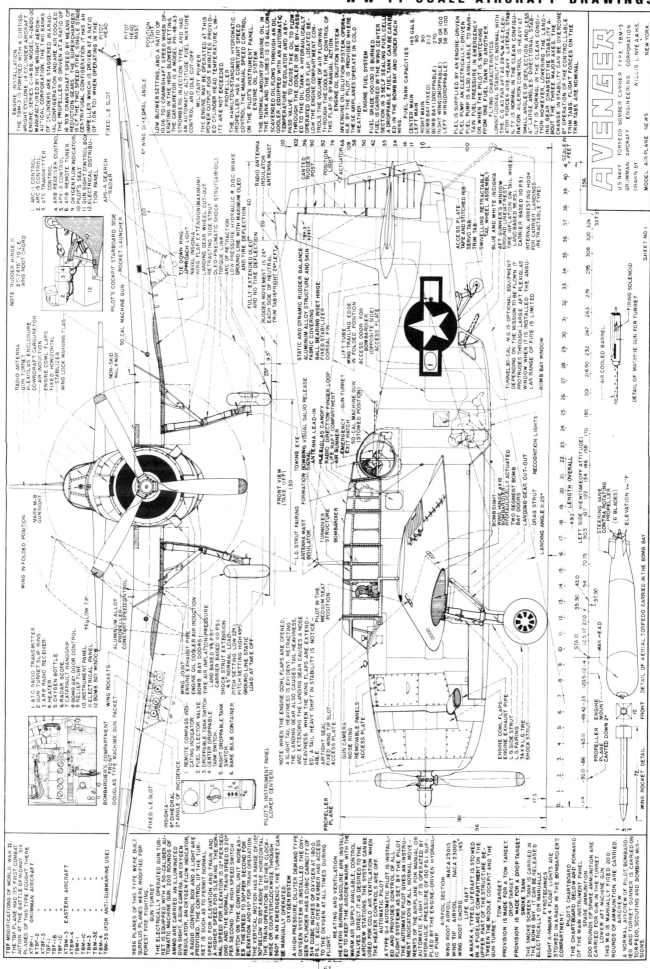

AVENGER

U.S. NAVY TORPEDO BOMBER CARRIER TYPE. TBM-3
GRUMMAN AIRCRAFT ENGINEERING CORPORATION
TBM-3, WILLIS L. NYE A.A.H.S.
MODEL AIRPLANE NEWS
New York.

SHEET NO. I

DETAIL OF MACHINE GUN FOR TURRET

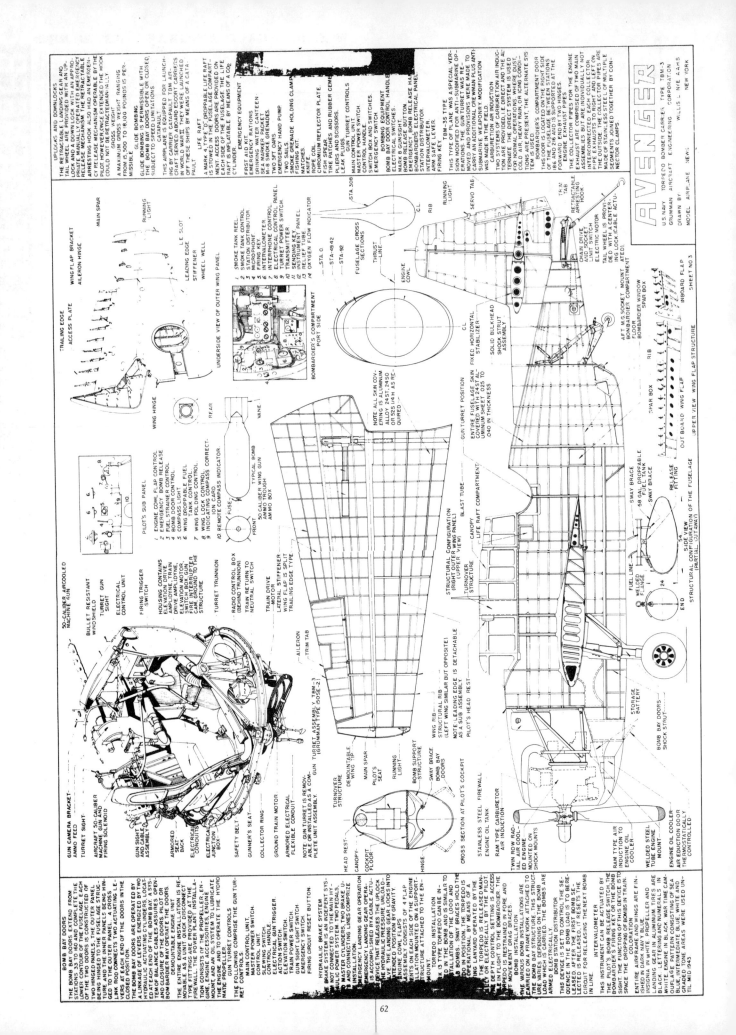

AVENGER

U.S. NAVY TORPEDO BOMBER CARRIER TYPE TBM-3

GRUMMAN AIRCRAFT ENGINEERING CORPORATION

DRAWN BY — WILLIS L. NYE, A.A.H.S.

MODEL AIRPLANE NEWS NEW YORK

SHEET No 3

GRUMMAN TBF AVENGER

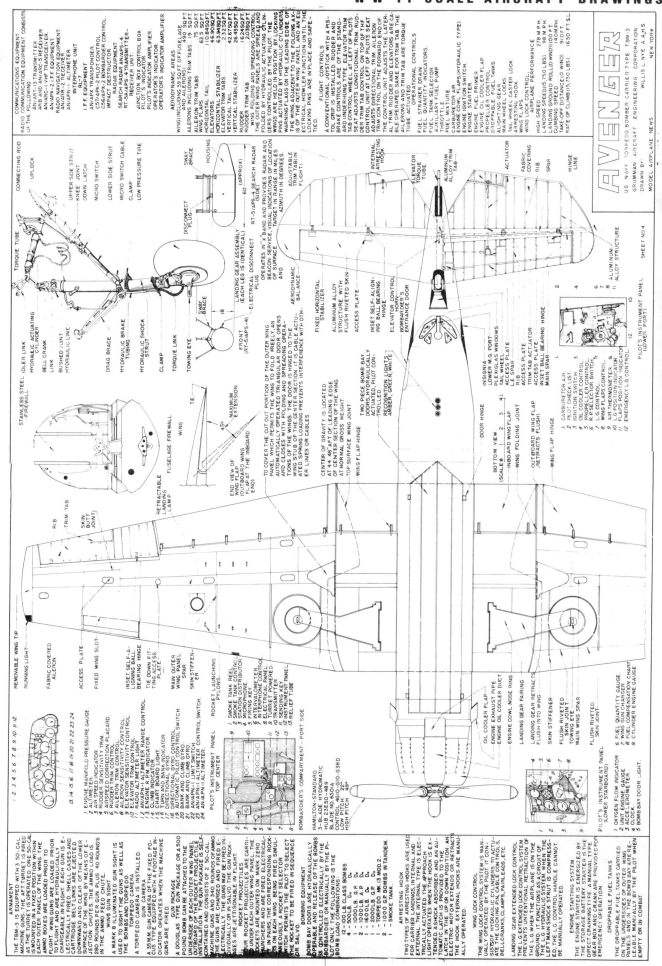

GRUMMAN F6F HELLCAT

An early production F6F-3 Hellcat with the two-tone gray camouflage that was still used in early 1943. Note the use of stars on both wings and the use of fairings around the muzzles of the six wing guns (later deleted).

AFTER studies convinced Grumman that the performance of the F4F Wildcat couldn't be improved by the installation of a larger engine, the company opted for an entirely new design—the Grumman 50. The model carried six .50-caliber machine guns and was powered by the 1,600hp Wright R-2600 Twin Cyclone engine. It differed most from the F4F in that its wing was lower and it had rearward-retracting landing gear, which was in the wing rather than in the fuselage. Also, the landing gear retracted aft while rotating 90 degrees to lay flat in the trailing edge of the wing in the same manner as the Curtiss P-40. Retained from the F4F was the manually folding wing with a 45-degree hinge.

A wooden mock-up of the new design was built for Navy inspection, which took place on January 12, 1941. In June, the Navy placed an order for two XF6F-1 prototypes with 1,700hp (T.O.) R-2600-10 engines.

F6F-5s on the deck of the USS Essex in April 1945. Note the belly tanks and underwing rockets on both airplanes, and the deck crew manually folding one plane's wing (center). The various white markings shown here were adopted in late 1943 to identify airplanes from different aircraft carriers.

As is often the case, many changes were made between the mock-up and the first flying prototype, most notably an increase in wingspan, from 31 feet, 4 inches to 33 feet, 6.5 inches; wing area, from 290 to 334 square feet; and length, from 41 feet, 6 inches to 42 feet, 10 inches. There were also many changes in installed equipment. The first XF6F-1, now officially named "Hellcat," flew on June 21, 1942. A notable detail not seen on the production Hellcats was a large propeller spinner.

The second prototype would have had a turbo-supercharged version of the R-2600 engine and been redesignated "XF6F-2." The Navy, however, directed a change to the 2,000hp (T.O.) Pratt & Whitney R-2800-10 engine, so the airplane was redesignated "XF6F-3" and became the prototype of the production articles. It first flew on July 30, 1942. After a crash caused by engine failure, the XF6F-3 was rebuilt as the XF6F-4 with an

Shown above is an F6F-3 with the short-lived red-bordered insignia and the new (since February 1943) camouflage that used dark blue-gray for top surfaces and graduated to glossy white for undersurfaces. Below: an F6F-5N (with a 20mm cannon and a wing-tip radar pod) that shows off the glossy, overall sea-blue camouflage that was adopted for carrier-based fighters in February 1944 and later expanded to cover most U.S. Navy tactical planes and some support planes.

R-2800-27 engine, and was later used to test cannon armament.

The abandoned XF6F-2 designation was revived in 1944 when the last production F6F-3 was fitted with a turbo-supercharged R-2800 engine with a four-blade propeller.

Delivery of the 4,402 production F6F-3s from Bethpage began early in 1943. The Hellcats entered combat on August 31, 1943, during an attack on Marcus Island in the Western Pacific. Later-production -3s had a rack under the right wing for up to 1,000 pounds of bombs.

Production variants of the F6F-3 were 150 F6F-3N night fighters with APS-6 radar in a pod built into the right wing; 18 similar F6F-3E night intruders with APS-4 radar; and several F6F-3Ps with long-focal-length cameras mounted vertically in the fuselage. All of these variants retained their six-gun wing armament and could also carry a 150-gallon drop tank under the fuselage. A total of 252 F6F-3s was provided to Britain's Fleet Air Arm

(FAA) under Lend-Lease. They were to have been designated "Gannet," but the British decided to use the American designation of "Hellcat I."

After the war, many F6F-3s were converted to unmanned, radio-controlled drones that were designated "F6F-3K" for use as anti-aircraft targets, for research into atom-bomb clouds and, in some cases, as guided bombs.

Although outwardly similar to the F6F-3, the 7,868 F6F-5s differed in that they had water-injected R-2800-10W engines, additional armor and revised engine cowlings and wind-shields. Racks for up to 1,000 pounds of bombs could now be carried under each wing, and late production articles could be fitted with racks for five 5-inch rockets under each wing. Deliveries began in April 1944.

Variants were as for the F6F-3, notably 1,189 F6F-5Ns with APS-6 radar pods. Some late -5Ns had their inboard .50-caliber machine guns replaced with 20mm cannon.

There were also F6F-5E night intruders and F6F-5P photoplanes. Britain received 925 F6F-5s.

It should be noted that by 1944, Britain had begun to use prefix letters to identify special-purpose variants of basic models. The 849 plain F6F-5s became Hellcat II, but the 76 F6F-5Ns became Hellcat N.F.II ("N.F." for Night Fighters).

The last of 12,275 Hellcats, all built at Bethpage, was delivered on November 21, 1944. After the war, some F6F-5s were converted to F6F-5K drones, while others became F6F-5D drone controllers. In later years, F6F-5s were provided to Argentina, France, Paraguay and Uruguay for their naval air forces. The U.S. Navy used F6F-5Ns as night fighters until 1953, and others were used by the reserve training squadrons into 1956.

The Hellcat was the Navy's most numerous carrier-based fighter and it quickly proved its superiority over the previously invincible Mitsubishi A6M Zero. It was also the Navy's most combat-effective fighter and is officially credited with 4,947 air-to-air victories by carrier-based units, with a further 209 credited to land-based and Marine Corps units. Some of the British Hellcats were modified in England to carry British rocket launchers and became Hellcat F.R. II fighter-reconnaissance models, while a few became P.R. II photo-reconnaissance versions. Put into service in December 1943, the British Hellcats saw action over the English Channel in April 1944. Eleven squadrons served in Southeast Asia seas until the end of the war. The last Hellcats left British service in August 1946 and were returned to the U.S. with the other Lend-Lease models.

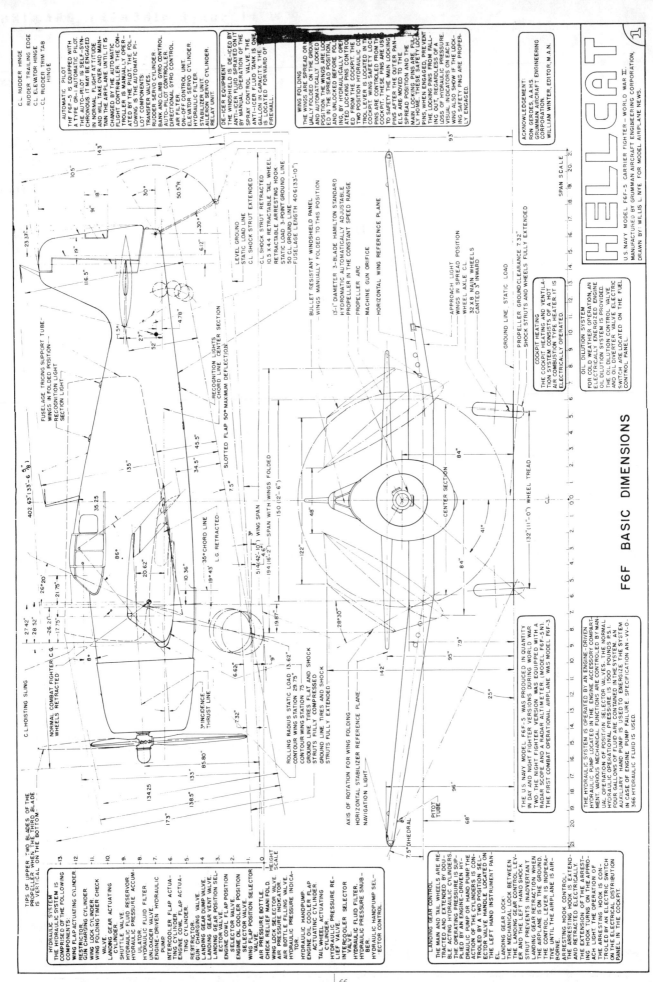

HELLCAT

F6F BASIC DIMENSIONS

U.S. NAVY MODEL F6F-5 CARRIER FIGHTER — WORLD WAR II.
MANUFACTURED BY GRUMMAN AIRCRAFT ENGINEERING CORPORATION.
DRAWN BY WILLIS L. NYE FOR MODEL AIRPLANE NEWS.

ACKNOWLEDGEMENT:
RON GERDES, A.A.H.S.
GRUMMAN AIRCRAFT ENGINEERING
CORPORATION.
WILLIAM WINTER, EDITOR, M.A.N.

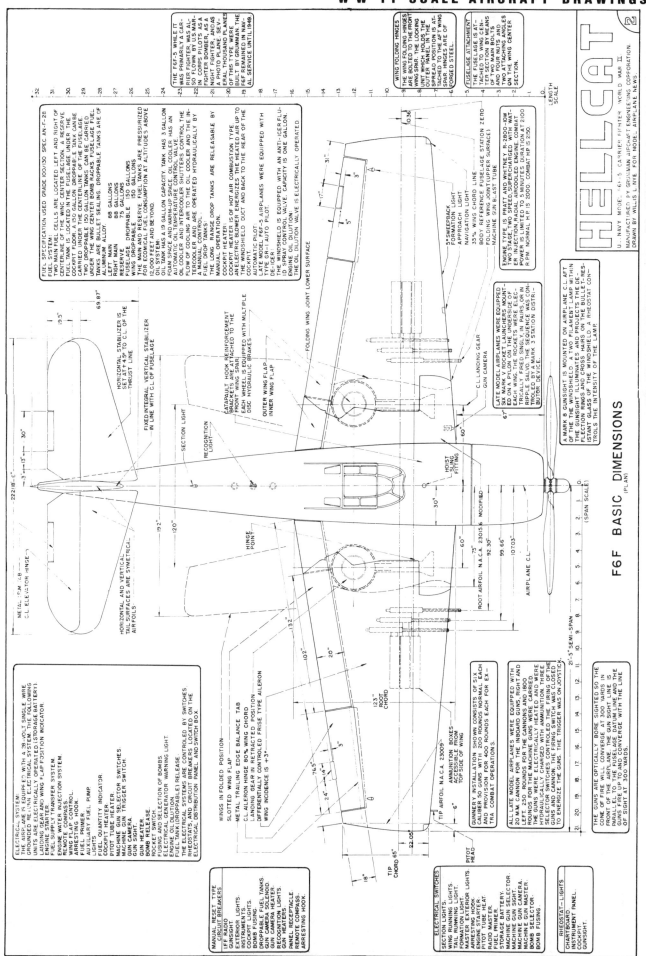

GRUMMAN F6F HELLCAT

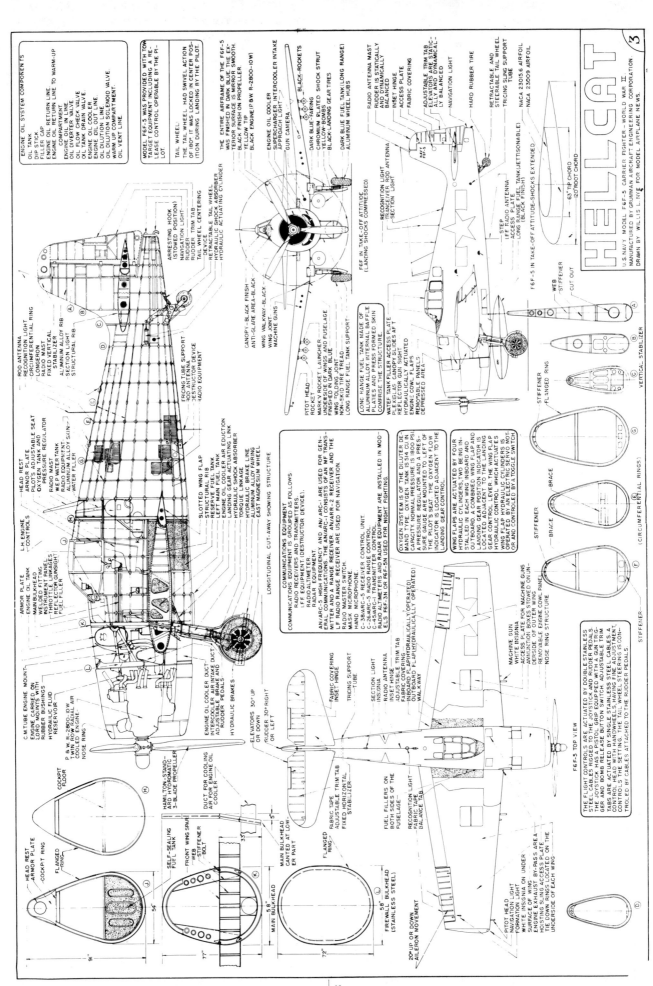

HELLCAT

U.S. NAVY MODEL F6F-5 CARRIER FIGHTER - WORLD WAR II.
MANUFACTURED BY GRUMMAN AIRCRAFT ENGINEERING CORPORATION.
DRAWN BY WILLIS L. NYE FOR MODEL AIRPLANE NEWS.

GRUMMAN F6F HELLCAT

HELLCAT

U.S. NAVY MODEL F6F-5 CARRIER FIGHTER WORLD WAR II
MANUFACTURED BY GRUMMAN AIRCRAFT ENGINEERING CORPORATION
DRAWN BY WILLIS L NYE FOR MODEL AIRPLANE NEWS

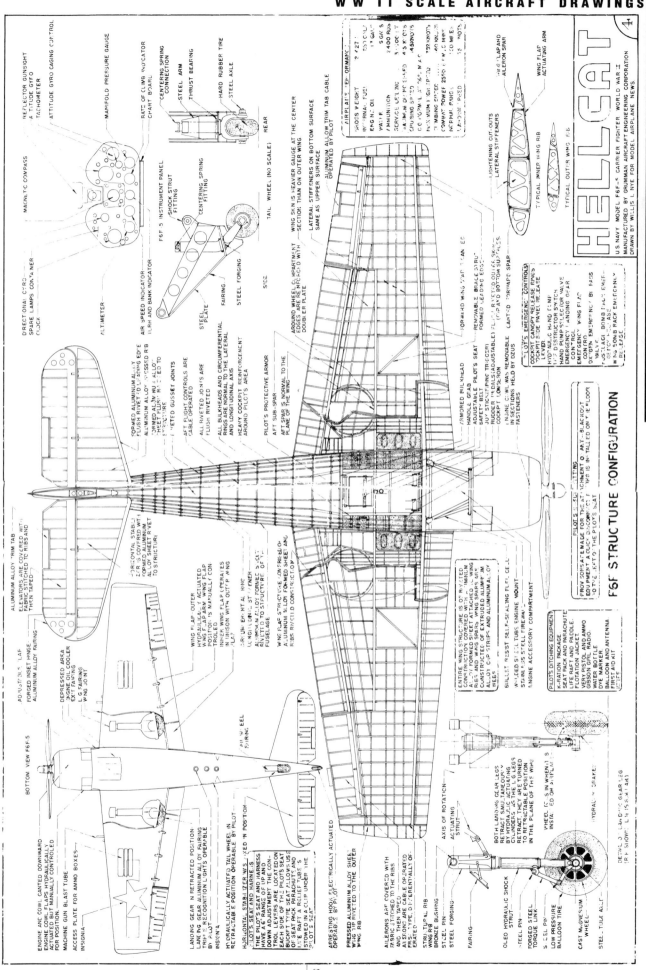

F6F STRUCTURE CONFIGURATION

HAWKER HURRICANE

A Hawker-built Hurricane IIC with a tropical air filter, two 44 Imperial Gallon drop tanks and four 20mm cannon.

THE Hawker Hurricane was a major milestone in the evolution of British fighter planes. Monoplanes weren't new to the type, but the Hurricane set new standards of armament and performance in one stroke. When it appeared in 1935, with eight guns, it was the world's most heavily armed fighter, and it was Britain's first to exceed 300mph.

Delivery of the Hurricane to the squadrons began at the end of 1937, and the plane went on to play a major role in the Battle of Britain in 1940. Although much of that glory must be shared with the Supermarine Spitfire, the Hurricane did the majority of the defensive work. There were 32 Hurricane squadrons in the battle (compared to 19 Spitfire squadrons), and the Hurricane's simple structure enabled damaged aircraft to be repaired more quickly. Its easy-maintenance features also reduced turnaround time.

Design of the Hurricane began as a private venture by the Hawker Aircraft Company of Kingston-On-Thames in January 1934, when Sidney Camm became aware of a new 910hp Rolls-Royce engine that was being developed. Camm sought to design a new monoplane to capitalize on this advanced engine, which was later ordered into production as the famous "Merlin."

Previous Hawker fighters had all been biplanes, and the new Hurricane was a prime example of a transitional design. The details of the fuselage, tail, nose and radiator of the monoplane closely resembled those of the biplanes, but its major difference was the fitting of a metal-frame, fabric-covered monoplane wing that contained an inward-retracting landing gear in place cf the biplane's lower wing. In September 1934, Hawker showed drawings of the new design (which used two nose guns and one gun in each wing) to the Air Ministry. An official specification was written to cover the design, and a contract for a prototype was awarded on January 10, 1934.

During construction, the armament was revised to use eight .303-rifle-caliber machine guns that were entirely enclosed in the thick wing (the guns noted on the drawings should be .303 rather than the stated .30 caliber). The prototype flew on November 1, 1935, and demonstrated a high speed of 315mph at 16,200 feet (5,000 meters). Production orders followed for a total of 3,759 Hurricane Is, and later models brought the total number of Hurricanes to 14,557.

Early production Hurricanes were fitted with 1,030hp Merlin II engines that drove two-blade, fixed-pitch,

The first production Hurricane I, with a fixed-pitch, wooden propeller. Note how orthochromatic film makes the red and yellow of the Type A.1 fuselage roundel appear dark, and the blue appear light.

The last Hurricane built: a Mark IIC. Note "The Last of the Many" painted below the cockpit. There's a Type C.1 roundel on the fuselage and a Type B roundel on the wing top.

wooden propellers, but these were soon replaced with variable-pitch, three-blade metal units. Production was increased by building Hurricanes at the Gloster Aircraft Company and the Austin Motor Company in England and at the Canadian Car and Foundry Company in Canada. Licenses to build Hurricanes were also granted to some "friendly" countries, but the outbreak of war cancelled most of these projects.

The Hurricane adopted several significant state-of-the-art improvements during the production of the Mark I. The wing structure was changed to all-metal; constant-speed propellers were adopted; and armor for the pilot and fuel tanks was added. For service in North Africa and in the Middle East, a "tropicalized" version was developed that featured dust filters for the engine air intake and other details which were dictated by operations and maintenance in desert conditions. Hurricanes were also adapted to naval operations from aircraft carriers by the fitting of arrester hooks, and operated under the name "Sea Hurricane."

The appearance of the 1,280hp Merlin XX engine with a two-stage supercharger resulted in the major Hurricane model—the Mark II—which had many variants, mostly in the arrangement of armament. Two different wings were built, one for 12 .303 guns (Mark IIB) and the other for four 20mm cannon, plus hard

points for up to 500-pound bombs (Mark IIC). The Mark IIA had the original eight-gun wing; the Mark IID had two 40mm cannon that were mounted below the wing.

There was to have been a British-built Hurricane III with the American Packard-Merlin engine, but it was never produced. The Hurricane IV (originally the "Mark IIE"), with a 1,620hp Merlin 27 engine, was designed for

A Gloster-built Sea Hurricane IB with an arrester hook extended (top), and a Hawker-built IIB carrying 250-pound bombs. Compare the color rendition of the roundels when photographed on panchromatic film with a yellow filter.

low-level attack missions with a wing that could be fitted with two 40mm cannons, bombs, drop tanks, or rockets. There were only two Hurricane Vs. These were Mark IVs that were fitted with 1,635hp Merlin 32 engines and four-blade propellers. After testing, they were reconverted to Mark IVs.

In Canada, use of the Packard-Merlin 28 engine and American Hamilton-Standard propellers in the basic Mark IIB

airframe resulted in the Mark X in 1941. The Mark XI was similar except for its Canadian equipment. The Mark XII used the Packard-Merlin 29 and had a 12-gun wing; the Mark XIIA had eight guns.

Altogether, Hawker built 9,900 Hurricanes; Gloster, 2,749; Austin, 300; Canadian Car, 1,606; and Avions Fairey (in Belgium), 2. The last Hurricane built, a Mark IIC, was delivered by Hawker in September 1944.

As a fighter, the Hurricane was generally surpassed by the German Messerschmitt Me 109. As the Hurricane was improved, so was the Me 109. The Hurricane was outclassed as an interceptor fighter by mid-1942, but with the new wing and heavier armament, it became a highly successful low-level fighter-bomber and tank buster.

Some 2,952 Mark IIs and IVs were supplied to Russia during the war, and this produced quite an oddity. Hawker sold 12 Hurricanes to Finland in January 1940 during that country's first war with Russia, and by the time of the second, or "Continuation," war, the Russians also had Hurricanes. Further, in a reversed Lend-Lease operation, Britain supplied Hurricanes to American fighter squadrons that arrived in Europe and North Africa but were not yet equipped with American fighters.

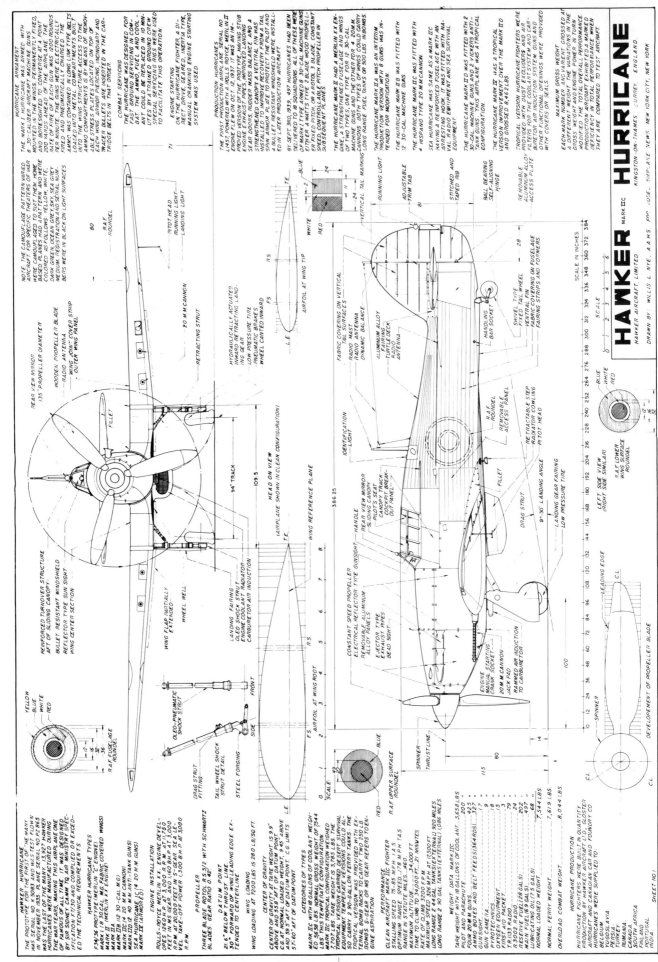

HAWKER HURRICANE

MARK IIC

HAWKER AIRCRAFT, LIMITED   KINGSTON-ON-THAMES   SURREY   ENGLAND

DRAWN BY: WILLIS L. NYE, A.A.H.S.   FOR MODEL AIRPLANE NEWS, NEW YORK CITY, NEW YORK

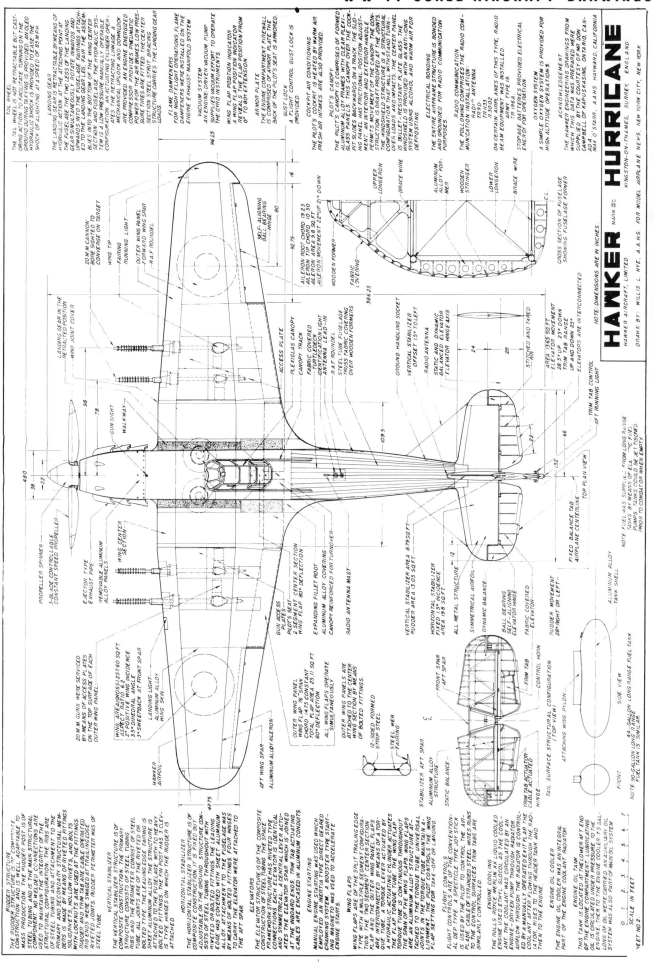

HAWKER HURRICANE

HAWKER MARK IIC **Hurricane**

HAWKER AIRCRAFT, LIMITED.

KINGSTON-ON-THAMES, SURREY, ENGLAND.

DRAWN BY: WILLIS L. NYE, A.A.H.S. FOR MODEL AIRPLANE NEWS, NEW YORK CITY, NEW YORK

NOTE: DIMENSIONS ARE IN INCHES

CROSS SECTION OF FUSELAGE SHOWING FUSELAGE FORMER

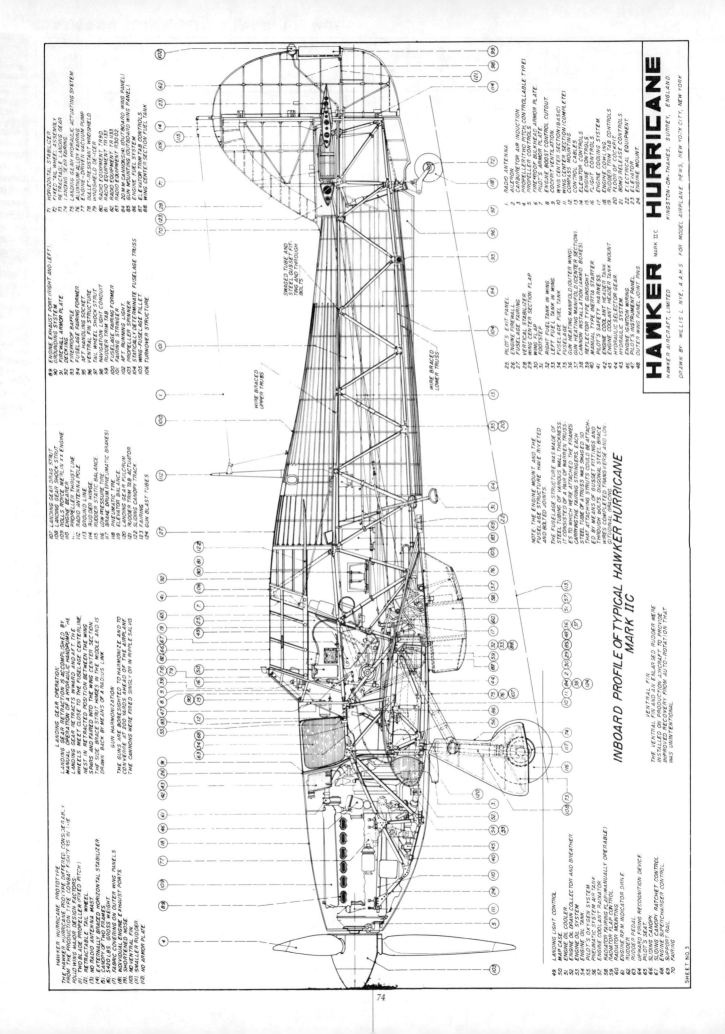

HAWKER HURRICANE MARK IIC

HAWKER AIRCRAFT, LIMITED
KINGSTON-ON-THAMES, SURREY, ENGLAND

DRAWN BY WILLIS L. NYE, A.A.H.S. FOR MODEL AIRPLANE NEWS, NEW YORK CITY, NEW YORK

INBOARD PROFILE OF TYPICAL HAWKER HURRICANE MARK IIC

THE VENTRAL FIN
THE VENTRAL FIN AND AN ENLARGED RUDDER WERE INSTALLED ON PRODUCTION AIRCRAFT TO PROVIDE IMPROVED RECOVERY FROM AUTO-ROTATION THAT WAS UNINTENTIONAL.

SHEET NO. 3

HAWKER HURRICANE

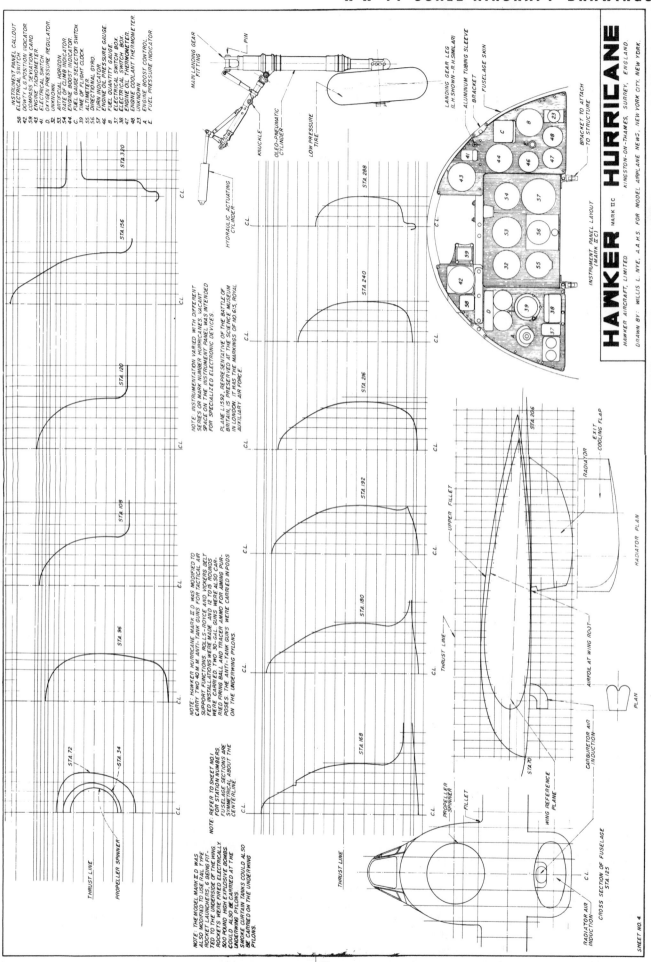

INSTRUMENT PANEL CALLOUT

58 ELECTRICAL SWITCH
42 DOWTY L.G. POSITION INDICATOR
59 COMPASS DEVIATION CARD
43 ENGINE TACHOMETER
41 ELECTRICAL SWITCH
D OXYGEN PRESSURE REGULATOR.
32 UNKNOWN
53 ARTIFICIAL HORIZON.
54 RATE OF CLIMB INDICATOR
44 ENGINE BOOST INDICATOR.
C FUEL GAUGE SELECTOR SWITCH
39 TIME OF FLIGHT CLOCK.
55 ALTIMETER
56 DIRECTIONAL GYRO.
57 TURN INDICATOR
46 FUEL QUANTITY GAUGE.
B ENGINE OIL PRESSURE GAUGE.
37 ELECTRICAL SWITCH BOX.
38 ELECTRICAL SWITCH BOX
47 ENGINE OIL THERMOMETER.
48 ENGINE COOLANT THERMOMETER.
23 UNKNOWN
A ENGINE BOOST CONTROL.
E FUEL PRESSURE INDICATOR

HAWKER HURRICANE MARK II C

HAWKER AIRCRAFT, LIMITED   KINGSTON-ON-THAMES, SURREY, ENGLAND.

DRAWN BY: WILLIS L. NYE, A.A.H.S. FOR MODEL AIRPLANE NEWS, NEW YORK CITY, NEW YORK.

INSTRUMENT PANEL LAYOUT (MARK II C.)

NOTE: INSTRUMENTATION VARIED WITH DIFFERENT SERIES OR MARK NUMBER HURRICANES. VACANT SPACE ON THE INSTRUMENT PANEL WAS INTENDED FOR SPECIALIZED ELECTRONIC DEVICES.

PLANE L1592, REPRESENTATIVE OF THE BATTLE OF BRITAIN, IS PRESERVED AT THE SCIENCE MUSEUM IN LONDON. IT HAS THE MARKINGS OF NO. 615, ROYAL AUXILIARY AIR FORCE.

NOTE: HAWKER HURRICANE MARK II D WAS MODIFIED TO CARRY TWO 40 M.M. ANTI-TANK GUNS FOR TACTICAL AIR SUPPORT FUNCTIONS. ROLLS-ROYCE AND VICKERS BELT FEED INSTALLATIONS WERE MADE, AND 12 TO 15 ROUNDS WERE CARRIED. TWO 30-GAL. GUNS WERE ALSO CARRIED FIRING BALL AND TRACER AMMO FOR AIMING PURPOSES. THE ANTI-TANK GUNS WERE CARRIED IN PODS ON THE UNDERWING PYLONS.

NOTE: THE MODEL MARK II D WAS ALSO MODIFIED TO USE RAIL TYPE ROCKET LAUNCHERS, 6 BEING FITTED TO THE UNDERSIDE OF THE WING. ROCKET'S WERE FIRED ELECTRICALLY. 500 POUND HIGH EXPLOSIVE BOMBS COULD ALSO BE CARRIED AT THE UNDERWING PYLONS.

SMOKE CURTAIN TANKS COULD ALSO BE CARRIED ON THE UNDERWING PYLONS.

NOTE: REFER TO SHEET NO. 1 FOR STATION NUMBERS FUSELAGE SECTIONS ARE SYMMETRICAL ABOUT THE CENTERLINE.

STA. 320
STA. 156
STA. 120
STA. 108
STA. 96
STA. 72
STA. 34

MAIN LANDING GEAR FITTING
PIN
KNUCKLE
OLEO-PNEUMATIC CYLINDER
LOW PRESSURE TIRE
HYDRAULIC ACTUATING CYLINDER

LANDING GEAR LEG (L.H. SHOWN—R.H. SIMILAR)
ALUMINUM TUBING SLEEVE
BRACKET
FUSELAGE SKIN
BRACKET TO ATTACH TO STRUCTURE

STA. 288
STA. 240
STA. 216
STA. 192
STA. 180
STA. 168

STA. 206
UPPER FILLET
RADIATOR
EXIT COOLING FLAP
RADIATOR PLAN

THRUST LINE
AIRFOIL AT WING ROOT
CARBURETOR AIR INDUCTION

WING REFERENCE PLANE
PLAN

PROPELLER SPINNER
FILLET

THRUST LINE
PROPELLER SPINNER

CROSS SECTION OF FUSELAGE STA. 125
RADIATOR AIR INDUCTION

SHEET NO. 4

KAWASAKI KI 61 TONY

A flight view of a Kawasaki Ki 61-I Tony that was captured by the Allies and tested after being repainted with non-standard coloring. The restored Japanese insignia was used for publicity purposes. Note the extremely clean design and radiator installation similar to the North American P-51.

THIS Kawasaki fighter, like other Japanese aircraft of WW II, is a source of confusion to Westerners because it has several designations. In the official sequential Kitai Army aircraft numbering system adopted in 1932, it's "Ki 61." It's also "Army Type 3 fighter" in the system where the number is the last digit of the Japanese dynastic Year 2603, (equivalent to 1940), the year in which the aircraft was designed. Further, the Allies, not knowing the true Japanese designations, assigned code names to all known Japanese airplanes. Believing that the Ki 61 was derived from an Italian design,

they code-named it "Tony."

While most Japanese fighters used air-cooled radial engines prior to the war, the Ki 61 used a Japanese version of the 1,050hp German Daimler-Benz DB-601A that the Kawasaki Aircraft Engineering Co. built under license as the Ha 40. Kawasaki then built the Ki 61 to utilize this engine. This aircraft was a major departure from traditional Japanese design, and was the first to incorporate features found essential in the first year of European WW II operations—armor, self-sealing fuel tanks and heavier firepower. The prototype Ki 61 first flew in December 1941.

SPECIFICATIONS AND PERFORMANCE KI 61-1b

Wingspan ..... 39 ft., 4 7/16 in.

Length .... 28 ft., 8 1/2 in.

Wing Area .... 215.2 sq. ft.

Empty Weight .... 4,872 lbs.

Gross Weight .... 6,504 lbs.
(7,165 lbs. with overload)

High Speed .... 368mph at
15,945 ft.

Service Ceiling .... 37,730 ft.

Max Range .... 684 miles

Its initial armament was a pair of 12.7mm machine guns on the nose, and two 7.9mm guns in each wing on Ki 61-1a or one 12.7mm gun in each wing on Ki 61-Ib. These more than doubled the firepower of Japanese fighters then in

service. Later versions adopted two and even four 20mm wing cannon. A few even had 30mm cannon.

The Tonys went into action in New Guinea in April 1943 and quickly became the principal Japanese Army fighter. Larger and heavier than the Japanese Navy's Mitsubishi Zeke, the Tony wasn't a dogfighter like the Zeke, but was better suited to the hit-and-run techniques that the Allies had developed to combat the Zeke. In any case, the

Tony was superior to the principal land-based fighters that initially opposed it: the Bell P-39 and the Curtiss P-40.

Improved versions of the Tony were developed but didn't achieve true mass production. A slightly enlarged Ki 61-II had a 1,500hp development of the Ha 40, designated "Ha 140," but this engine was plagued with problems to the point where 275 of the Ki 61-IIs were completed as "Ki 100," with 1,500hp Mitsubishi Ha 112 radial engines. Peak production of the Tony (254 a month) was achieved in July 1944.

The final operations of the Tony were against Allied aircraft that were attacking the Japanese home islands. Only Ki 61-IIs with the altitude-rated Ha 140 engine could reach, and

This ground view of a Ki 61-I shows the wide-track landing gear and basic natural-metal finish. Various camouflage patterns were often applied in the field.

were effective against, the operating altitude of the B-29. Others did well against carrier-based fighters and were outclassed only by the U.S. Army P-51s operating from nearby Iwo Jima.

Production of the Tony ended in January 1945, owing to Allied bombing of the airframe and engine factories. Altogether, 3,078 Tonys were built: 2,654 Ki 61-Is (per the drawing), plus 12 prototype and pre-production Ki 61-Is and 412 Ki 61-IIs.

KAWASAKI KI 61 TONY

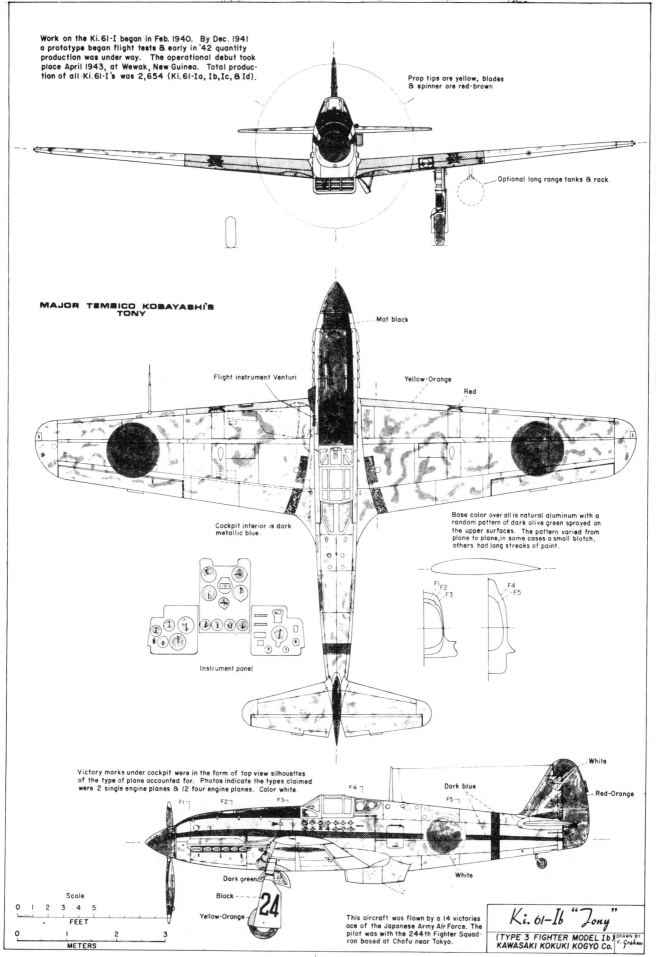

Work on the Ki.61-I began in Feb. 1940. By Dec. 1941 a prototype began flight tests & early in '42 quantity production was under way. The operational debut took place April 1943, at Wewak, New Guinea. Total production of all Ki.61-I's was 2,654 (Ki.61-Ia, Ib, Ic, & Id).

Prop tips are yellow, blades & spinner are red-brown

Optional long range tanks & rack.

MAJOR TEMBICO KOBAYASHI'S TONY

Mat black

Flight instrument Venturi

Yellow-Orange

Red

Cockpit interior is dark metallic blue.

Base color over all is natural aluminum with a random pattern of dark olive green sprayed on the upper surfaces. The pattern varied from plane to plane, in some cases a small blotch, others had long streaks of paint.

Instrument panel

F1 F2 F3   F4 F5

Victory marks under cockpit were in the form of top view silhouettes of the type of plane accounted for. Photos indicate the types claimed were 2 single engine planes & 12 four engine planes. Color white.

F4

F5

White

Dark blue

Red-Orange

F1   F2   F3

Dark green

Black

Yellow-Orange

White

This aircraft was flown by a 14 victories ace of the Japanese Army Air Force. The pilot was with the 244th Fighter Squadron based at Chofu near Tokyo.

Ki. 61-Ib "Tony"

(TYPE 3 FIGHTER MODEL Ib)
KAWASAKI KOKUKI KOGYO Co.

DRAWN BY C. Graham

Scale
0 1 2 3 4 5
FEET

0   1   2   3
METERS

LOCKHEED HUDSON

THE Lockheed Hudson is an outstanding example of a successful transport plane—the 1937 14-passenger Lockheed Model 14—that became an even more successful bomber. The airliner was offered with a variety of radial engines in the 750-1,100hp range, and 112 were sold. Ironically, some planes, with a manufacturing license, were sold to Japan. During the war, the Allies code-named the Japanese versions "Thelma" and the imports "Toby."

In February 1938, aware of an upcoming visit by a British purchasing commission interested in obtaining American bombers, Lockheed rushed to produce a wooden mock-up of a Model 14 bomber fuselage. The British liked what they saw, but it didn't fully meet their needs. They wanted a reconnaissance bomber that would have a navigator as a key crew member. He needed to be close to the pilot and have an excellent field of view. Within 24 hours, Lockheed had modified the mock-up by increasing the number of windows in its nose.

Following two months of intensive discussion about

A Lockheed Hudson I displays the early 1940 form of the British fin flash, which ran the full height of the fin.

SPECIFICATIONS AND PERFORMANCE LOCKHEED HUDSON

Wing Area	551 sq. ft.
Empty Weight	11,630 lbs.
Gross Weight	17,500 lbs.
Top Speed	246mph at 6,500 ft.
Cruising Speed	170mph
Ceiling	25,000 ft.
Range	1,700 miles

aircraft details and equipment, the Air Ministry ordered 200 Lockheed B-14Ls under the British designation "Hudson I" (at a cost of $25,000,000), and as many more as could be delivered by December 1939.

The Hudson's airframe was the same as the airliner's, and it marked the first military use of the new Fowler wing flap that had been introduced on the Model 14. It extended rearward and down, which increased wing area. An advanced feature, by U.S. military standards, was a British Boulton & Paul powered dorsal gun turret, which contained two British .303-caliber Vickers machine guns. Two fixed .303 guns were installed in the nose, and a bomb bay for up to 1,400 pounds of bombs or depth charges was located beneath the airliner floor. The powerplant for the Hudson I was the 1,100 takeoff hp Wright GR-1820-G302A Cyclone single-row engine.

The first flight of the Hudson was on December 10, 1938, and in February the first plane was shipped to England, where armament was installed. In the absence of a British turret in the U.S., the first Hudson was tested with a wooden mock-up of the turret.

The earliest Hudsons were shipped to England from California, or flown to New York and loaded aboard ships. Later Hudsons were sent to Canada for delivery to England by air, but because of U.S. neutrality at the time, they couldn't be flown across the Canadian border. They were flown by U.S. crews to airports right on the border, towed across the line, and flown on by Canadian crews.

Altogether, 2,940 Hudsons were built under six basic designations for British Commonwealth forces, two U.S. Army designations and one U.S. Navy designation, as follows:

BRITISH HUDSONS

Hudson I—The original 200 on the British direct-purchase order, plus an additional 150, all with Cyclone engines. Australia complicated the picture by ordering 50 Lockheed B-14Ss as "Hudson I" but specified the 1,100hp Pratt & Whitney R-1830-SC3G Twin Wasp, a twin-row engine. In recognition of the identity problem, a further 50 Australian Hudsons were ordered as "Hudson II," and the Australian Hudson Is were redesignated "Hudson IV."

Hudson II— Distinguishing

A Hudson V without a turret on a factory test flight in June 1941. Compare the cowling for the Pratt & Whitney engines with those of Wright-powered models in the drawing and other photos. Also note the rearward as well as the downward extension of the Fowler flaps.

external details of these twin-row engine Hudsons were deeper cowlings fitted with cooling flaps. The Australian Mark IIs differed from the Mark Is in that they had constant-speed propellers and a strengthened airframe.

Hudson III—The 428 Hudson IIIs had the airframe and propellers of the Mark II, upgraded 1,200 takeoff hp GR-1820-G205A engines, and three additional .303-caliber machine guns (one on each side of the rear fuselage and another in a ventral station).

Hudson IIIA—The 616 Mark IIIs obtained under the Lend-Lease program were

This U.S. Navy PBO-1, formerly a Hudson IIIA, carries early 1942 Navy markings, is fitted with the British Boulton & Paul gun turret and retains its original British "Sand and Spinach" camouflage.

designated "Hudson IIIA" to reflect their closer conformity to U.S. Army specifications and equipment. Because they were procured with U.S. funds through U.S. Army channels, they were given U.S. Army designations (in this case, "A-29"). The civil Cyclone engines were redesignated as Army R-1820-87s.

Hudson IV—Redesignation of the original Australian Mark Is and Mark IIs as "Hudson IV." An additional 30 were

sent to England.

Hudson IVA— 52 Mark IVs supplied to Australia under Lend-Lease with the U.S. Army designation "A-28." The engines were now R-1830-45.

Hudson V—The 408 Hudson Vs with Twin-Wasp engines were the last Hudsons procured on British direct-purchase contracts. They had the same equipment as the Mark IIIs.

Hudson VI—Improved Mark Vs with 1,200 takeoff hp R-1830-67 engines built by Chevrolet; 450 were procured through the U.S. Army as "A-28A."

U.S. HUDSONS

Even before Lend-Lease and the assignment of U.S. designations to the Hudsons, the Army "drafted" some undelivered Hudsons from British contracts to meet its own increasing need for new aircraft. Most of these were used in unarmed transport and training roles. Because

they didn't meet U.S. Army specifications at the time, they operated as "Lockheed Model 414" under their original British serial numbers, and they often used British insignia. Under Lend-Lease, new Army specifications were written to fit the existing airplanes so that they could be given the standard Army designations A-28 and A-29.

A-28—Lend-Lease designation for the Hudson IVA. Many were retained by the U.S. Army for use as bomber-trainers.

A-28A—Improved Mark Vs delivered as "Hudson VI."

A-29—Eight hundred Mark IIIAs built under Lend-Lease. Late in 1941, some were taken from the British order, armed and used to patrol the U.S. coastline. With no British turrets available, the armed A-29s were fitted with a single, hand-swung, .50-caliber machine gun in an open cockpit that replaced the turret.

A U.S. Army AT-18 gunnery trainer with a molded Plexiglas Martin gun turret. The rubber de-icer boots on the wings and tail are prominent on this unpainted airplane.

A-29A—The 184 A-29As were A-29s with cabins modified for alternative use as unarmed troop transports.

A-29B—Twenty-four A-29s that were modified for use as photo-survey planes.

AT-18—The only Hudsons built from scratch for the U.S. Army were the AT-18 Advanced Trainers. The 217 AT-18s were gunnery trainers fitted with American Martin turrets that used .50-caliber Browning machine guns. The engines were R-1820-87s.

AT-18A—The 83 unarmed AT-18As were navigation trainers (with the cabins arranged for trainee navigators and their instructors).

PBO-1—The U.S. Navy acquired 20 Hudson IIIAs with British turrets late in 1941 and designated them "PBO-1" ("PB" for "Patrol Bomber" and "O" for "Lockheed"). Engines were Navy (even dash number) R-1820-40s. Equipped with four 325-pound depth bombs, one PBO-1 sank a German U-boat on March 1, 1942, and another sank one on March 15. These were the first U.S. aircraft sinkings of U-boats.

Over the entire Hudson series, gross weight varied from 17,500 pounds (I) to 22,360 pounds (AT-18A); top speeds varied from 246 (I) to 261 (AT-18A).

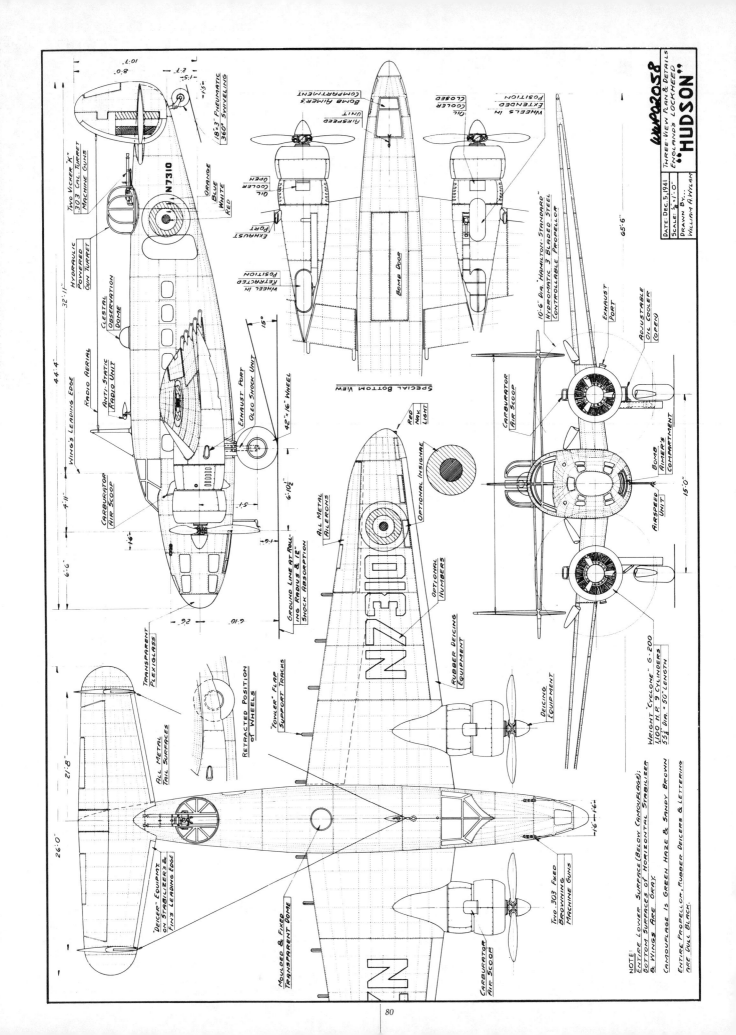

LOCKHEED HUDSON

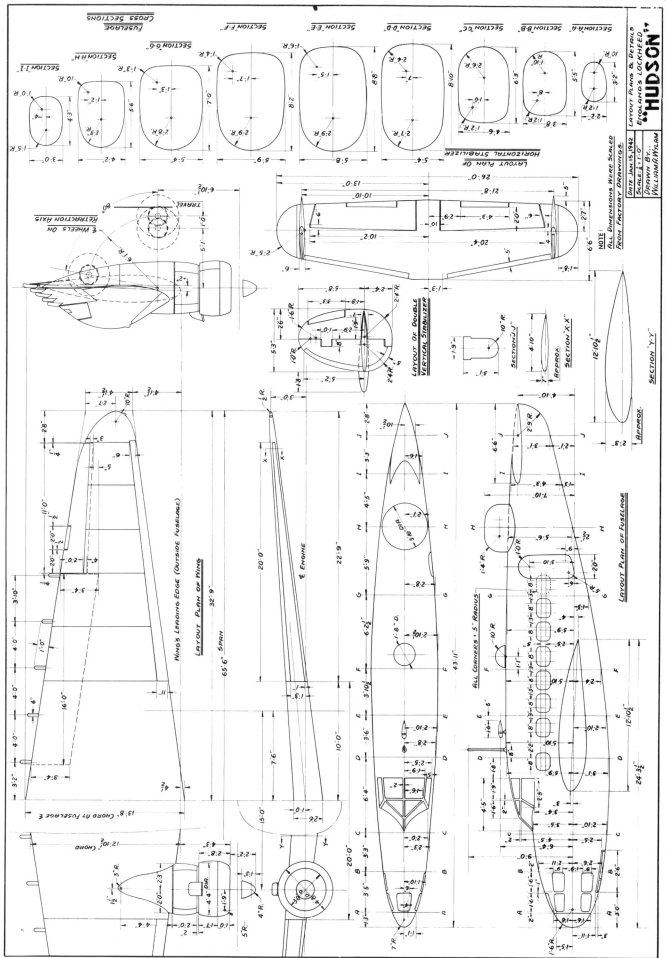

England's Lockheed "HUDSON"

Layout Plans & Details

Date	Jan. 15, 1942
Scale	1:1'-0"
Drawn By	WILLIAM A. WYLAM

NOTE: ALL DIMENSIONS WERE SCALED FROM FACTORY DRAWINGS.

FUSELAGE CROSS SECTIONS

LAYOUT PLAN OF HORIZONTAL STABILIZER

LAYOUT OF DOUBLE VERTICAL STABILIZER

SECTION "X-X"

SECTION "J-J"

SECTION "Y-Y"

LAYOUT PLAN OF WING

WING'S LEADING EDGE (OUTSIDE FUSELAGE)

LAYOUT PLAN OF FUSELAGE

ALL CORNERS = 5" RADIUS

MARTIN PBM MARINER

FOUNDED in 1918, the Glenn L. Martin Company was one of the oldest American aircraft manufacturers. Martin was a major builder of flying boats, beginning in 1930 with the Navy-designed PM-1 and P3M-1 models built in its new plant in Baltimore, MD. The most famous Martin flying boat of original design was the four-engine "China Clipper" (Model 130), that opened trans-Pacific mail and passenger routes in 1935.

In June 1937, Martin was awarded a U.S. Navy contract for a single twin-engine flying boat: the Martin Model 162, designated "XPBM-1." It was intended as a follow-up and possible replacement for the Consolidated PBY model that was then in production. While the XPBM-1 had double the gross weight, and a wing that was only 14 feet longer than the PBY's, it had more powerful 1,600hp Wright R-2600-6 engines. In a very unusual move, Martin built a manned, quarter-scale flying model (Model 162A) for aerodynamic testing of the unique gull-wing design. The first flight of the XPBM-1 was on February 18, 1939.

The notable features of the XPBM-1 were its gulled wing; a powered nose turret with a single gun; a two-gun, powered dorsal turret just aft of the wing; a single gun in the tail cone; and single guns in hemispherical, hand-swung blister turrets on each side of the hull aft of the wing. Twin

fins and rudders were at the ends of a straight, horizontal stabilizer, and the wing-tip floats retracted inward to lay flush against the underside of the wing. Up to 2,000 pounds of bombs or depth charges could be carried.

In a rare move of its own, the Navy ordered 20 production PBM-1s in December 1937, 14 months before the prototype flew. They were outwardly identical to the XPBM-1 except for the dihedral in the horizontal tail. An odd feature here was that the fins and rudders, instead of being vertical, were mounted perpendicular to the stabilizer. Wind-tunnel tests had revealed that there was less aerodynamic drag from a right-angle intersection between the fins and rudders and the stabilizer than when the fins were vertical to pro-

duce one acute and one obtuse angle of intersection.

The single XPBM-2, ordered at the same time, was similar to the PBM-1, except that it had increased fuel capacity and was stressed for catapult landing. Production PBM-1s

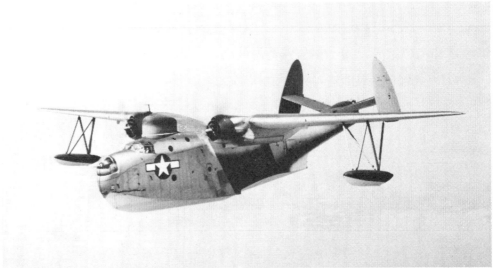

The Martin PBM-3D Mariner with late 1943 color and markings. Note the two-gun nose and tail turrets, the large radome on top of the hull and flush panels enclosing the side guns.

began to reach the fleet in September 1940 and were given the name "Mariner" in October 1941.

PBM-3—True mass production of the Mariner began with the PBM-3, 379 of which were ordered in November 1940. They had 1,700hp R-2600-12 engines in lengthened nacelles that contained completely enclosed bomb bays. Armament was two .50-caliber guns in the nose turret and one each in the dorsal, tail and side positions. The side blister turrets of the PBM-1 were eliminated and the side

guns then fired through flat panels that opened when required. The most notable outward change was the replacement of the retractable wing floats with the fixed type on five long struts.

PBM-3 Variants

PBM-3B—Six PBM-3B were supplied to the R.A.F. as "Mariner I," but they didn't measure up to British requirements and were returned to the U.S. Navy.

PBM-3C—The 274 PBM-3Cs had increased protective armor and could carry up to 4,000 pounds of bombs. Some were fitted with a large radome for search radar on top of the hull between the cockpit and the wing.

PBM-3D—Greater changes came with the 201 PBM-3Ds. They had 1,900hp R-2600-22 engines driving four-blade

This PBM-3 with prewar silver coloring was photographed in late 1942 or early 1943. Note the unpowered tail machine-gun turret and flush panels for side gun stations. The red bands on the wings and hull (later changed to green) identify an instrument trainer.

propellers; twin guns in the nose; dorsal and tail turrets; and single side guns. Bomb capacity was now 8,000 pounds, and some Ds had the large radome that was introduced on the PBM-3C.

PBM-3R—The 20 PBM-3Rs were unarmed transports with seating for 20 passengers and a reinforced cabin floor for heavy cargo.

PBM-3S—The 156 PBM-3Ss were specialized antisubmarine versions that carried four 325-pound depth bombs, extra fuel, and only four guns.

PBM-4—There were to have been 180 PBM-4s

(essentially PBM-3s upgraded to use new, four-row 23,000hp Wright R-3350-8 engines). They weren't produced because the PBM-5 was built instead.

PBM-5—The 631 PBM-5s were outwardly similar to the PBM-3D, but they used 2,100hp Pratt & Whitney R-2800-22 or -34 engines. Six were converted to PBM-5A amphibians, and one was completed as the single-tail XP5M-1, of which 239 P5M-1 and -2 models were built after the war.

PBM-5 Variants
PBM-5E—PBM-5s fitted with search radar were techni-

cally designated "PBM-5E," but because the use of special-mission suffix letters was just beginning, the designation was seldom used in airplane paperwork or by the crews.

PBM-5G—During the war, several PBM-5s were transferred to the U.S. Coast Guard without a change of designation. After the war, these and other Navy transfers acquired the suffix letter "G" (as "PBM-5G"), which identified modifications made for specialized Coast Guard missions, most notably air-sea rescue.

PBM-5A—The final production model of the Mariner was the PBM-5A amphibian, with 36 built to complete the production of 1,366 Mariners by March 1949. The last Mariners were

withdrawn from squadron use in July 1956.

It's odd that the amphibious version of the Mariner appeared so late in its career. If the feature had been added earlier, it might have added greatly to the airplane's utility

The first and the last: the XPBM-1 in its original form with a straight, horizontal tail and side gun blisters, and the PBM-5A amphibian that ended the Mariner line in 1949. The red bars were added to the insignia in January 1947.

(as it had done with the PBY) and given the Mariner a greater role in WW II naval aviation.

One of six PBM-3Bs sent to England as "Mariner I," painted in the British Coastal Command's white and gray color scheme. The Mariners didn't meet British requirements and were returned to the U.S. Navy.

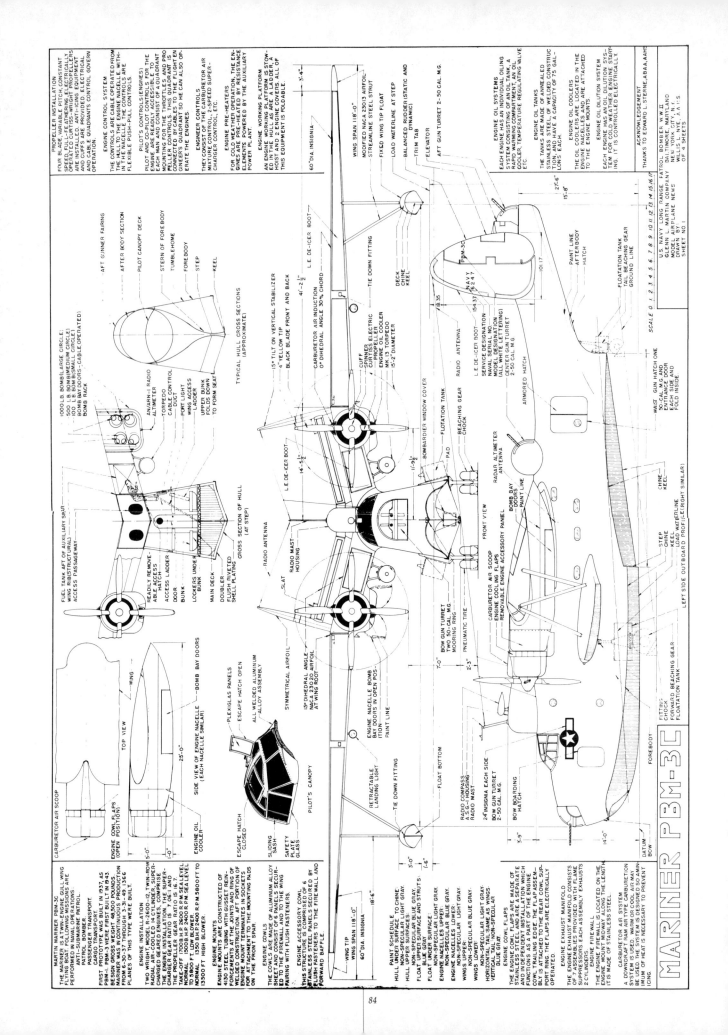

MARINER PBM-3C

U.S. NAVY LONG RANGE PATROL BOMBER, W.W.II
GLENN L. MARTIN COMPANY
BALTIMORE, MARYLAND
MODEL AIRPLANE NEWS
DRAWN BY:
WILLIS L. NYE, A.A.I.'S
SHEET NO. 1
of 4 SHEETS

ACKNOWLEDGEMENT
THANKS TO EDWARD L. STERNE, ABAA, AAHS

84

MARTIN PBM MARINER

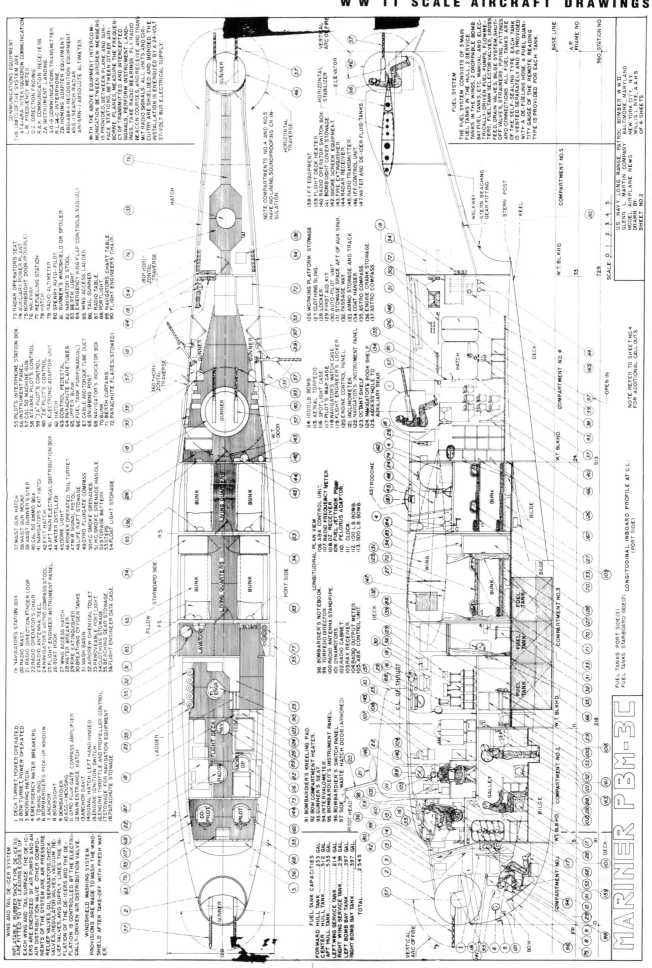

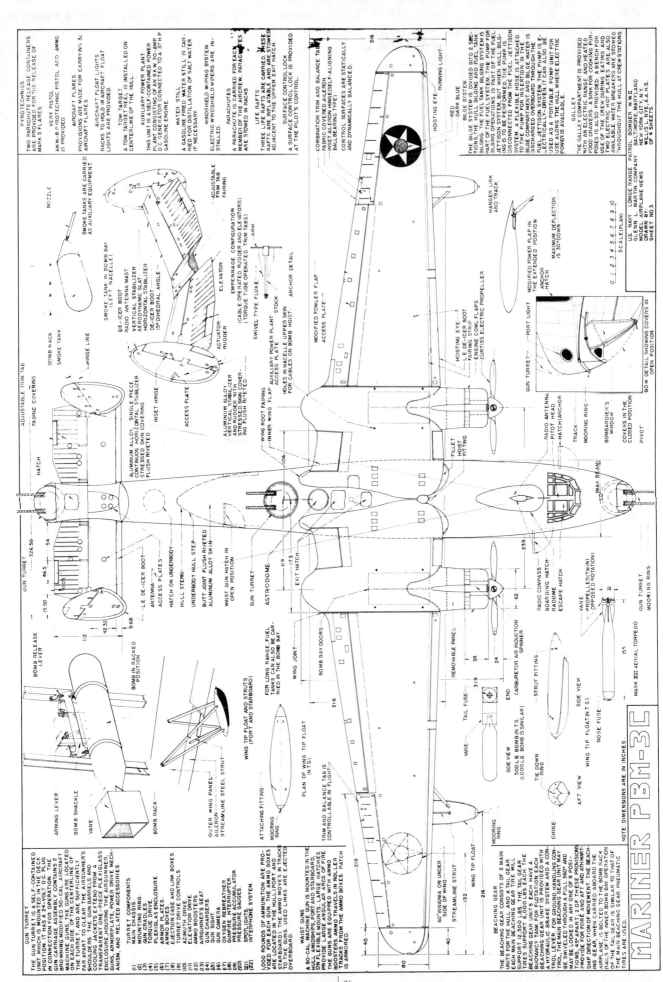

MARINER PBM-3C

NOTE: DIMENSIONS ARE IN INCHES

U.S. NAVY LONGE RANGE PATROL BOMBER W.W.II
GLENN L. MARTIN COMPANY BALTIMORE, MARYLAND
MODEL AIRPLANE NEWS NEW YORK CITY, N.Y.
DRAWN BY: WILLIS L. NYE, A.A.H.S.
SHEET NO.3 OF 4 SHEETS

86

MARTIN PBM MARINER

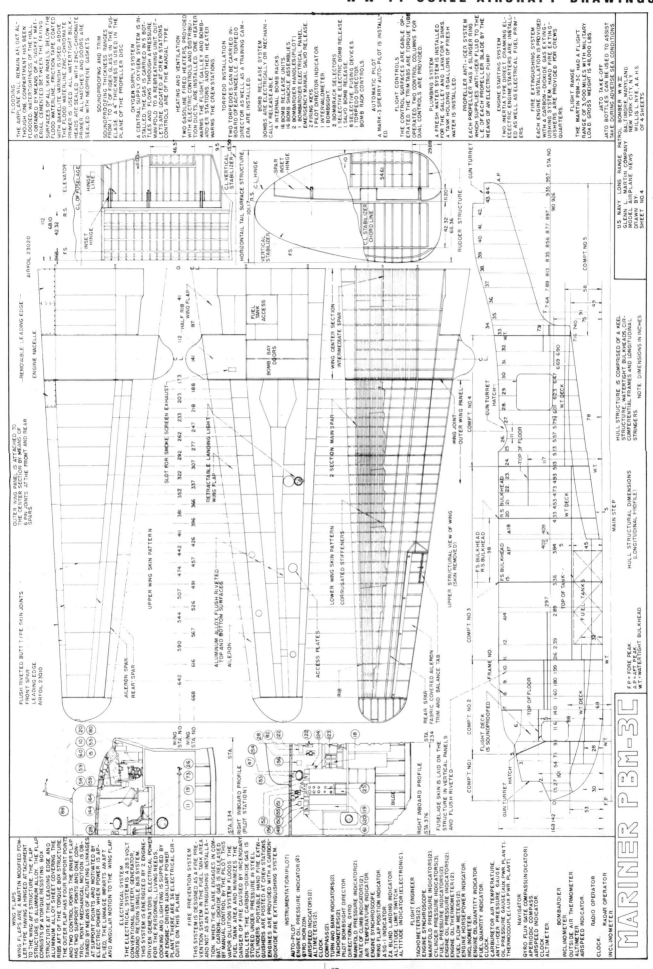

MARTIN B-26 MARAUDER

IN addition to its impressive record as a warplane, the Martin B-26 Marauder should be considered an historic U.S. Army design for another reason: it was the first warplane ever to be ordered into mass production "right off the drawing board" without having a prototype tested first. In January 1939, the U.S. Army, foreseeing an immediate need for new, high-performance airplanes, asked for proposals from the aircraft industry for a new medium bomber that would have an unprecedented high speed for the industry and carry five crew men, four .30-caliber machine guns and 2,000 pounds of bombs. By omitting requirements for low-speed handling characteristics, the Army implied that it was willing to accept a "hot" airplane to get the desired top-end performance. The Glenn L. Martin Co. submitted its paper Model 179 on July 5, 1939. After evaluating it

against other proposals, the Army awarded Martin a contract for 201 production bombers and designated them "B-26."

B-26—First flown on November 25, 1940, the new B-26 was powered with 1,850hp Pratt & Whitney R-2800-5 engines. Its initial armament was a single flexible, .30-caliber machine gun in the nose and another in a manned tail position, and two .50-caliber guns in a powered, Martin-designed dorsal turret—the first such device to be installed in a U.S. bomber. The B-26 was also the first U.S. warplane to have been designed from the start with self-sealing fuel tanks. The bomb load was 4,800 pounds.

A wingspan of only 65 feet with an area of 602 square feet combined with the 32,000-pound gross weight to create the highest wing loading ever used on an Army airplane to that time. This horri-

fied the pilots—and time was to justify their fears. The early models used for crew training soon earned the nickname "Widow Maker," and they almost lived up to the derisive reference "One a Day in Tampa Bay" at a Florida training center.

Later models had more span and area, but the wing loading didn't decrease, because the gross weight was increased. The early "Short Wing" B-26s were the fastest of all, with top speeds of 317mph at 15,000 feet.

B-26A—The B-26s were

This early B-26 shows the initial installation of a .30-caliber tail machine gun. The photo was taken late in 1941, before the U.S. Army serial number was added to the vertical tail.

★　　★　　★

followed by 139 B-26As with minor refinements and a fuselage that was lengthened by 2 feet, 3 inches. All four guns were now .50 caliber, and provision was made for carrying naval torpedoes and bombs.

B-26B—There were 1,883 B-26Bs, but a major change was made with the B-26B-10 that tamed it, and almost made it a different airplane. The wingspan was increased

Note: *While Bill Wylam's drawing is titled "B-26D," the airplane shown is actually representative of late B-26B models. Although detailed photos were released to the public during the war, accurate designations weren't given. For security reasons, all information relative to the B-26 was given under the designation "Marauder," without reference to the particular stage of model development. This was a major reason for the use of "popular" names for U.S. military airplanes. Mr. Wylam made as close a guess as he could for the designation based on the information that was available to him.*

A B-26F-1-MA in the natural metal finish adopted for most U.S. Army combat planes early in 1944. Note the external "package guns" on the lower fuselage.

by 6 feet to make it 71 feet; the wing area increased to 659 square feet; and the height of the vertical tail was increased. Other changes common to all B-26Bs were a 24-volt (rather than a 12-volt) electrical system, 2,000hp R-2800-41 engines and increased protective armor.

For defense, the single hand-swung tail gun was replaced with two .50 calibers in a ball turret, and two .50 calibers were mounted in the lower waist. The drawing shows these in socket fittings ahead of the "openable" panel, but they fire through the panels (as shown in the photo). For ground attack, a fixed, .50-caliber gun was installed inside the nose, and four others were added as "package guns" on the outside of the fuselage.

The normal gross weight of the B-26B increased to only 34,000 pounds, but the bomb load was reduced to 3,000 pounds. Overloads were common, however, and with a 5,200-pound bomb load, the gross weight rose to 36,500 pounds.

The tail number on the Wylam drawing is accurate for a B-26B-25-MA ("MA" identifies the main Martin plant in Baltimore).

B-26C—The 1,235 B-26Cs were similar to the B-26Bs except that they were built in a

new Martin plant in Omaha, NE, where slightly different manufacturing methods were used. The designation became "B-26-MO." Gross weight increased to 38,200 pounds; the top speed dropped to 282mph.

B-26D and E—These two production B-26Bs were modified for experimental projects.

B-26F—The 300 B-26F-MAs were similar to the B and

C models except that the angle of incidence of the wing was increased 3 1/2 degrees to further improve the takeoff and landing characteristics.

B-26G—The 893 B-26G-MAs were similar to the F model except that they had only 11 .50-caliber machine guns. A further 57 were built as unarmed crew trainers, and were designated "TB-26G."

This close-up flight view of the B-26B-30-MA shows the ball tail turret, waist gun ports with the guns extended, and the double-hinged doors of a bomb bay containing 500-pound bombs.

REDESIGNATED B-26s

Some production Marauders were modified for use as crew trainers and redesignated: 208 former B-26Bs became "AT-23A Advanced Trainers," while 350 B-26Cs became "AT-23B." These were soon redesignated "TB-26B" and "C" after 203 of the AT-23Bs were transferred to the Navy as unarmed JM-1s ("J" for "Utility," "M" for "Martin"). The Navy also received 47 of the TB-26Gs as JM-2. The JMs were used primarily as tow-target tugs.

ROYAL AIR FORCE MARAUDERS

The R.A.F. received 544 B-26s under Lend-Lease as follows: 52 B-26As as Marauder I; a further 19 B-26As as Marauder IA; 123 B-26Cs as Marauder II; and a combination of 350 B-26Fs and Gs as Marauder III.

MARAUDERS IN ACTION

The first few B-26s were retained for testing, but the squadrons began to get B-26s in the spring of 1941. They served in every theater of U.S. Army Air Force operations, starting in New Guinea in April 1942, where the distance between targets and U.S. bases required a reduction of the bomb load because of the extra fuel tanks that were carried in the bomb bays. B-26As were used as torpedo planes in the Battle of Midway in June 1942.

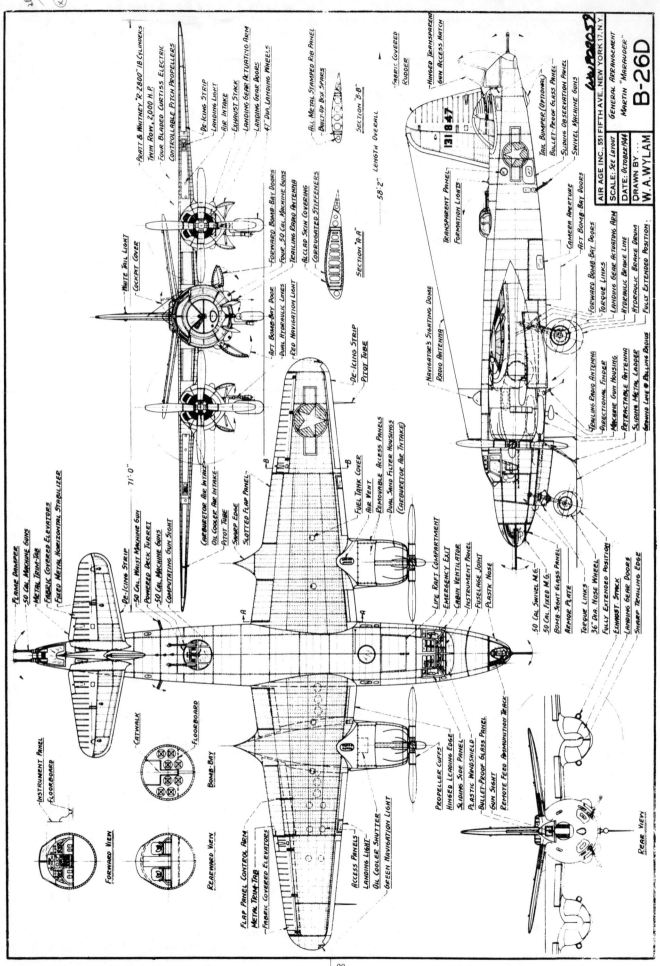

264/1535
(X.138.31)

Pratt & Whitney "R-2800" 18 Cylinders
Twin Row, 2,000 H.P.
Four Bladed Curtiss Electric
Controllable Pitch Propellers
De-Icing Strip
Landing Light
Air Intake
Exhaust Stack
Landing Gear Actuating Arm
Landing Gear Doors
47" Dia. Landing Wheels
All Metal Stamped Rib Panel
Built-Up Box Spars
Section "B-B"
Fabric Covered Rudder
Hinged Transparent Gun Access Hatch

Forward Bomb Bay Doors
Four .50 Cal. Machine Guns
Trailing Radio Antenna
Alclad Skin Covering
Corrugated Stiffeners
Section "A-A"

White Tail Light
Cockpit Cover

Aft Bomb Bay Door
Dual Hydraulic Lines
Feed Navigation Light

De-Icing Strip
Pitot Tube

Navigator's Sighting Dome
Radio Antenna

Transparent Panel
Formation Light

Tail Bumper (Optional)
Bullet-Proof Glass Panel
Sliding Observation Panel
Swivel Machine Guns

131847

Camera Aperture
Aft Bomb-Bay Doors

Forward Bomb-Bay Doors
Torque Links
Landing Gear Actuating Arm
Hydraulic Brake Line
Hydraulic Brake Drum
Fully Extended Position

Trailing Radio Antenna
Directional Finder
Machine Gun Housing
Retractable Antenna
Sliding Metal Ladder
Ground Line & Rolling Radius

AIR AGE INC., 551 FIFTH AVE., NEW YORK 17, N.Y.
GENERAL ARRANGEMENT
MARTIN "MARAUDER"
SCALE: See Layout
DATE: October 1944
DRAWN BY...
W. A. WYLAM
B-26D

Frame Damper
.50 Cal. Machine Guns
Metal Trim-Tab
Fabric Covered Elevators
Fixed Metal Horizontal Stabilizer

De-Icing Strip
.50 Cal. Waist Machine Gun
Powered Deck Turret
.50 Cal. Machine Guns
Computating Gun Sight

71' 0"

Carburetor Air Intake
Oil Cooler Air Intake
Pitot Tube
Sharp Edge
Slotted Flap Panel

Fuel Tank Cover
Air Vent
Removable Access Panels
Dual Sand Filter Housing
(Carburetor Air Intake)

Life Raft Compartment
Emergency Exit
Cabin Ventilator
Instrument Panel
Fuselage Joint
Plastic Nose

.50 Cal. Swivel M.G.
.50 Cal. Fixed M.G.
Bomb Sight Glass Panel
Armor Plate

Torque Links
36" Dia. Nose Wheel
Fully Extended Position
Exhaust Stack
Landing Gear Doors
Sharp Trailing Edge

Instrument Panel
Floorboard
Forward View

Catwalk
Floorboard
Bomb Bay

Rearward View

Flap Panel Control Arm
Metal Trim-Tab
Fabric Covered Elevators

Access Panels
Landing Light
Oil Cooler Shutter
Green Navigation Light

Propeller Cuffs
Hinged Leading Edge
Sliding Side Panel
Plastic Windshield
Bullet-Proof Glass Panel
Gun Sight
Remote Feed Ammunition Track

58' 2" Length Overall

Rear View

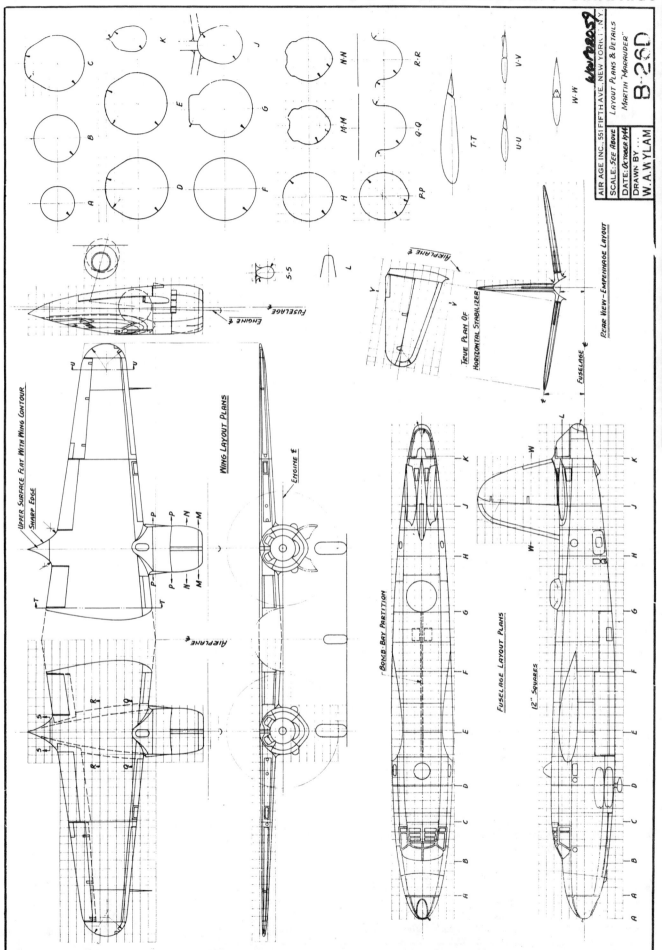

MARTIN B-26 MARAUDER

AIR AGE INC., 551 FIFTH AVE., NEW YORK, N.Y.

SCALE: See Above

DATE: October 1944

Layout Plans & Details

Martin "Marauder"

DRAWN BY ....
W. A. WYLAM

B-26D

Wing Layout Plans

Upper Surface Flat With Wing Contour

Sharp Edge

Engine ₵

Airplane ₵

Engine ₵

Fuselage ₵

Rear View—Empennage Layout

True Plan Of Horizontal Stabilizer

Airplane ₵

Fuselage ₵

Bomb-Bay Partition

Fuselage Layout Plans

12" Squares

MESSERSCHMITT ME 109

An Me 109B-2 in 1938 camouflage and markings. Note the white circle around the swastikas, the narrow white borders for all crosses, and the wing crosses close to the wing tips.

The Me 109 was one of the world's great fighter planes and it enjoyed the distinction of having been built in greater numbers than any other—some 33,000 were built. It was mass-produced in Germany from 1936 through 1945 and it was built in other countries after the war, serving in Spain until 1967.

The Me 109 was designed in 1934 in a four-way design competition for a modern fighter to be used by the brand-new Luftwaffe. Although it was designed to use the new 610hp Junkers Jumo inverted V-12 engine, the Me 109V-1 prototype had to use an upright 625hp British Rolls-Royce Kestrel engine when it flew in September 1935. While it differed little in outline from the new monoplane fighters that were being developed in other countries, the Me 109 was almost revolutionary in its use of a greatly simplified, all-metal structure for mass production and ease of maintenance in the field.

The design was also suitable for "stretch"—the use of higher power, heavier armament and other state-of-the-art changes that kept it competitive with later Allied fighters until the war's end. About the only serious deficiency of the Me 109 was the design of the landing gear. The gear was on a narrow track and the wheels weren't 90 degrees to the ground. This often gave the pilots serious problems when they landed.

PROTOTYPES

Three Me 109 prototypes were ordered in 1934 and designated "Me 109V-1" through "V-3" ("Versuchs," or "Experimental"). These were followed by 10 more prototypes mixed with pre-production Me 109B models. Designated V models continued to appear until late in the war (reaching V-55). Most of these were adapted from production models rather than built from scratch as experimental models.

Me 109B—This was the first production model because there was no Me 109A as such. It used the 635hp Jumo 210 engine and drove a fixed-pitch wooden propeller, which was later replaced by a two-blade metal controllable-pitch type. Its initial armament was a pair of 7.9mm machine guns that fired through the propeller, with a third gun that fired through the hollow propeller shaft. Early combat experience was gained by 45 109Bs that were sent to the German Condor Legion, which was fighting in the Spanish Civil War. The Me 109B's gross weight was 4,740 pounds and its top speed was 289mph at 13,120 feet (4,000 meters).

Me 109C—This model was outwardly similar to the B, but it had an improved Jumo 210C engine and two additional guns in the wings. Some Cs were used to test a 20mm cannon that fired through the propeller shaft, but this wasn't

Note: The "Me 109J" designation that's used on the Wylam drawing never officially existed. It was an in-house designation used by Messerschmitt for some Me 109G models that were being built for Spain late in the war. The drawing shows the configuration of the prewar Me 109B through D models fitted with the three-blade propeller of the Me 109E. The markings are for early Me 109Bs as seen in 1938. The "J" was just a guess on Mr. Wylam's part, as accurate designations for many German aircraft weren't readily available to the Allies in 1940, when the drawing was made.

Also, note that the abbreviations "Bf" and "Me" are both used in reference to the Messerschmitt airplanes. Although the planes were designed by Willi Messerschmitt and were referred to as such, they were the product of the Bayersche Flugzeug Werke (Bavarian Airplane Works) of Augsburg and were officially designated "Bf." The name of the firm was changed to Messerschmitt in July 1938, so "Me" became the official abbreviation, but "Bf" also remained in use almost until the war's end. Because "Me" is the most commonly used term today, it's used here even for the early, "true" Bf models.

An Me 109E-4/B, in 1940 coloring, carrying a 550-pound bomb. Note the wide white borders on the fuselage and the underwing crosses, and the wing crosses now located farther from the wing tip.

The major change in the appearance of the Me 109F resulted from the larger propeller spinner and round wing tips. Shown here is an early Me 109F-0.

The Me 109G was outwardly similar to the F model, except for the bulges for larger nose-gun ammunition drums located ahead of the cockpit (which started with the G-3). Shown here is an ME 109G-10/R1.

yet standard equipment.

Me 109D—The Me 109D, which kept the Jumo engine and two-blade propeller, was the first true mass-produced model, with several hundred built. Although it rapidly became obsolete, some D models saw action during the German invasion of Poland in September 1939. They were then "retired" to fighter-pilot schools.

Me 109E—A major change came with the Me 109E, which used the 960hp Daimler-Benz DB 600 engine, (an inverted V-12 like the Jumo) but had a three-blade propeller and a notably different radiator arrangement under the nose. Production Es with 1,100hp DB 600A engines entered service with the Luftwaffe early in 1939. A great variety of armament was incorporated in the E over its production life, and the nose-mounted cannon was standard equipment. Some other Es had cannon installed in the wings. Provision was also made for the installation of racks under the wings for bombs, and either a 300-liter drop tank or a 550-pound bomb could be carried under the fuselage.

In combat, the Me 109E was slightly superior to the British Hurricane I and far better than the Curtiss Kittyhawk. It was about even in performance with the early British Spitfires.

Me 109F—Major changes in appearance came in late 1940 with the Me 109F. Most notable were a greatly en-

larged, nearly hemispherical propeller spinner, rounded (instead of squared) wing tips, and a horizontal cantilever tail that eliminated the bracing struts. From the F-3 model on, the engine used was the 1,350hp DB 601E. Its gross weight was 6,063 pounds and its high speed was 391mph at 19,680 feet (6,000 meters).

Me 109G—The Me 109G of 1942 was the most-produced model. Some featured cockpit pressurization (a new feature for fighters at the time), and from the G-3 on, the nose guns were 13mm. The larger ammunition drums required for these guns caused conspicuous bulges on each side of the fuselage ahead of the cockpit. Again, wing armament varied between cannons,

extra machine guns and rockets. Its gross weight was 6,945 pounds; the high speed was 387mph at 22,967 feet (7,000 meters).

Me 109H, J—A small series of Me 109H prototypes (which were intended to be high-performance fighters) was started, using F-4 airframes for prototypes and G-5s for early production models. Only a few were delivered before the program was cancelled. The "J" designation was used by Messerschmitt as its own designation for 25 G airframes that were shipped to Spain without engines.

Me 109K—The final production model, which was similar to the late 109G, appeared late in 1944. The Me 109K used the 1,500hp DB 605L engine with a two-stage supercharger that could deliver up to 2,000hp for short dashes.

Its gross weight was 7,400 pounds, and its high speed was 452mph at 19,606 feet. These were figures that emphasized the ability of the 1934 design to grow and remain competitive with later fighter designs.

POSTWAR PRODUCTION
The Avia plant in Czechoslovakia had been building Me 109Gs, and after the war, it continued to build them for the new Czech Air Force, using both DB 605 and Jumo engines. Spain also built Me 109Gs after the war, using Hispano-Suiza engines, which were later replaced by British Rolls-Royce Merlins.

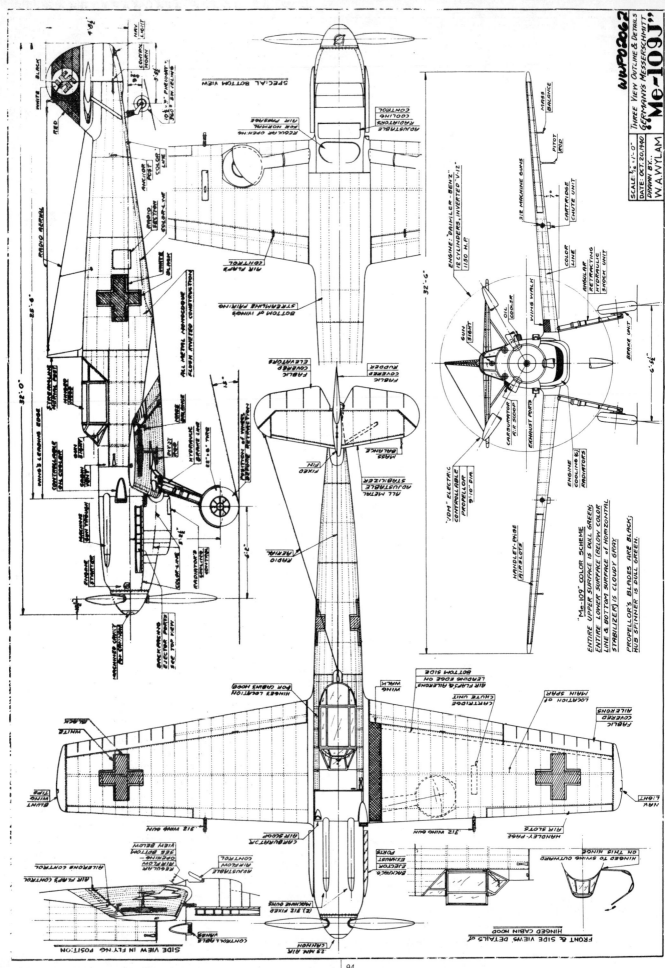

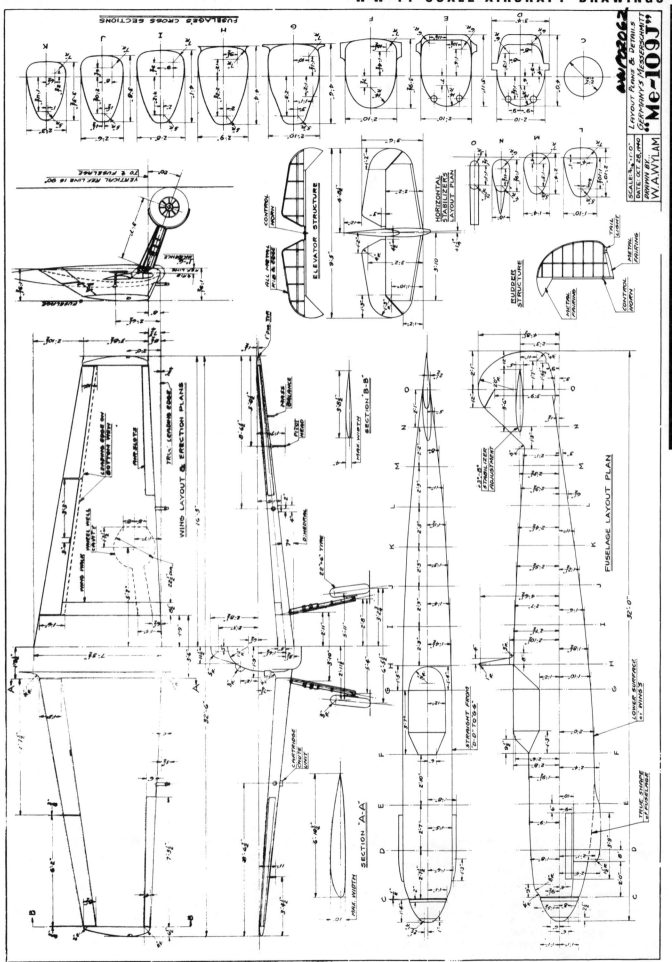

MESSERSCHMITT ME 109

SCALE: ⅜"=1'-0"
DATE: OCT 28, 1940
DRAWN BY:
W.A.WYLAM

Layout Plans & Details
Germany's Messerschmitt
"Me-109J"

FUSELAGE CROSS SECTIONS

HORIZONTAL STABILIZERS LAYOUT PLAN

ELEVATOR STRUCTURE

ALL METAL RIB & FRAME

CONTROL HORN

RUDDER STRUCTURE

METAL FAIRING

TAIL LIGHT

CONTROL HORN

WING LAYOUT & ERECTION PLANS

FUSELAGE LAYOUT PLAN

SECTION 'B-B'

SECTION 'A-A'

MESSERSCHMITT ME 262 SWALLOW

An Me 262A-1a tested in the U.S. after the war. The original German fuselage markings had been painted out, but erroneous crosses in WW I style were painted on later for publicity purposes.

THE German Messerschmitt Me 262 has the distinction of being the first turbojet airplane to see combat. It wasn't the first fighter without propellers to do so, however. That honor went to the Messerschmitt Me 162 Komet, which was powered by a liquid-fuel rocket engine and went into action on August 14, 1944. Although the Me 262 didn't go to war until October 3, 1944, its impact on aircraft design was great. Rocket propulsion wasn't adopted for subsequent fighters, but all of today's fighters are powered by turbojets.

It was fortunate for Allied air power that deployment of the Me 262 was held up, first by delays in jet-engine development and then by official indecision as to how it should be used. The initial planning for its use as a fighter was faulty, and then Adolph Hitler ordered that it be produced as a bomber rather than a fighter.

In 1938, the German Air Ministry encouraged the development of jet and rocket powerplants for military aircraft. As a result, the newly named Messerschmitt A.G. ("A.G." for "Aktien Geselleschaft," or Proprietary Company) was invited to design a jet-powered fighter. Messerschmitt's preliminary design study received the Ministry's Project No. P.1065, which appeared as a wooden mock-up in March 1940. Approval of this resulted in an order for three all-metal prototypes, designated "Me 262." The new fighter eventually received the name "Schwalbe" (Swallow).

As a fighter airframe, the Me 262 was a relatively conventional design, but it featured a slightly swept-back wing to reduce compressibility at high speeds. Two axial-flow turbojet engines were installed in nacelles on the underside of the wing, outboard of the inward-retracting landing gear.

A detail new to fighters at the time, but soon to be widely adopted, was the use of a cockpit canopy that was entirely above the fuselage, not faired into it as on the Me 109 and its contemporaries.

The first four Me 262s (Me 262V-1 through V-4) featured conventional tail-wheel landing gear. This was quickly changed to the tricycle type, and for good reason. The jet blast hit the pavement, damaging it, and also bounced upward to scorch the tail surfaces while further damaging them with blown-up debris. Significantly, all subsequent jet airplanes used tricycle landing gear with their jets parallel to the ground (notable exceptions are latter-day vertical takeoff types such as the British Harrier).

Airframe development got far ahead of jet-engine development, so the Me 262V-1 was hurriedly fitted with a

Me 262A-1as in Germany. Note that the tail swastika is black with a white border, but that the fuselage cross consists only of a white outline over the fuselage camouflage pattern.

1,200hp Junkers Jumo piston engine in a modified nose. It made its first flight on April 18, 1941. Later attempts to fly it and other prototypes with early developmental jets failed because the engines weren't delivering sufficient thrust (1 pound of thrust equals 1hp at approximately 375mph; 1 pound of thrust equals more than 1hp above that speed and less below it).

Finally, powered by two 1,848-pound-thrust (static) Junkers 109-004A engines, the first all-jet Me 262 flight was made by the V-3 on July 18, 1941. Orders were then placed for production Me 262A-0 and -1 fighters, but for a while, it looked like they wouldn't be delivered as such. Hitler saw a demonstration flight of the Me 262V-6 in November 1943 and, impressed by its speed, decided that it was just the thing for hit-and-run bombing raids on England. He ordered that the new jets be built as bombers in-stead of fighters. A redesign program got under way, and the Me 262A-2 version could carry two 500kg (1,100-pound) bombs under the fuse-lage. The bomber version was named "Sturmvogel" (Storm Bird). Reason prevailed in the Air Ministry, however, and Hitler was persuaded to allow simultaneous production of both the Me 262 bomber and the fighter. The fighter was usually fitted with four 30mm cannon in the nose, but other armament arrangements were also used.

By April 1944, 12 proto-types and 10 Me-262A-0 pre-production models had been built. Initial production models went to fighter-pilot schools, not to the front, because con-siderable training was needed for experienced fighter pilots during their transition to the new jets. The first Me 262 combat mission against U.S. daylight bomber formations was on October 3, 1944.

The performance of the Me 262 handed the Allies a nasty sur-prise: it was more than 80mph faster than the best Allied fighters of the time. Its speed was an asset in hit-and-run attacks on the bomber streams and allowed it to avoid mixing with the de-fending fighters. The powered gun turrets of the bombers couldn't follow the Me 262's high-speed passes. Most of the Me 262s that were shot down were victims either of their own pilots' errors or of slowing down for more careful aim or for landing. Some Me 262s were designed with a single 50mm (2-inch) cannon in the nose to permit the Me 262s to attack the bombers while safely out of range of their .50-caliber guns. This version, however, was never produced.

The increasing need for night fighters resulted in the installation of specialized night-fighting radar into some single-seat Me-262A-1s, com-plete with an impressive array of antennas on the nose. Two-seat Me 262Bs were devel-oped specifi-cally as night fighters.

Altogether,

A two-seat Me 262B-1a/U1 night fighter tested in the U.S. after the war. Note the nose radar antennas and the auxiliary fuel tanks where bombs were carried on the bomber versions.

1,430 Me 262s were built out of thousands ordered, and then they were a classic ex-ample of too little, too late. Had they been available a year and half earlier (before long-range fighters began to ac-company the bombers), the outcome of the Allied strategic bombing program might have been different.

☆   ☆   ☆

Note: The designations "FE" and "T2" on the rear fuselages of German aircraft photo-graphed in the U.S. during and after the war aren't origi-nal German markings. "FE" means "Foreign Equipment," and "T2" is the number of the particular Technical Intelli-gence office that tested the aircraft.

Me 262 nose details. At left, an Me 262A-2a with two 250kg (550-pound) bombs under the fuselage. At right, an Me 262A-1a fighter. Note the ports for the 30mm cannon in the upper nose.

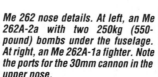

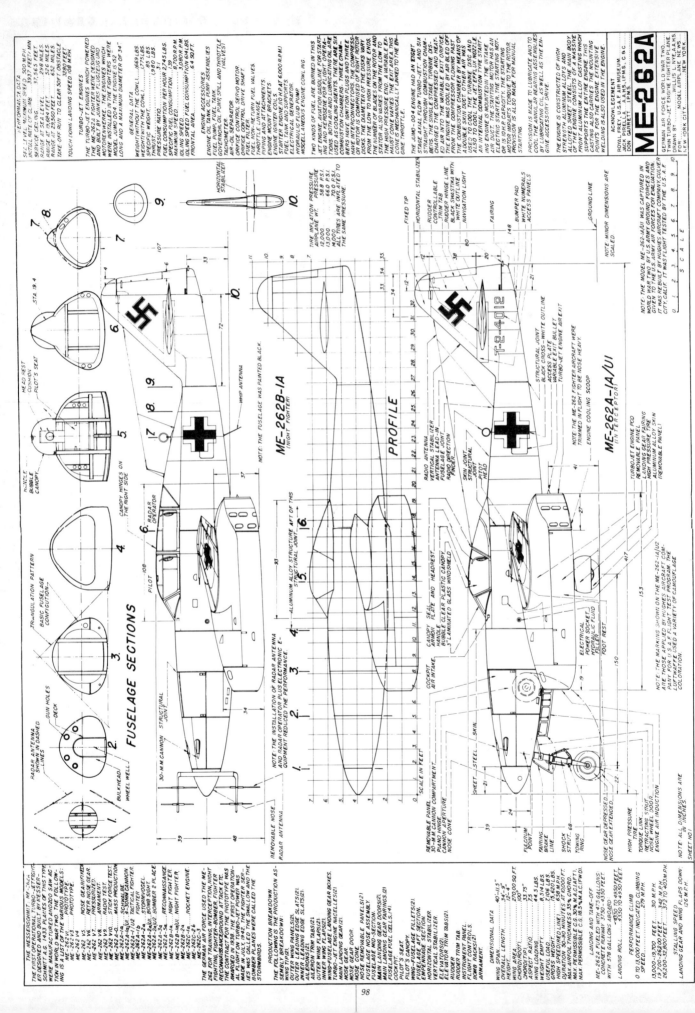

ME-262A

ACKNOWLEDGEMENT
ROYAL FREY, U.S.A.F. AIR MUSEUM
JACK PIRELLA, A.A.H.S., I.P.M.S., C.B.C.
DON GARRETT, I.P.M.S.

GERMAN AIR FORCE WORLD WAR TWO.
TURBO-JET INTERCEPTOR-FIGHTER PLANE.
DRAWN BY . . . . WILLIS L. NYE, A.A.H.S.
MODEL AIRPLANE NEWS,
NEW YORK CITY.

MESSERSCHMITT ME 262 SWALLOW

ME-262A

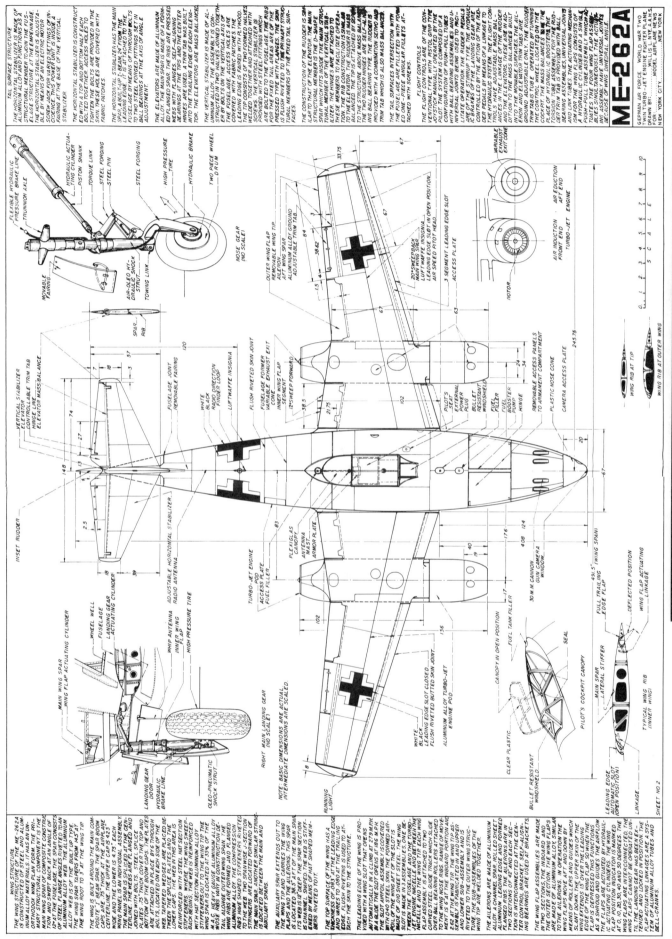

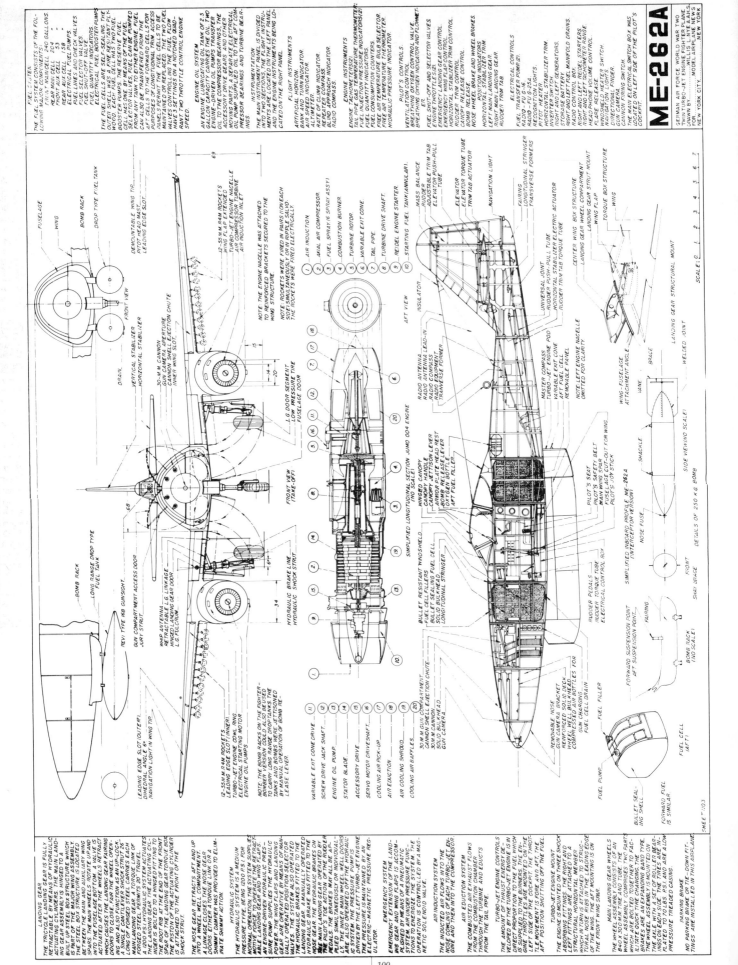

ME-262A

GERMAN AIR FORCE WORLD WAR TWO
TWIN TURBO-JET ENGINE FIGHTER PLANE.
DRAWN BY: WILLIS T. NYE A.A.H.S.
NEW YORK CITY. MODEL AIRPLANE NEWS,
NEW YORK.

MESSERSCHMITT ME 262 SWALLOW

ME-262A

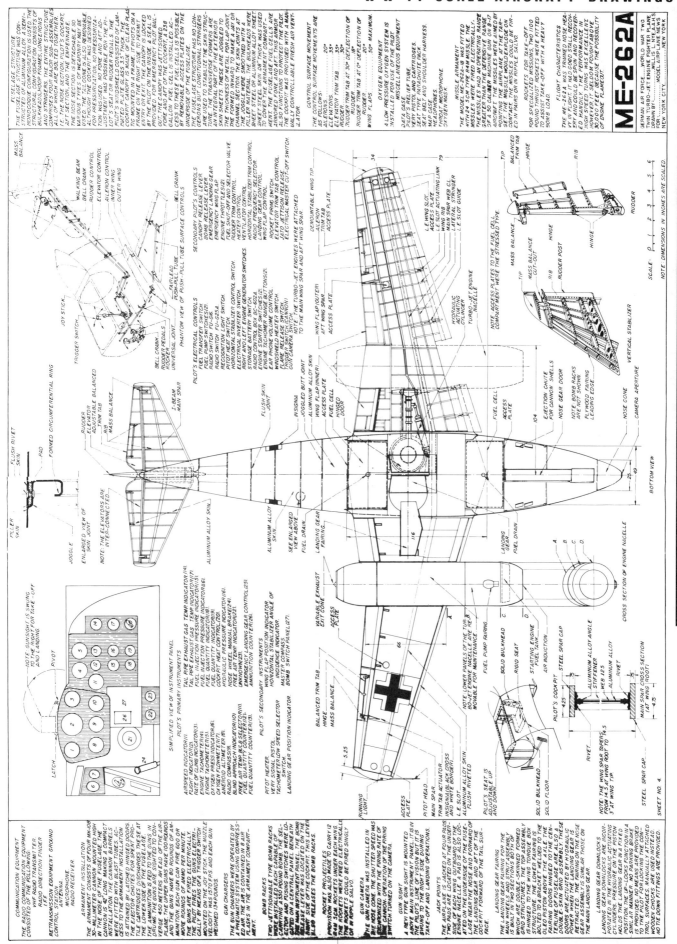

101

MITSUBISHI A6M ZERO

A restored Mitsubishi A6M-5C Zeke 52. Its markings are more accurate than on most restorations, but the rear fuselage doesn't match the drawing.

THE Mitsubishi A6M, called "Zero", "Zeke" and "Hamp" by the Allies, was one of the major technological surprises sprung by the Japanese in WW II. Because they had long been contemptuously regarded as being capable only of copying foreign airplane designs, their highly original, carrier-based fighter was startling.

The designation "Zero" came from the Japanese Navy practice of designating airplane types by the last two digits of the Japanese Dynastic calendar. The Japanese year 2600 matched our calendar year 1940, so "00," was shortened to "Type 0" for the A6M, which was named "Raiden." The naval model designation of "A6M" reflected the sixth A-model built by Mitsubishi (M). The sub-designation for the A6M-1 was

Model 11, while the A6M-2 became Model 21, and the A6M-3 became Model 32, etc. The Allies also referred to it broadly as "The Zero," but when code names were applied to Japanese military aircraft, the standard models were called "Zeke," and the short-wing Model 32 was called "Hamp."

The prototype, which was powered by a 780hp Mitsubishi Zuisei engine, flew

April 1, 1939, and was quickly ordered into production as Type 0 fighter Model 11. It entered combat in China in July 1940. Allied Intelligence reported on its capabilities, but the warnings were disregarded, which caused later regrets.

For two years, the Zero was superior to any plane it fought. It was fast and highly maneuverable and, thanks to its auxiliary fuel tanks, it had long

range. Its shortcomings included a lack of armor protection for the pilot, a light structure and fuel tanks that weren't self-sealing. The Zero was also highly vulnerable to the .50-caliber guns of U.S. fighters—when they were able to hit it.

Its initial armament was two 7.7mm machine guns in the nose and two 20mm cannon in the wings. Armament varied during production to a maximum of a single 13.2mm gun in the nose, two more in the wings, plus the two cannon. Its bomb load ranged from two 132-pound bombs to a single 1,102-pounder, or up to eight 22-pounders. Late -6 and -8 versions could also be fitted with rockets.

Although it was obsolete by mid-1943, when new Allied fighters opposed it, the Zero remained in production until the end of the war, with 3,879 built by Mitsubishi and 6,570 built under license by Nakajima, for a total of 10,449.

Most Zeroes—Models 11, 21, 52 and 64 (AM6-1, -2, -5 and -8)—had wingspans of 12 meters (39 feet, 4 inches), but Model 32 (A6M-3) had its span shortened by 1 meter to 36 feet. Other data for Zero Model 52 (A6M-5): powerplant: 1,130hp Nakajima Sakae 21; wing area: 229.27 square feet; empty weight: 4,136 pounds; gross weight: 6,025 pounds; high speed: 351mph at 19,685 feet.

No, the Luftwaffe didn't use Zeroes. This A6M-2 Zeke 21, photographed in China just after the war, carries the green cross on a white marking used by some of the Japanese airplanes that were allowed to continue flying during the surrender negotiations. Note that a souvenir hunter has cut the unit marking off the rudder.

MITSUBISHI A6M ZERO

MODEL	ENGINE	H.P.	SPEED	AT ALTITUDE OF
A6M2	SAKAE 12 (Ha. 35/12)	925	317	16,400 FT.
A6M3	SAKAE 21 (Ha. 35/21)	1,130	341	20,500
A6M5	" "	"	358	22,000
A6M5c	" "	"	346	19,600

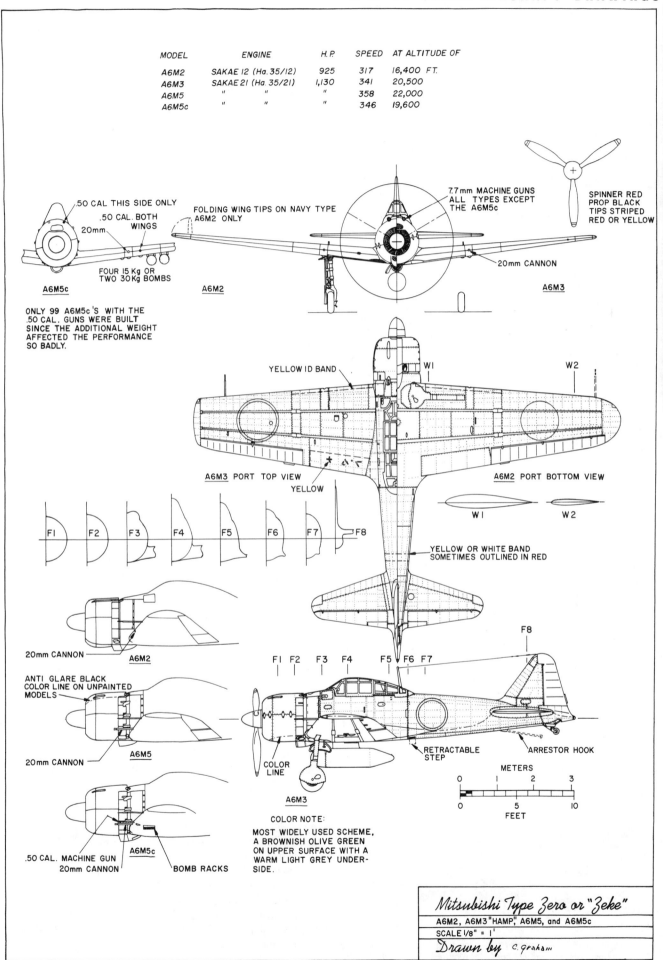

.50 CAL THIS SIDE ONLY

.50 CAL. BOTH WINGS

20mm

FOUR 15 Kg OR TWO 30 Kg BOMBS

A6M5c

FOLDING WING TIPS ON NAVY TYPE A6M2 ONLY

A6M2

7.7 mm MACHINE GUNS ALL TYPES EXCEPT THE A6M5c

20mm CANNON

A6M3

SPINNER RED PROP BLACK TIPS STRIPED RED OR YELLOW

ONLY 99 A6M5c'S WITH THE .50 CAL. GUNS WERE BUILT SINCE THE ADDITIONAL WEIGHT AFFECTED THE PERFORMANCE SO BADLY.

YELLOW ID BAND

W1

W2

A6M3 PORT TOP VIEW

YELLOW

A6M2 PORT BOTTOM VIEW

W1

W2

F1 F2 F3 F4 F5 F6 F7 F8

YELLOW OR WHITE BAND SOMETIMES OUTLINED IN RED

20mm CANNON

A6M2

ANTI GLARE BLACK COLOR LINE ON UNPAINTED MODELS

20mm CANNON

A6M5

.50 CAL. MACHINE GUN 20mm CANNON

A6M5c

BOMB RACKS

F1 F2 F3 F4 F5 F6 F7

F8

RETRACTABLE STEP

ARRESTOR HOOK

COLOR LINE

A6M3

COLOR NOTE:

MOST WIDELY USED SCHEME, A BROWNISH OLIVE GREEN ON UPPER SURFACE WITH A WARM LIGHT GREY UNDER-SIDE.

METERS

0   1   2   3

0   5   10

FEET

Mitsubishi Type Zero or "Zeke"

A6M2, A6M3 "HAMP", A6M5, and A6M5c

SCALE 1/8" = 1'

Drawn by C. Graham

MITSUBISHI G4M BETTY

This view of the Mitsubishi G4M-2 Betty bomber shows the powered upper turret and four-blade propellers added to this model. The color is dark green on the upper surfaces and silvery gray underneath.

THE Japanese Naval Air Arm was unusual in that it made extensive use of land-based bombers, and used them for long overland flights deep into enemy territory in what would usually be considered an Army-type operation.

The Mitsubishi G4M, code-named "Betty" by the Allies but not officially named in Japan, did acquire the unofficial nickname of "Hamaki," or "Cigar," in an obvious reference to the shape of its fuselage. The G4M prototype flew in September 1939, but its production was delayed in favor of the G6M-1, which had the same airframe but was equipped as a long-range escort fighter. This was necessary for raids deep into China, because Japan had no conventional fighters that were capable of escorting the

bombers then in use for the full distance. The G6M-1 concept didn't work out, so the 30 planes that were built in 1940 were converted to trainers and transports.

Production Bettys, which were designated Navy Type 1 Attack Bomber Model 11 (G4M-1), were first delivered in April 1941. Its initial powerplants (contrary to the drawing) were 1,530hp Mitsubishi MK4A Kasei 11 engines; the bomb load was 1,764 pounds or one standard naval torpedo; defensive armament was four 7.7mm machine guns—one in the nose, one in a topside blister, one each in side blisters, and a 20mm cannon in the tail turret. The G4M-1's range was 3,256 nautical miles (3,749 statute miles), and its top speed was 266mph at

13,780 feet.

The G4M-1s enjoyed great success on raids into China as far inland as Chungking, and their lack of armor and heavy defensive armament wasn't a handicap when they faced the weak Chinese fighter resistance. It did, however, cause serious problems when they encountered even the second-rate but determined fighters that the U.S. and British defenses first put up against it.

Improvements were made on the G4M-2 Model 22. The top blister was replaced with a powered turret that contained a 20mm cannon. The nose guns were doubled, the side blisters were removed and replaced with flat hatches (still containing 7.7mm guns), and a revised tail turret retained its 20mm cannon. Bomb load

increased to 2,205 pounds, and power was increased to 1,800hp (takeoff), with Kasei 21 MK4P engines driving four-blade propellers (the G4M-1 had three-bladers). A new wing with laminar airfoil was used; gross weight increased to 27,588 pounds, but high speed increased to only 272mph at 15,090 feet. The final production version of the Betty was the G4M-3, which had a redesigned tail turret and dihedral in the horizontal tail.

Bettys were in production until the war's end, and they operated everywhere there were targets for land-based bombers (either land targets or ships at sea). An unusual conversion was made on the G4M-2e, which had its bomb bay modified to carry the MXY-7 Ohka ("Cherry Blossom," but called "Baka," or "Fool," by the Allies) single-seat suicide bomber. Carrying the Ohka greatly reduced the performance of the Betty, and made it an easy target for U.S. and British fighters. Sixteen were shot down during a single attack.

Altogether, 1,200 G4M-1s, 1,154 G4M-2s and 60 G4M-3s were built.

SPECIFICATIONS AND PERFORMANCE G4M-2

Wingspan	82 ft., 1/4 in.
Length	65 ft., 7 in.
Wing Area	840.9 sq. ft.
Empty Weight	17,199 lbs.
Gross Weight	27,588 lbs.
High Speed	272mph at 15,090 ft.
Range	3,765 statute miles

This view of the G4M-2 Betty bomber shows the flush hatches that replaced side machine gun blisters, and the tail turret redesigned with two vertically aligned transparent clam shells that opened to permit movement of the 20mm cannon.

MITSUBISHI G4M BETTY

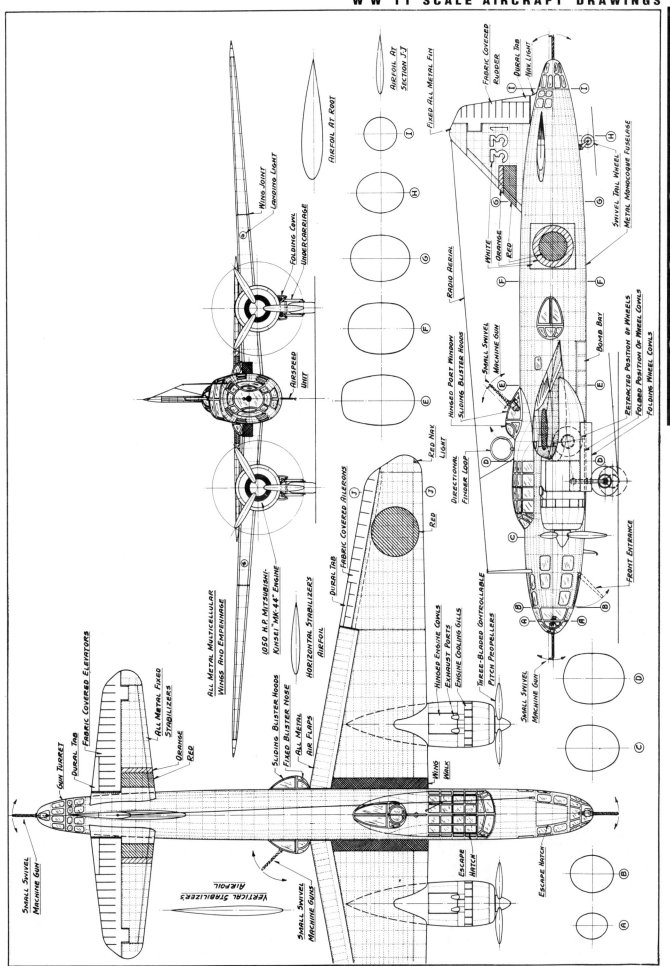

NAKAJIMA KI-84 FRANK

A Nakajima Ki-84 "Frank" of the 11th Sentai (group), captured in the Philippines. Note the lightning-flash Sentai marking on the tail and the plane's well-worn appearance. The numeral "46" on the rudder is an allied inventory number for captured airplanes.

THE best all-around Japanese fighter developed in response to the new U.S. models was the Nakajima Ki-84 Hayate ("Gale"). It was code named "Frank" by the Allies, but its official designation was Type 4 (for the Japanese year 2604) Model 1A Fighter. It was designed and built by the Nakajima Aeroplane Company, Ltd.; the prototype flew in April 1943.

The engine was a 1,800hp Nakajima Ha-45 Type 11, and the airplane's lines were similar to Nakajima's Ki-43 "Oscar" and Ki-44 "Tojo".

The prototype had provision for a single drop-tank under the fuselage, but the production models could carry two 44-gallon tanks, or up to two 550-pound bombs under the wings. Its initial armament was a pair of 12.7mm machine guns in the nose and two 20mm cannon in the wings. The Ki-84 was up-to-date in its use of heavy armor and protection for the fuel tanks, and it featured special "Butterfly Flaps" that could be lowered to improve maneuverability in combat.

The Ki-84 wasn't quite as fast as the latest U.S. P-51s and P-47s, but it could out-maneuver and out-climb them. "Franks" first went into combat against the U.S. 14th Air Force (the former Flying Tigers), in China in March 1944. Soon after, 10 three-squadron fighter groups that were equipped with Franks were stationed in the Philippines to resist the impending Allied invasion. The Franks didn't live up to their potential there, because they were badly outnumbered, and also because they suffered from fuel and hydraulic-system malfunctions and the failure of less-than-standard landing gear.

Improved versions of the Ki-84 quickly followed the Ki-84-Ia. The Ki-84-Ib eliminated the two machine guns and used four cannon. The few Ki-84-Ics (specialized bomber interceptors) had two 20mm cannon and two 30mm cannon.

Because of the serious shortage of aluminum in Japan, wood was substituted for many parts of the Ki-84. The resulting composite model had a 1,990hp Ha-45 Type 23 engine and was designated the "Ki-84-II." Production was also seriously hampered by the B-29 raids on Japan, and an engine shortage after the engine factory was bombed. As in Germany, much of Nakajima's fighter production was forced into underground factories.

Altogether, 3,509 Ki-84s were built (contrary to the drawing)—127 prototypes, service test and pre-production models; and 3,382 production Ki-84-Is and -IIs by Nakajima and the Mansyu Aeroplane Manufacturing Co. in Manchuria. The drawing total includes derivative designs with other designations, such as the Ki-87 variant with a turbo-supercharger and the lightweight Ki-116.

SPECIFICATIONS AND PERFORMANCE KI-84-IA

Wingspan	36 ft., 10 7/16 in.
Length	32 ft., 6 9/16 in.
Wing Area	226.04 sq. ft.
Empty Weight	5,864 lbs.
Gross Weight	7,955 lbs.
Overload Weight	8,576 lbs.

A wooden-fuselage Nakajima Ki-84-II on display at Wright Field after the war. The coloring is standard U.S. Army olive drab and gray. Unbordered and undersized Hinomaru markings have been re-applied for display purposes.

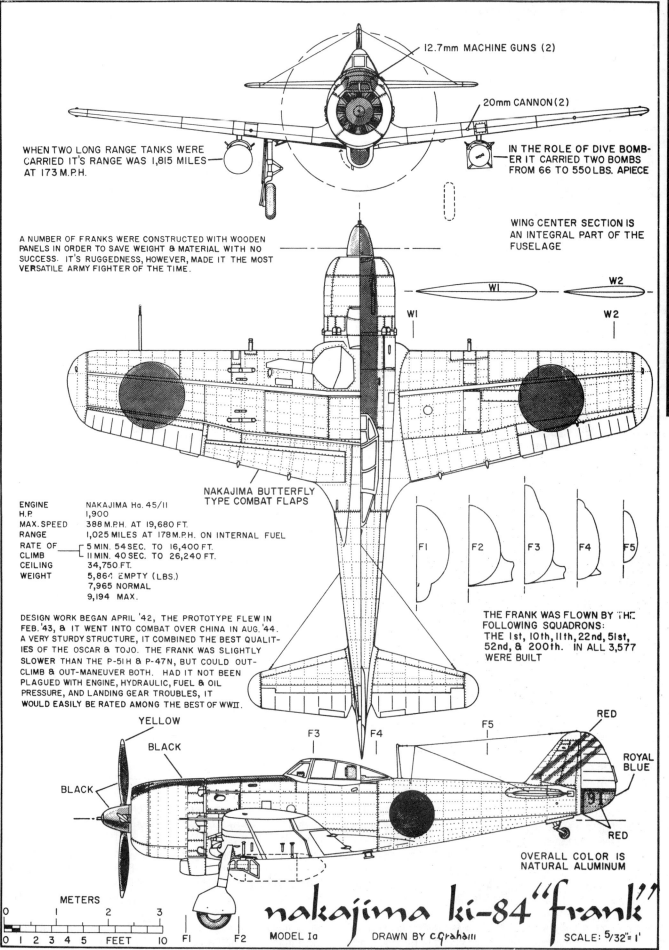

NAKAJIMA KI-84 FRANK

12.7mm MACHINE GUNS (2)

20mm CANNON (2)

WHEN TWO LONG RANGE TANKS WERE
CARRIED IT'S RANGE WAS 1,815 MILES
AT 173 M.P.H.

IN THE ROLE OF DIVE BOMB-
ER IT CARRIED TWO BOMBS
FROM 66 TO 550 LBS. APIECE

A NUMBER OF FRANKS WERE CONSTRUCTED WITH WOODEN
PANELS IN ORDER TO SAVE WEIGHT & MATERIAL WITH NO
SUCCESS. IT'S RUGGEDNESS, HOWEVER, MADE IT THE MOST
VERSATILE ARMY FIGHTER OF THE TIME.

WING CENTER SECTION IS
AN INTEGRAL PART OF THE
FUSELAGE

W1   W2

W1   W2

NAKAJIMA BUTTERFLY
TYPE COMBAT FLAPS

ENGINE   NAKAJIMA Ha. 45/11
H.P.   1,900
MAX. SPEED   388 M.P.H. AT 19,680 FT.
RANGE   1,025 MILES AT 178 M.P.H. ON INTERNAL FUEL
RATE OF   5 MIN. 54 SEC. TO 16,400 FT.
CLIMB   11 MIN. 40 SEC. TO 26,240 FT.
CEILING   34,750 FT.
WEIGHT   5,864 EMPTY (LBS.)
                7,965 NORMAL
                9,194 MAX.

F1   F2   F3   F4   F5

DESIGN WORK BEGAN APRIL '42, THE PROTOTYPE FLEW IN
FEB. '43, & IT WENT INTO COMBAT OVER CHINA IN AUG. '44.
A VERY STURDY STRUCTURE, IT COMBINED THE BEST QUALIT-
IES OF THE OSCAR & TOJO. THE FRANK WAS SLIGHTLY
SLOWER THAN THE P-51H & P-47N, BUT COULD OUT-
CLIMB & OUT-MANEUVER BOTH. HAD IT NOT BEEN
PLAGUED WITH ENGINE, HYDRAULIC, FUEL & OIL
PRESSURE, AND LANDING GEAR TROUBLES, IT
WOULD EASILY BE RATED AMONG THE BEST OF WWII.

THE FRANK WAS FLOWN BY THE
FOLLOWING SQUADRONS:
THE 1st, 10th, 11th, 22nd, 51st,
52nd, & 200th. IN ALL 3,577
WERE BUILT

F3   F4   F5   RED

YELLOW
BLACK   ROYAL
                                                 BLUE
BLACK

RED

OVERALL COLOR IS
NATURAL ALUMINUM

METERS
0   1   2   3

0 1 2 3 4 5   FEET   10   F1   F2

nakajima ki-84 "frank"

MODEL Ia   DRAWN BY c.Graham   SCALE: 5/32"=1'

NORTH AMERICAN P-51B MUSTANG

A camouflaged P-51B-5-NA Mustang, photographed with the Ninth Air Force in England. The letters "AX" identify the 12th Squadron of the 67th Reconnaissance Group, identified by the letter "M."

IN 1940, the British Purchasing Commission (in the U.S.) wanted North American (NAA) of Inglewood, CA, to build the Curtiss P-40 under license. NAA engineers had been researching a new fighter design that would overcome some of the notorious deficiencies of the designs used early in the war. The design would also incorporate a new aerodynamic feature: the laminar-flow wing.

In 120 days, NAA built a prototype that used the same 1,100hp Allison V-1710-F3R engine then being used in the P-40. The first flight of the NA-73 (the company-funded prototype with civil registration NX19998) was made on October 25, 1940. Production models with British-specified armament of six .303-caliber guns were flying in May 1941. NAA had originally called it the "Apache," but this was soon changed to "Mustang." The initial British contract was for 320 Mustang Is, and this was soon increased by another 300. Some of these were ac-

quired by the U.S. Army, but they weren't yet called P-51s.

The U.S. Army wasn't particularly interested in the new design, but it did direct that the fourth and tenth production Mustang Is be tested by the Army as "XP-51." Despite good maneuverability and high speed, the Army still wasn't interested in production. The 150 supplied to Britain as "Mustang IA" under Lend-Lease with four 20mm cannon were designated "P-51" though their armament and other details differed from the XP-51s. These carried both U.S. Army and British serial numbers.

The first Army order to NAA was for 500 examples of an odd type—a single-seat dive-bomber variant designated "A-36A." This had dive brakes, racks for two 500-pound bombs and an armament of six .50-caliber machine guns (four in the wings and two in the lower nose). The engine was the 1,325hp V-1710-87.

The A-36A first flew on September 21, 1942, and pro-

duction models took part in the invasions of North Africa and Sicily. The dive-bombing tactic, however, was soon abandoned, and the dive brakes were wired shut.

The first Army fighter order was for 310 P-51As with 1,200hp V-1710-81 engines. Armament was four .50-caliber guns in the wings. Britain obtained 50 P-51As under Lend-Lease as "Mustang II." At this time, the Army didn't send P-51As overseas for combat.

The Mustang's only serious shortcoming was its lack of performance at altitude, which was attributable to the Allison engine. The British were sufficiently concerned about this to upgrade four Mustangs with Rolls-Royce

Merlin engines. The performance gain was impressive, and the U.S. Army and NAA were encouraged to try Merlins in P-51s on their own. Two four-cannon P-51s were fitted with 1,380hp Packard-built V-1650-3 Merlins... and the rest is history.

Production orders followed for 1,998 P-51B-NAs at Inglewood and 1,750 similar P-51C-NTs from a new factory in Dallas, TX. Armament was the same as in the P-51A. The P-51Bs and Cs through B-10 and C-3 had 1,380hp V-1650-3 engines, while higher dash numbers of each had 1,490hp V-1650-7 engines.

The British designated their 275 P-51Bs "Mustang III," but they made no distinction for 636 P-51Cs, which carried the same name.

There were also camera-carrying versions of the P-51. Such P-51s were designated "F-6A"; P-51As became "F-6B"; and both P-51Bs and Cs became "F-6C."

Because the Wylam drawing shows the P-51B with high turtle deck, the later bubble-canopy variants (P-51D through P-51K) won't be detailed here, but the British called them all "Mustang IV."

SPECIFICATIONS AND PERFORMANCE P-51 B	
Wingspan	37 ft.
Length	32 ft., 3 in.
Wing Area	237.7 sq. ft.
Empty Weight	17,199 lbs.
Gross Weight	11,000 lbs.
High Speed	440mph at 30,000 ft.
Armament	Four .50-caliber guns, plus two 1,000-lb. bombs

NORTH AMERICAN MUSTANG P-51B

WORLD'S FINEST PURSUIT PLANE

william a. wylam

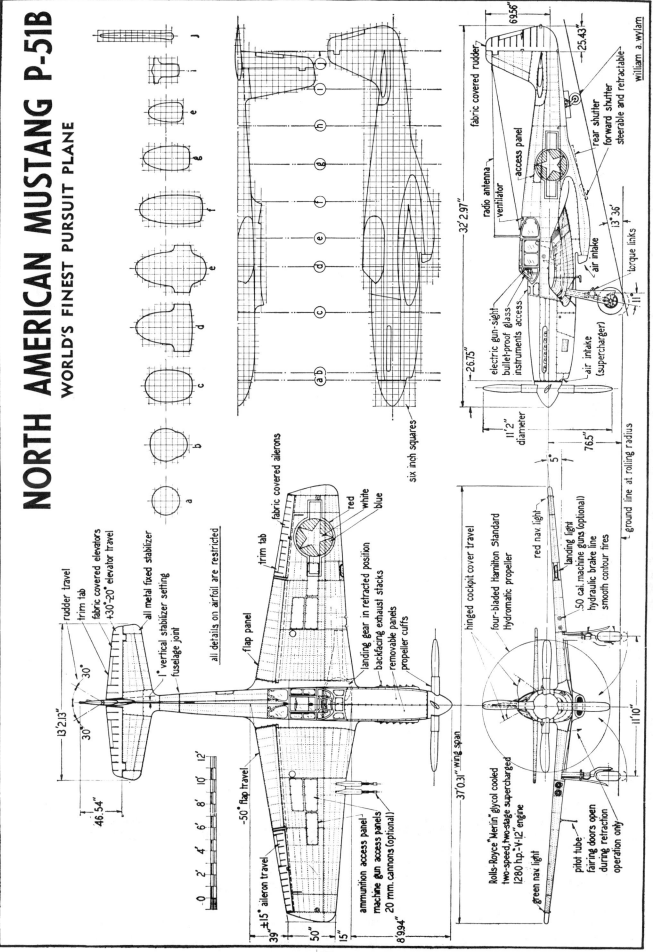

six inch squares

all details on airfoil are restricted

fabric covered ailerons

red
white
blue

trim tab

flap panel

landing gear in retracted position
backfacing exhaust stacks
removable panels
propeller cuffs

rudder travel
trim tab
fabric covered elevators
+30°-20° elevator travel
all metal fixed stabilizer
1° vertical stabilizer setting
fuselage joint

30°
30°
30°

13'2.13"

46.54"

-50° flap travel

±15° aileron travel

ammunition access panel
machine gun access panels
20 mm. cannons (optional)

39" 50" 15"
8'9.94"

0 2' 4' 6' 8' 10' 12'

fabric covered rudder
access panel
rear shutter
forward shutter
steerable and retractable

69.56"
25.43"

radio antenna
ventilator

32'2.97"

13'.36'

air intake
torque links

1'1"

electric gun-sight
bullet-proof glass
instruments access

26.75"

air intake
(supercharger)

11'2" diameter

76.5"

ground line at rolling radius

hinged cockpit cover travel

four-bladed Hamilton Standard
Hydromatic propeller

red nav. light
landing light
.50 cal. machine guns (optional)
hydraulic brake line
smooth contour tires

5°

37'0.31" wing span

11'10"

Rolls-Royce "Merlin" glycol cooled
two-speed, two-stage supercharged
1280 h.p. V-12 engine

pitot tube
fairing doors open
during retraction
operation only

green nav light

NORTHROP P-61 BLACK WIDOW

The glossy black Northrop P-61B on a factory test flight. Note the radar antenna alongside the cockpit. The army serial number below the fin is painted in red, which is standard for black night fighters.

MOST of the night fighters used in the war were adapted from existing designs for a specific mission. The only fighter that was specifically designed for night missions was the three-seat, twin-engine Northrop P-61. It was named "The Black Widow" because of its overall glossy black coloring.

The U.S. Army became interested in specialized night fighters as a result of British experience with German night raiders in 1940. Northrop Aircraft, Inc., of Hawthorne, CA, responded to an Army request and submitted a design with four fixed, forward-firing, 20mm cannon in the belly; British-designed radar in the nose to detect and track the enemy; and four .50-caliber machine guns in a powered turret for defense.

The engines were 2,000hp Pratt & Whitney R-2800-10s. The plane's most unusual feature was its twin-boom layout, with the crew in a short pod rather than in a full-length fuselage. The radar operator sat alongside the pilot. Two XP-61 prototypes were ordered, followed by 13 YP-61 service test models.

The first XP-61 had a matte-black finish and flew on May 26, 1942. Satisfactory tests resulted in an order for 200 production P-61As with glossy instead of dull paint, and deliveries began late in 1943. From the 38th aircraft on, the top turret was deleted in the belief that added speed was a better defense at night than manually aimed guns. The P-61As were sent to the Pacific and scored their first night victory on July 7, 1944. Others were sent to Europe and participated in the Normandy invasion.

The P-61As were followed by 450 improved P-61Bs in July 1944. Most of these restored the top turret and could carry either four 1,600-pound bombs or two 300 gallon drop tanks under their wings. Final production versions of the Black Widow were 41 P-61Cs with 2,800hp R-2800-77 engines.

Subsequent P-61 designations were for conversions.

Two XP-61Ds were former P-61As with R-2800-77 engines, and two XP-61Es were P-61Bs that were converted to day fighters with four cannons in the nose, no radar or top turret and the two-man crew seated in tandem under the longest one-piece bubble canopy built to that time. A P-61C conversion to XP-61F was cancelled. Sixteen P-61Bs were converted to unarmed P-61G Weather Reconnaissance planes. The first XP-61E was converted to the XF-15 "photo plane" with cameras in the nose, along with one P-61A that became the XF-15A. Thirty-six production F-15As followed, but they were out of service by 1952.

SPECIFICATIONS AND PERFORMANCE P-61 B	
Wingspan	66 ft.
Length	49 ft., 7 in.
Wing Area	664 sq. ft.
Gross Weight	29,700 lbs.
High Speed	366mph at 20,000 ft.

P-61As (with black and white "Invasion Stripes") over Europe after the invasion of July 6, 1944. The wartime censor has left the serial numbers on the airplanes but has blacked out the radar antennas. Note the "Shark Face" painted on the nearest plane.

NORTHROP P-61 BLACK WIDOW

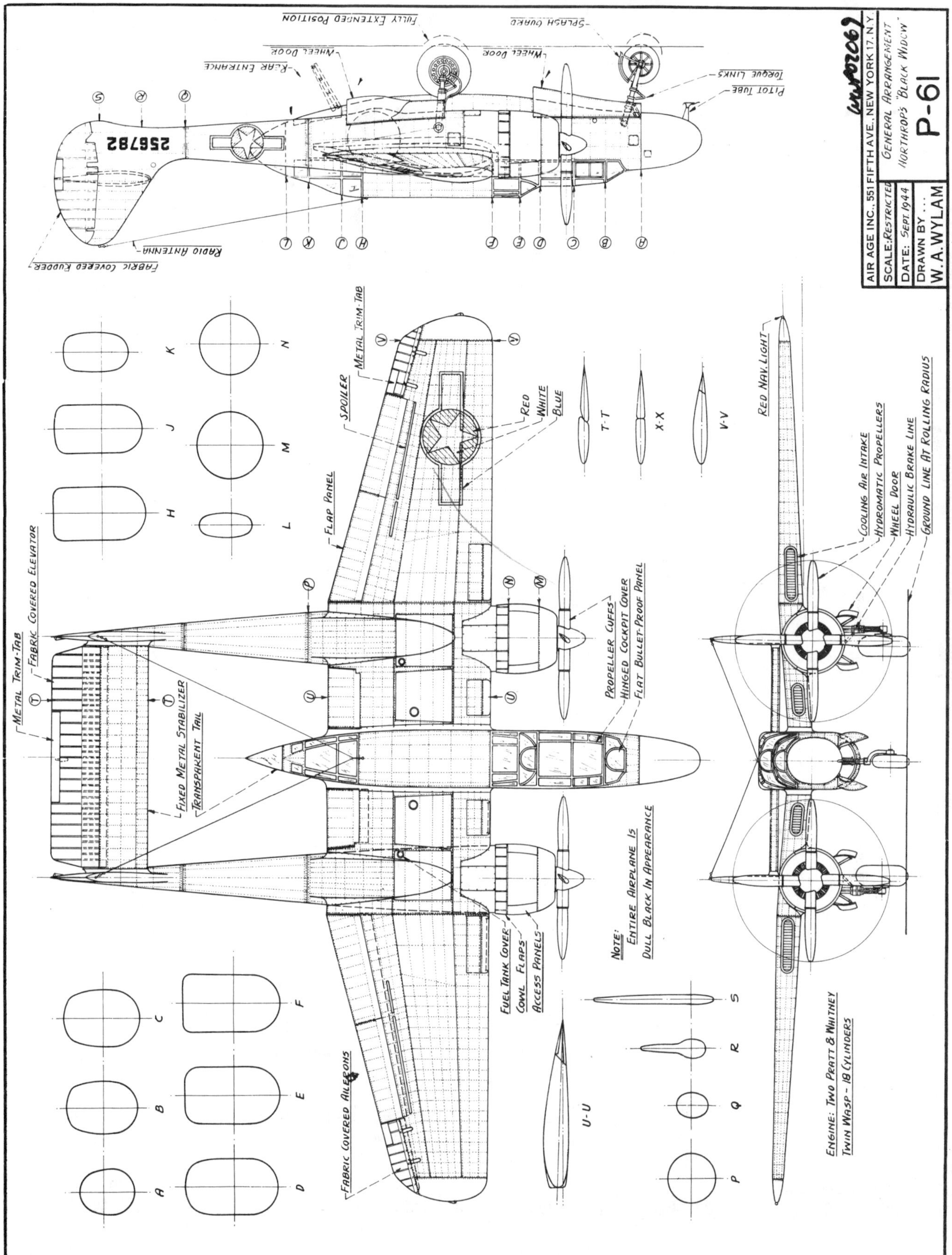
AIR AGE INC., 551 FIFTH AVE., NEW YORK 17, N.Y.
SCALE: RESTRICTED
DATE: SEPT. 1944
DRAWN BY ...
W. A. WYLAM
GENERAL ARRANGEMENT
NORTHROP'S "BLACK WIDOW"
P-61
FULLY EXTENDED POSITION
SPLASH GUARD
WHEEL DOOR
REAR ENTRANCE
WHEEL DOOR
TORQUE LINKS
PITOT TUBE
256782
RADIO ANTENNA
FABRIC COVERED RUDDER
METAL TRIM-TAB
FABRIC COVERED ELEVATOR
FIXED METAL STABILIZER
TRANSPARENT TAIL
SPOILER
METAL TRIM-TAB
RED
WHITE
BLUE
FLAP PANEL
PROPELLER CUFFS
HINGED COCKPIT COVER
FLAT BULLET-PROOF PANEL
NOTE:
ENTIRE AIRPLANE IS
DULL BLACK IN APPEARANCE
FUEL TANK COVER
COWL FLAPS
ACCESS PANELS
FABRIC COVERED AILERONS
ENGINE: TWO PRATT & WHITNEY
TWIN WASP - 18 CYLINDERS
T-T
X-X
V-V
U-U
RED NAV. LIGHT
COOLING AIR INTAKE
HYDROMATIC PROPELLERS
WHEEL DOOR
HYDRAULIC BRAKE LINE
GROUND LINE AT ROLLING RADIUS

REPUBLIC P-47 THUNDERBOLT

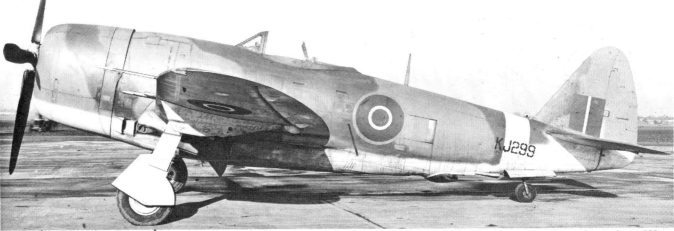

A Republic P-47D-25 in service with the Royal Air Force as "Thunderbolt II." The streamlined shape under the wing is a rack for either a drop tank or a 500- or 1,000-pound bomb. Note the absence of a dorsal fin.

THE Republic P-47 Thunderbolt, commonly called "The Jug," is an excellent example of a successful fighter that evolved through a series of designs from the same design team.

The Jug's distinctive configuration can be traced back to the 1933 appearance of the Seversky SEV-3 twin-float amphibian. The plane's distinctive features were its all-metal construction, its fuselage with a nearly circular cross-section, and its wing planform (straight sweepback on the leading edge and an elliptical trailing edge and wing tips). This trademark wing planform (shared with the Supermarine Spitfire) was retained for all subsequent Seversky and Republic fighters through the P-47 and some of its experimental derivatives.

Alexander Seversky, a former Imperial Russian Air Force pilot, didn't have a factory when he started business.

His first airplane was built by Edo of College Point, NY, a famous builder of all-metal seaplane pontoons. Now, with a successful design to sell, Seversky established a factory in Farmingdale, Long Island, NY. The second Seversky airplane, which was similar to

A P-47C shows off the sharp-topped fuselage structure behind the cockpit that earned models before the P-47D-25 the nickname "Razorback."

the first, was initially tested as a two-seat, land-plane fighter with fixed landing gear. It was soon modified (for a U.S. Army fly-off design competition) to a single-seater with an 850hp Pratt & Whitney R-1830 Twin Wasp engine and

backward-retracting gear. Seversky won a production order for 77 P-35s with 950hp R-1830-9 engines, backward-retracting gear and an armament of one .30-caliber and one .50-caliber machine gun. Deliveries began in 1937, and the last production aircraft

was fitted with a turbo-supercharger in the belly, and a new wing of the same span and area as the XP-41, but with a different center section and inward-retracting landing gear.

By that time, Seversky had been ousted, and the company

was renamed "Republic." The new features of the XP-41 were incorporated into a new model, the P-43, which used the 1,200hp R-1830-35 engine and a standard armament of two .30-caliber and two .50-caliber machine guns. The fuselage had refined lines and was nearly 2 feet longer than the P-35/XP-41. There were 272 P-43s and P-43As built. Meanwhile, Republic had been selling export versions of the P-35. Of 120 ordered by Sweden, 60 were drafted by the U.S. after the Arms Embargo went into effect, and they were designated "P-35A." Most were shipped to the Philippines, where they soon fell victim to the Japanese Zero.

There was to have been a P-44—essentially the P-43 fitted with the new 1,850hp Pratt & Whitney R-2800 engine—but it was decided that the engine was too big for the existing airframe. A new Republic model that was then being designed (the light-

This P-47D-30 with a dorsal fin and 150-gallon drop tanks has the dark blue stripes of the First Air Commando Group, which was based in Southeast Asia in 1944-45.

weight XP-47) was cancelled, and the designation "XP-47B" was given to an enlarged development of the P-43 that would use a big engine and eight .50-caliber machine guns (the heaviest armament then fitted to a single-seat fighter). The XP-47B, with a 2,000hp XR-2800-21 engine, flew on May 6, 1941, and it was followed by P-47 production models through P-47N (to a total of 15,683 planes), which are detailed here.

P-47B—This was the first production model, and 171 were built. Deliveries started late in 1942, and some went into action in Europe on April 8, 1943. In combat, the P-47B-RE had inadequate climb and maneuverability, but it had plenty of speed and firepower. It also had excellent diving ability, and its heavy structure could absorb terrific punishment. Its wingspan was 40 feet, 9 inches; area, 300 square feet; gross weight, 13,360 pounds; high speed, 429mph at 27,800 feet.

P-47C—The 602 P-47Cs were refined P-47Bs that had their noses lengthened 13 inches and were equipped to carry a 200-gallon drop tank under the fuselage. Although it wasn't quite as fast as the P-47B, its greater range enabled it to be used on long-range escort missions.

P-47D—This model was the major production version, and 6,315 were built. The initial improvement was a water-injected version of the 2,000hp R-2800-21 engine, which gave it a top speed of 433mph at 30,000 feet. Provision was made for two

150-gallon drop tanks under the wings or a 250- to 1,000-pound bomb on the same streamlined rack, plus a 500-pound bomb under the fuselage. A new Republic plant was built in Evansville, IN, and 2,350 P-47D-RAs were built there.

There were two notable external changes during P-47D production: a cut-down rear fuselage and a bubble canopy (as tested on the XP-47K) became standard on the P-47D-25 and on, and a long, shallow dorsal fin was added to the P-47D-27 and on. Because of the two different fuselage configurations, the P-47 models prior to D-25 became known as "Razorbacks."

The P-47D proved to be more effective as a fighter-bomber than as an escort fighter, and from P-47D-30 on, provision was made for

carrying 10 rockets under the wings in addition to the bombs. England received 240 Razorback P-47Ds as "Thunderbolt I," and 590 P-47D-25s and on as "Thunderbolt II." The gross weight of the P-47D-25 was 19,400 pounds; its high speed was 428mph at 30,000 feet.

XP-47E—The last P-47B tested with a pressurized cockpit.

XP-47F—One P-47B tested with a laminar-flow wing.

P-47G—Duplicates of the P-47B built by Curtiss to compensate for the cancelled P-60A contract.

XP-47H, J, K and L—Experimental conversions which tested new features and equipment. The XP-47J tested a new, liquid-cooled, 2,300hp, 16-cylinder Chrysler XIV-2220-1 engine; the lightened XP-47J with a 2,100hp R-2800-61 engine became the

first piston-engined plane to exceed 500mph; the XP-47K tested the bubble canopy; and the XP-47L had increased internal fuel capacity.

P-47M—A need for a fast, high-altitude fighter was met with the P-47M. Only 150 were built after three P-47Ds were modified as YP-47M prototypes. The bomb and rocket racks were deleted, and special 2,800hp R-2800-57 engines gave a top speed of 473mph at 32,500 feet. Most of the P-47Ms were in combat in Europe in the closing months of the war.

P-47N—The final production model, P-47, was produced solely for action in the Pacific. Its new wing had a span of 42 feet, 10 inches, an area of 322 square feet and squared-off wing tips. With additional internal fuel (as tested on the XP-47L), two 93-gallon drop tanks under the wings and a 100-gallon drop tank under the fuselage, the P-47N had a total fuel capacity of 1,266 gallons and a range of 2,350 miles, which was enough to enable it to escort B-29s to Japan in the last months of the war. With a 2,800hp R-2800-77 engine, the P-47N had a gross weight of 20,700 pounds and a high speed of 467mph at 32,500 feet.

Republic built 1,667 P-47Ns in Farmingdale and 149 in Evansville. A further 5,934 planes were cancelled. The P-47 was retired as a first-line fighter right after the war, but bubble-canopy P-47Ds and P-47Ns stayed in the reserve training squadrons until 1955.

This is the final "Jug" model, the P-47N, with a lengthened and square-tipped wing. This plane is in fighter-bomber configuration, with two 1,000-pound bombs and 10 rockets.

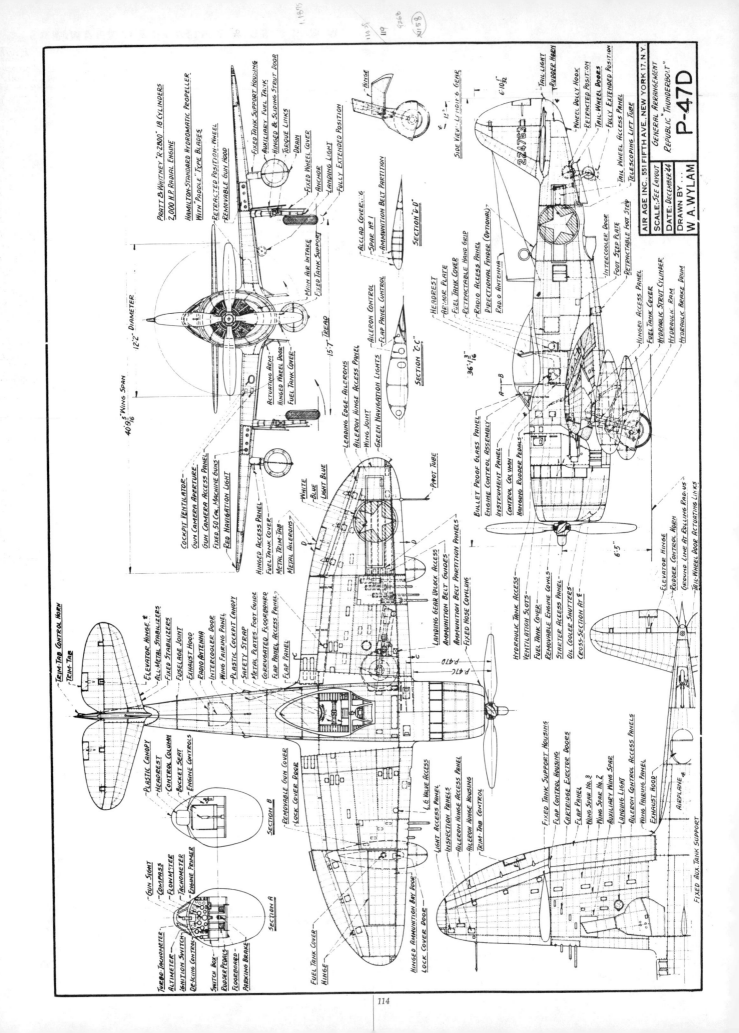

AIR AGE INC. 551 FIFTH AVE. NEW YORK 17. N.Y.

General Arrangement
Republic "Thunderbolt"

P-47D

SCALE : See Layout
DATE : December 44
DRAWN BY ...
W. A. WYLAM

REPUBLIC P-47 THUNDERBOLT

P-47D

AIR AGE INC. 551 FIFTH AVE. NEW YORK 17, N.Y.
LAYOUTS & CROSS-SECTIONS
REPUBLIC "THUNDERBOLT"
SCALE: *Above*
DATE: *December 44*
DRAWN BY ... W. A. WYLAM

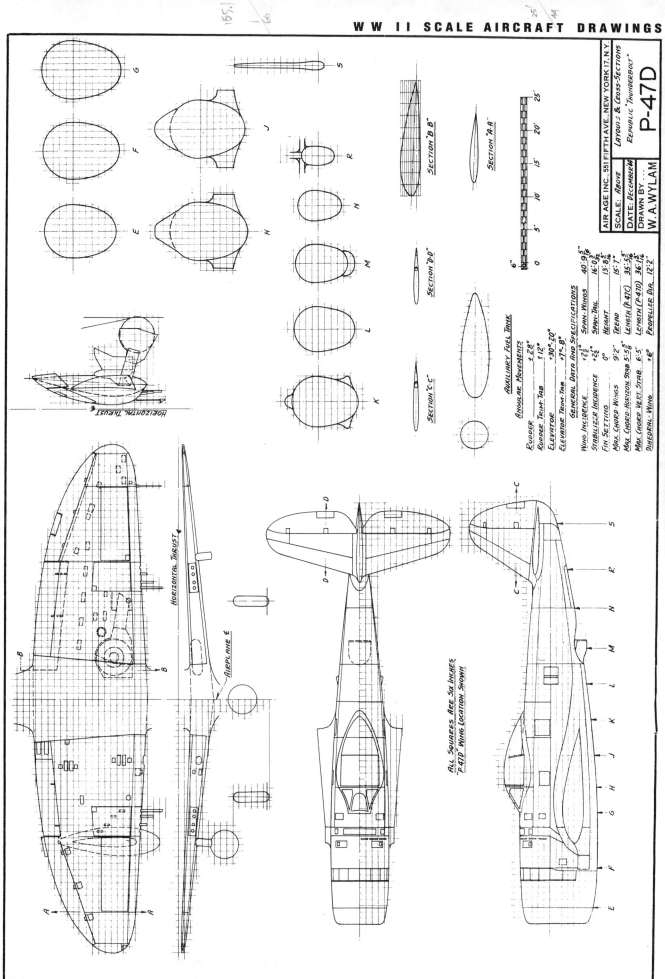

SECTION "B-B"

SECTION "A-A"

AUXILIARY FUEL TANK

SECTION "D-D"

SECTION "C-C"

ANGULAR MOVEMENTS

RUDDER	±28°
RUDDER TRIM-TAB	±12°
ELEVATOR	+30°-20°
ELEVATOR TRIM-TAB	+7°-8°

GENERAL DATA AND SPECIFICATIONS

WING INCIDENCE	+2½°
STABILIZER INCIDENCE	+2½°
FIN SETTING	0°
MAX. CHORD-WINGS	9'2"
MAX. CHORD-HORIZON. STAB.	5'-5⅝
MAX. CHORD VERT. STAB.	6'5
DIHEDRAL-WING	+6°
SPAN-WINGS	40'-9⅝"
SPAN-TAIL	16'-0 3/32
HEIGHT	13'-8 3/16
TREAD	15'-7"
LENGTH (P-47C)	35'-5 5/16
LENGTH (P-47D)	36'-1 1/16
PROPELLER DIA.	12'2"

HORIZONTAL THRUST

HORIZONTAL THRUST

AIRPLANE ₵

ALL SQUARES ARE SIX INCHES
"P-47D" WING LOCATION SHOWN

STEARMAN KAYDET

THE Kaydet was the most used U.S. military primary trainer of WW II, but there's often confusion surrounding it because it had two builders' names—Stearman and Boeing. In 1934, after the breakup of the United Aircraft and Transport companies, the Stearman Aircraft Company of Wichita, KS became a wholly owned subsidiary of Boeing. It became Boeing's Stearman Division in 1938, and the Wichita Division of Boeing in 1941, when the airplanes officially became Boeings, even though the old Stearman model and serial numbers were continued. However, all those associated with the airplanes—builders and users alike—stubbornly continued to call the planes Stearmans, and today they're still referred to as such in the antique airplane movement.

In the case of the Stearman/ Boeing Model 75, the use of the name "Kaydet" made it readily identifiable, even though there were eight manufacturers' sub-designations, four U.S. Army model designations and five U.S. Navy N2S series designations (see table).

The original Stearman Model 70 trainer, with a welded-steel tube fuselage and wooden-frame wings, flew late in 1933. The U.S. Navy bought 61 improved Model 73s in 1934 as NS-1 ("N" for trainer, "S" for Stearman) and had them fitted with 220hp Wright J-5 engines that had been out of production since 1929, but were still plentiful in Navy

A Stearman PT-13A banked over to reveal the underside detail. The U.S. Army lettering is 24 inches high; the star insignia is 30 inches in diameter under the wing and 42 inches above.

warehouses.

Model 75, which was introduced in October, 1934, was similar to Model 73, but it used three different 220hp radial engines and won large orders from both the Army and the Navy. Altogether, 8,504 biplanes were built in the Model 70-76 series, with spare parts raising the widely publicized total to 10,346 (only the U.S. military Model 75s are shown in the table). Unit prices, less such government-furnished equipment

(GFE) as engines and instruments, ranged from $7,713 to $10,412.

Until the spring of 1942, the Army Kaydets had colorful blue fuselages, chrome-yellow wing and tail surfaces, and the distinctive Army rudder stripes that had been used since 1926. Subsequent Army deliveries were all silver and without stripes. The winterized PT-27s supplied to Canada under Lend-Lease were all yellow, and some had cockpit canopies. Early Navy Kaydets were all yellow. Most of the later models were all silver, but a few were delivered all yellow.

Before inter-service standardization with the E-75 model, the Army and Navy frequently exchanged their Kaydets. Oddly, the different Navy dash numbers weren't equally significant; the difference between the N2S-1 and -2 was the same as between the Army PT-17 and PT-13, with entirely different engines, while the N2S-1, -3 and -4 differed only in the dash numbers of the same Continental R-670 engine.

Stearman Model	U.S. Army Designation	U.S. Navy Designation	Engine	No. Built
75	PT-13	-	Lycoming R-680	26
A75	PT-13A, B	-	Lycoming R-680	268
A75J-1	PT-18	-	Jacobs R-755	150
A75N-1	PT-17, 17A	N2S-1, -4	Continental R-670	3,769
B75	-	N2S-2	Lycoming R-680	125
B75N-1	-	N2S-3	Continental R-670	1,875
D75N-1	PT-27	-	Continental R-670	300
E75	PT-13D	N2S-5	Lycoming R-680	1,786

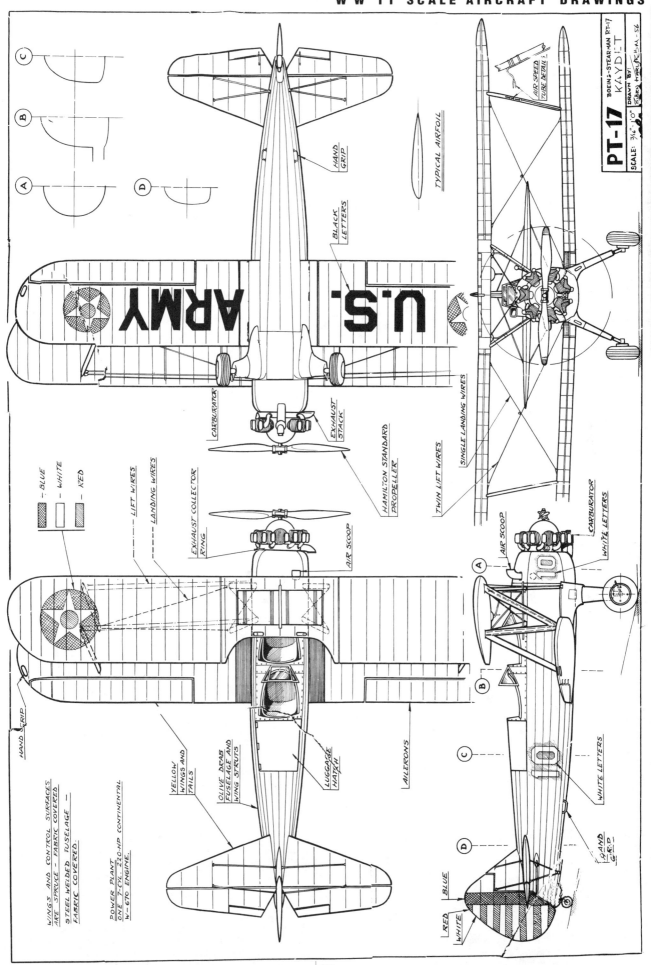

STEARMAN KAYDET

PT-17 BOEING-STEARMAN PT-17
KAYDET
SCALE: ³/₄"=1'0"
DRAWN BY:

HAND GRIP

TYPICAL AIRFOIL

BLACK LETTERS

CARBURATOR

EXHAUST STACK

AIR SPEED TUBE DETAIL

HAMILTON STANDARD PROPELLER

TWIN LIFT WIRES

SINGLE LANDING WIRES

LIFT WIRES

LANDING WIRES

EXHAUST COLLECTOR RING

AIR SCOOP

CARBURATOR

WHITE LETTERS

AIR SCOOP

BLUE
WHITE
RED

HAND GRIP

YELLOW WINGS AND TAILS

OLIVE DRAB FUSELAGE AND WING STRUTS

LUGGAGE HATCH

AILERONS

WHITE LETTERS

HAND GRIP

RED
WHITE
BLUE

WINGS AND CONTROL SURFACES ARE SPRUCE - FABRIC COVERED.
STEEL WELDED FUSELAGE - FABRIC COVERED.

POWER PLANT
ONE 7-CYL. 220-HP CONTINENTAL
W-670 ENGINE.

U.S. ARMY

SUPERMARINE SPITFIRE

THE British Supermarine "Spitfire" was one of the greatest all-around fighters of the war. Its lines and performance, however, weren't the result of a long line of pedigreed fighters, in the way that the Hawker Hurricane evolved from Hawker and Sopwith fighters dating back to WW I. Rather, the Spitfire evolved from a line of monoplane seaplane racers that was started by designer Reginald J. Mitchell in 1925. His S-4 model changed the development of high-speed aircraft from biplanes to low-wing monoplanes. Later S-models set new speed records. The S-6B of 1931 retired the Schneider Trophy with a

An early Spitfire I with a fixed-pitch wooden propeller and a straight top canopy. Note the Type A roundel under the wing and the Type A.1 roundel on the fuselage.

speed of 340.8mph around a triangular course, and it later set a new absolute speed record of 407.5mph.

Mitchell's racers were masterpieces in the way they fit the slimmest possible fuselage around a pilot and a liquid-cooled engine. This practice continued with the Spitfire, which was built in response to a 1934 Air Ministry request for an eight-gun fighter. The prototype used a 990hp Rolls-Royce Merlin C engine, and featured an elliptical wing

planform for maximum aerodynamic efficiency, which was supposed to offset the handicap of added structural complexity. The narrow landing gear retracted outward into the wing, which, in its initial form, contained eight .303-caliber machine guns. The semi-monocoque metal fuselage was so narrow at the pilot's shoulder level that it was necessary to install a hinge-down door on the left side for access.

The prototype flew on March 5, 1936, and production orders soon followed. Spitfire Is with 1,030hp Merlins driving fixed-pitch, wooden two-blade propellers began to reach the squadrons

A Mk V Spitfire with a fin flash and an A.1 roundel on the fuselage, as used from December 1940 through June 1942. The Type B roundel was retained on the wings almost until the war's end. Note the rear-view mirror above the windshield and the tape over the gun muzzles.

A Spitfire H.F.VII with extended triangular wing tips (above) and a Spitfire VB with clipped wing tips (below).

in May 1938. Later articles featured three-blade, controllable-pitch metal propellers. Nine squadrons of Spitfires were in service by the start of the war, and 19 were in service when the Battle of Britain started in August 1940. Spitfires fought in all theaters where the R.A.F. operated.

The early Spitfires were slightly superior to the German Me 109E in speed and maneuverability, but the Me 109 could out-climb and out-dive them, and its guns had greater range. To meet the competition, the Spitfire was continually improved throughout the war years, using two different engines and a variety of wing planforms and structures to accommodate varying armament. It also used different fuselages and tail shapes.

In 1940, three of the famous Eagle Squadrons, manned by American volunteer pilots, flew Spitfires. Because of the shortage of American fighters in 1943, the British provided two U.S. Army Air Force fighter groups in England with Spitfires.

Altogether, the U.S. obtained 600 Spitfires under Reverse Lend-Lease out of the 21,767 built. These weren't given standard U.S. Army designations or serial numbers. Instead, they flew with British designations, serial numbers, equipment and coloring, with only the U.S. star insignia to identify them as being operated by the USAAF.

Although the accompanying drawings show the Spitfire V

with the standard wing and fuselage, the following text and photos cover all of the variants through the postwar Spitfire 24, and identify the significant configuration changes. The higher Mark (Mk) numbers are out of sequence because the Spitfires with Merlin engines are grouped separately from those with Griffon engines. It should be noted that Spitfires through Mk XX were identified by Roman numerals, while later ones were identified with Arabic figures.

SEA-GOING SPITFIRES

It was inevitable that a successful land-based fighter would be considered for use

A Spitfire Mk VB of the 309th Fighter Squadron, 31st Fighter Group, with U.S. insignia. Note the bulge on the wing over the cannon breech and the hinge-down door necessary for pilot access to the narrow cockpit.

on aircraft carriers. This was done with the Spitfire, which then became the "Seafire." (The basic Seafire and its variants are described following the Griffon Spitfire write-ups.)

SPITFIRE WINGS

The basic Spitfire wing had an elliptical planform, a span of 36 feet, 10 inches and an area of 242 square feet. It was built in three types: A, B and C. The A-Wing had provision for four or eight .303-caliber machine guns entirely enclosed within it. The B-Wing had provision for two 20mm cannon in place of two machine guns. The C-Wing was called the "Universal Wing," and it could carry two 20mm cannons and either two or four .303 guns. The final wing was the E-Wing, which had only 1 inch more span but 2 feet more area, because of its different root and tip shapes. This wing was fitted with four 20mm cannons.

SUPERMARINE SPITFIRE

A Spitfire F.Mk XIV with a Rolls-Royce Griffon engine, four-blade propeller, cut-down rear fuselage with bubble canopy, and an enlarged vertical tail.

In all cases, the structure of the A-, B- and C-wings allowed for planform variations. The wing-tip panels could be removed and the ends covered to produce a "clipped wing" with a 32-foot, 7-inch span. The span could also be increased to 40 feet, 2 inches by adding new triangular tips in place of the ellipticals. These span changes could be made within the various Spitfire Marks without affecting the Mark numbers. Some of the Spitfire Mark numbers mentioned below were assigned to Seafires.

MERLIN-POWERED SPITFIRES

Mark I—This was the initial production model, with a 1,030hp Merlin II engine and a non-retractable tail wheel. The early straight-top canopy changed to the bulged type to increase the pilot's headroom and visibility. There were four .303 guns in the Mk I because of a shortage; but there were eight in the

Mk IA. It had no protective armor. The Mk 1B had a B-Wing.

Mark II—This was just like the Mk I but had a 1,050hp Merlin XII engine and 73 pounds of armor. The Mk IIB had two 20mm cannons and four .303 guns in the B-Wing. A few flew in the Battle of Britain, and some were later converted to Mk V with more armor and a Merlin 45 engine.

Mark III—This was a single prototype, strengthened to take the two-stage Merlin XX engine that delivered 1,280hp for takeoff and 1,480hp at 12,250 feet. It had additional armor, a strengthened structure, a retractable tail wheel and clipped wings. The 1,000 production versions ordered were completed as "Mks V" and "IX," and a further 120 were cancelled.

P.R. Mark III—Unrelated to the Mk III prototype, many Mks I and II were fitted with cameras in the fuselage and redesignated "P.R. Mk III" (for "Photoreconnaissance").

P.R. Mark IV—This unarmed photoreconnaissance variant appeared in September 1941. Extra range was obtained by building fuel tanks into the leading edge of the wing, thereby eliminating the guns. Various cameras were in the fuselage, as they were on the P.R. Mk III.

Mark V—A major advance, using the Merlin 45, 50, or 50A (1,470hp at 9,250 feet), or the -46 engine that delivered 1,415hp at 14,000 feet. Mks VB and VC could carry 115 or 175 Imperial gallon auxiliary tanks under the fuselage and either two 250- or one 500-pound bomb. The Mk VC introduced the C-Wing and entered service in March 1941. Some were modified for low-altitude work with 1,585hp Merlin 45M, 50M, or 55M engines, and were redesignated "L.F. Mk V" (for "Low-Altitude Fighter").

Mark VI—This high-altitude

fighter with a pressurized cockpit and 1,415hp Merlin 47 engine was developed from the Mk VB. This model introduced the extended, pointed wing tips. Gross weight: 7,178 pounds; high speed: 364mph at 22,000 feet.

Mark VII—A designed-for-the-purpose high-altitude fighter with a two-stage, 1,710hp Merlin 64 engine, a C-Wing and a retractable tail wheel. It was delivered in April 1942. Gross weight: 7,875 pounds; high speed: 408mph at 25,000 feet.

F. Mark VIII—This was similar to the Mk VII, but didn't have the pressurization. The high-altitude version with an extended wing was designated "H.F. Mk VIII"; the low-altitude version with clipped wings was designated "L.F. Mk VIII." Several Mk VIIIs were used for experimental modifications, but retained their "Mk VIII" designation.

Mark IX—With the Mk V outclassed by later Me 109s and the new Focke-Wulf Fw 190, Mk V airframes were refitted with 1,720hp Merlin 66 engines and redesignated "Mk IX." There were three versions—standard F, H.F. and L.F.—all with the Mk V's fixed tail wheel. Deliveries began in July 1942. H.F. Mk IX gross weight: 7,500 pounds; high

The first Spitfire Mk 22, with a Griffon engine, five-blade propeller, bubble canopy and enlarged tail. Note the bulges in the nose to cover the cylinder banks of the larger engine.

The final variant of the Spitfire line: the Seafire Mk 46 with contra-rotating propellers. Note the extension of the rudder carried by the stinger-type arrester hook. The later Mk 47 was very similar, except for its greater fuel capacity and folding wings.

speed: 416mph at 27,500 feet.

P.R. Mark X—A pressurized photo-reconnaissance version of the Mk IX.

P.R. Mark XI—Just like the P.R. Mk X but without pressurization. It was delivered in 1942.

Mark XVI—Similar to the Mk IX; some had a C-Wing, and later versions had an E-Wing and an enlarged vertical tail. Others had a cut-down rear fuselage and a bubble canopy. It was delivered in 1944 with a low-altitude, American-built Packard Merlin engine.

GRIFFON-POWERED SPITFIRES

The need for greater performance resulted in the installation of the 1,735-2,050hp Rolls-Royce Griffon engine. This was larger than the Merlin (2,240-cubic-inch displacement vs. 1,650). The larger size resulted in prominent bulges in the longer nose to cover the cylinder banks. Four- and five-blade propellers were used, and some variants used two three-blade counter-rotating propellers. Altogether, 2,053 Spitfires were delivered with Griffon engines.

Mark IV—The Griffon prototype, with a 1,735hp engine, a four-blade propeller and an extensively reinforced structure. A mock-up wing was fitted with six 20mm cannon, but no six-cannon Spitfire was ever produced. To avoid confusion with the Merlin-powered P.R. Mk IV, the Mk IV prototype was redesignated "Mk XX."

Mark XII—Built in two ver-sions: a strengthened Mk VC airframe for low-altitude fighting with a fixed tail wheel; and a Mk VIII airframe with retractable tail wheels. All entered service early in 1943 and had larger vertical tails and four-blade propellers. Gross weight: 7,400 pounds; high speed: 393mph at 18,000 feet.

Mark XIV— These had Mk VIII airframes with five-blade propellers. Some late articles had cut-down rear fuselages and bubble canopies. The F.R. Mk XIVE was a fighter-reconnaissance variant with fuselage cameras and a 2,050hp Griffon 65 engine. Gross weight: 8,500 pounds; high speed: 448mph at 26,000 feet.

Mark XVIII—Built from scratch in two versions: the F.Mk XVIII fighters and the F.R. Mk XVIII fighter-reconnaissance planes. Both versions had a reinforced fuselage and wing, and carried additional fuel. They were delivered too late to serve in the war.

P.R. Mark XIX—Unarmed Mk XIV airframes with a Mk VC wing. The first 20 weren't pressurized, but the final 225 were. They were operational in the closing months of the war.

Mark XX—The Mk IV prototype redesignated.

Mark 21—A major redesign with new E-Wing and fuselage structure but old-style cockpit canopy. Its powerplant was a 2,050hp Griffon 61 engine driving a five-blade propeller. It had four-cannon armament.

This design was made too late for combat; only 122 of the 1,500 Mk 21s ordered were built. Gross weight: 9,200 pounds; high speed: 454mph at 26,000 feet.

Mark 22—This was similar to the Mk 22, except for its cut-down rear fuselage and bubble canopy. Some had contra-rotating propellers.

Mark 24—The last of 21,767 Spitfires and Seafires built was the Mk 24, which was similar to the Mk 22, but had increased fuel capacity. The last one was delivered to the R.A.F. in October 1947.

SEAFIRES

Mark IB—This was a conversion of A-Wing Mk VB Spitfires with A-frame arrester hooks (see "Hawker Sea Hurricane"). They were put into service in June 1942. Seafires participated in the invasion of North Africa in November 1942.

Mark IIC—These were built as new airframes similar to the Mk VC Spitfires with C-Wings. It came in two versions, the F. Mk IIC and the L.F. Mk IIC; the latter had a 1,645hp Merlin 32 engine and four-blade propeller. Some L.F. IICs were fitted with cameras and operated as "P.R. Mk IIC."

Mark III—A disadvantage of the early Seafires was their lack of folding wings for shipboard storage. On the designed-for-the-purpose Mk III, the outer wing panels folded upward near the root, and the tips folded downward to re-duce the height and clear the ceiling of the below-deck hangars. Its armament was two 20mm cannon and four .303 guns. The fuselage was reinforced for catapult launching, and up to 500 pounds of bombs could be carried. Variants were the L.F. Mk III and F.R. Mk III. Engine: 1,470hp Merlin 55; gross weight: 7,100 pounds; high speed: 352mph at 12,250 feet.

Mark XV—This was essentially a sea-going variant of the Mk XII Spitfire, with a 1,850hp Griffon VI engine and a four-blade propeller. After the first 50, the arrester hook was changed from the A-frame type to a stinger type below the rudder which was fitted with a fairing that continued the rudder contour. Gross weight: 8,000 pounds; high speed: 383mph at 13,500 feet.

Mark XVII—Similar to the Mk XV except for the bubble canopy.

Mark 45—The postwar equivalent of the Spitfire Mk 22, with non-folding wings and a Griffon 61 engine with a five-blade propeller.

Mark 46—Similar to the Mk 45, except that it was powered by a Griffon 87 engine driving co-axial propellers. Also, it had the fuselage structure and bubble canopy of the Spitfire Mk 22.

Mark 47—Similar to the Mk 46, except that its wings folded upward outboard of the cannon, and it wasn't necessary to fold the wing tips.

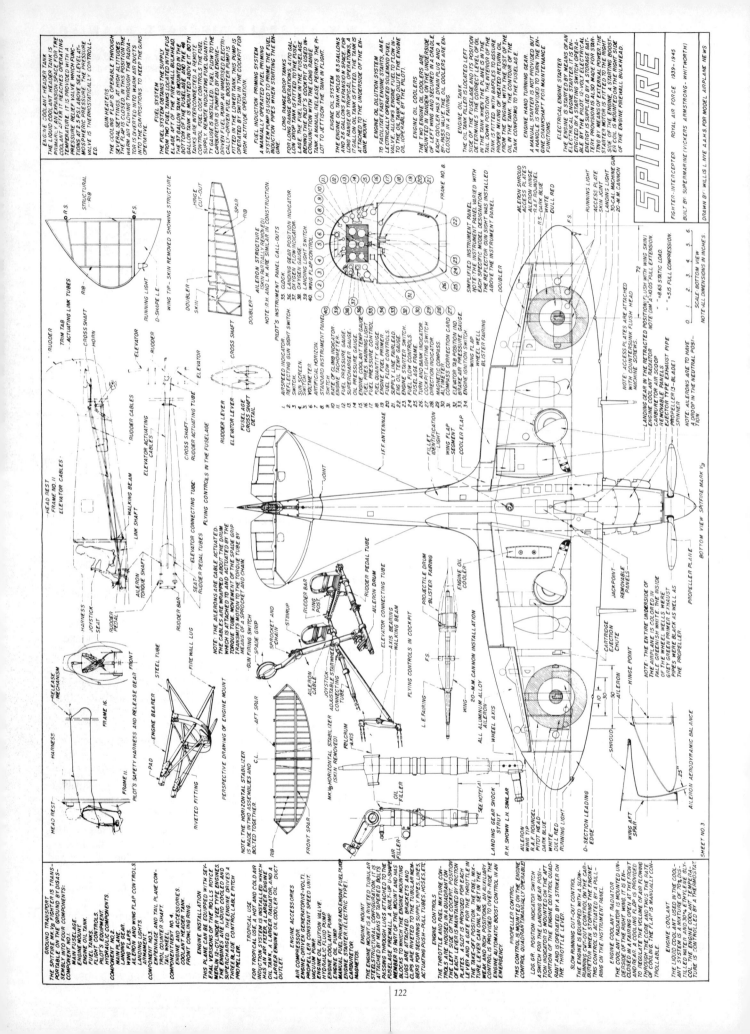

SPITFIRE

FIGHTER-INTERCEPTER   ROYAL AIR FORCE 1939-1945
BUILT BY: SUPERMARINE (VICKERS ARMSTRONG - WHITWORTH)
DRAWN BY: WILLIS L NYE A.A.H.S. FOR MODEL AIRPLANE NEWS

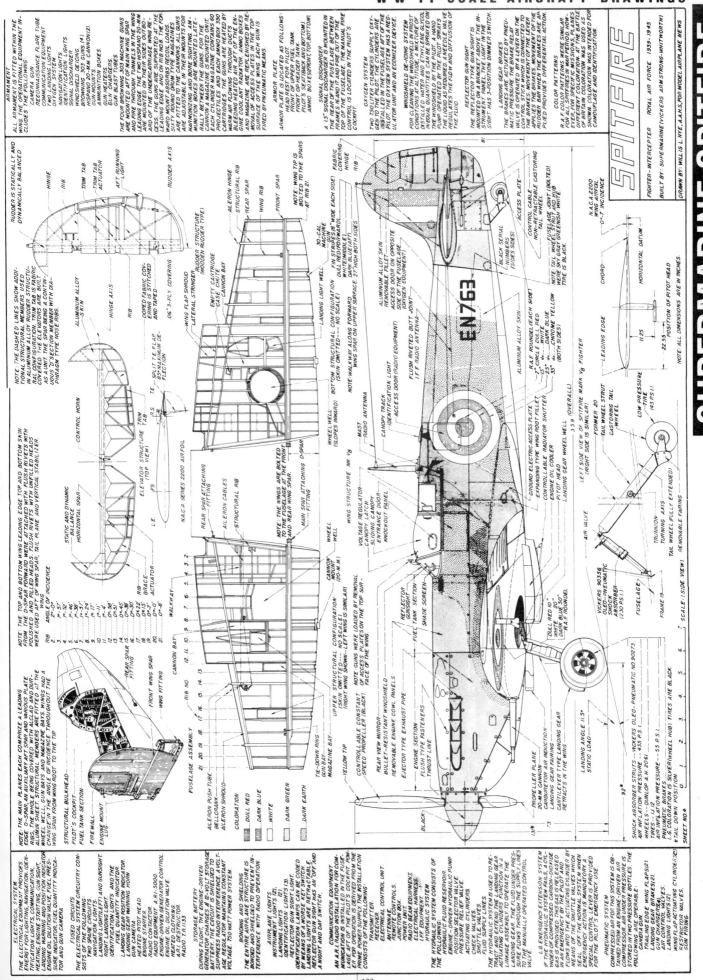

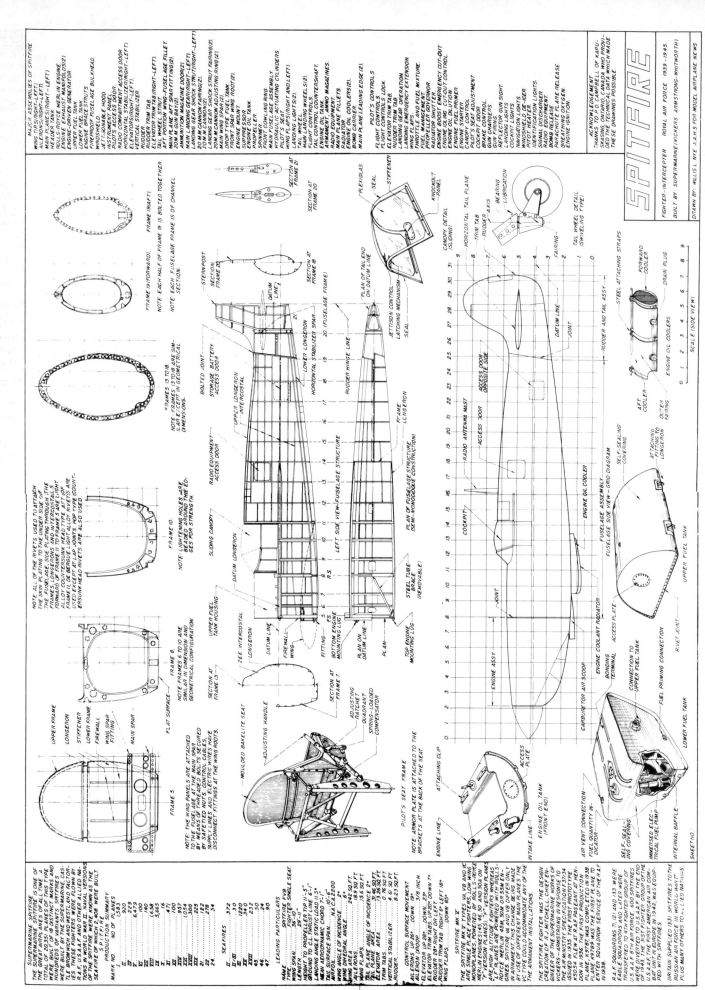

SPITFIRE

FIGHTER-INTERCEPTER   ROYAL AIR FORCE 1939-1945.

BUILT BY: SUPERMARINE (VICKERS ARMSTRONG-WHITWORTH)

DRAWN BY: WILLIS L. NYE S.A.H.S. FOR MODEL AIRPLANE NEWS

ACKNOWLEDGEMENT -
THANKS TO R. G. CAMPBELL, OF KAPU-
SKASING, ONTARIO, CANADA WHO PROVI-
DED THE TECHNICAL DATA WHICH MADE
THESE DRAWINGS POSSIBLE.

SHEET NO. I

124

SUPERMARINE SPITFIRE

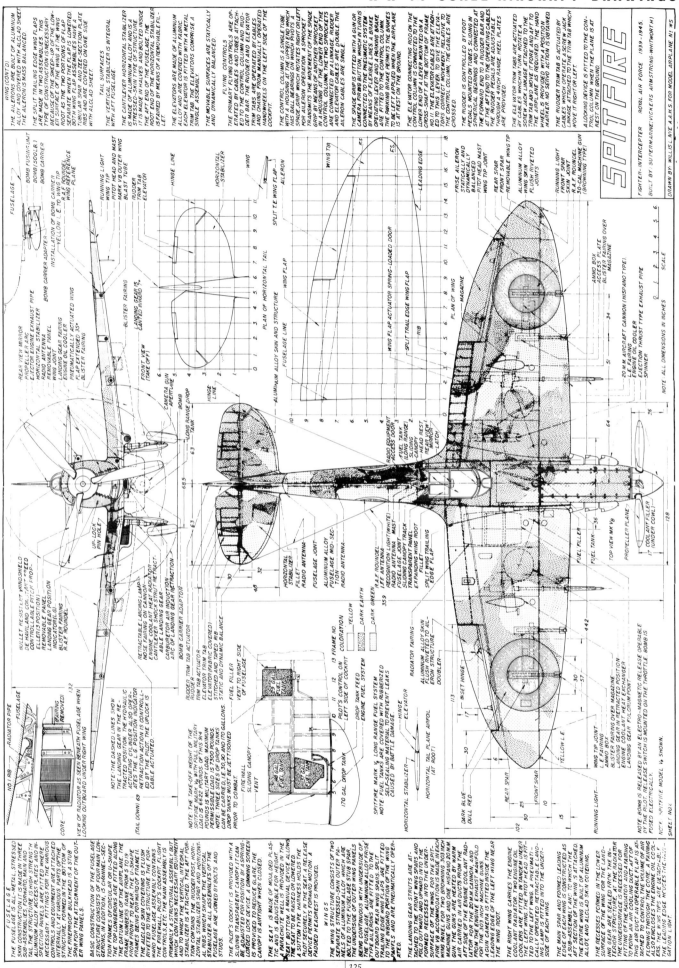

SPITFIRE

FIGHTER-INTERCEPTER   ROYAL AIR FORCE 1939-1945.

BUILT BY SUPERMARINE-VICKERS ARMSTRONG-WHITWORTH)

DRAWN BY: WILLIS L NYE A.A.H.S. FOR MODEL AIRPLANE N.º WS

THE VEGA VENTURA

The first Ventura I ordered by Britain on a factory test flight. The British turret is installed, but the guns aren't in yet. Note the step-up forward of the tail for the ventral gunner's station.

IN 1938, Lockheed introduced an improved version of its Model 14 airliner as the "Model 18 Lodestar." The British were pleased with the Hudson bomber conversion of the Model 14, and they asked Lockheed to do the same with the Model 18, but with more major changes.

The principal change was the use of the new 1,850hp Pratt & Whitney S1A4-G (R-2800) Double Wasp engine in place of the 875 to 1,200hp airliner powerplants. The R-2800s used wide-blade, or "paddle," propellers because the location of the engine nacelles on the Lodestar wing precluded larger diameters, and four-blade units weren't desirable. A bomber nose and a bomb bay similar to those on the Hudson were fitted, but the lower rear fuselage was modified to accommodate a ventral gunner's station, which resulted in a distinctive upward step toward the tail. A powered dorsal turret was installed farther forward than the one on the Hudson.

Lockheed gave the new bomber a new model number (37), and the British, after placing an initial order for 300 in May 1940, named it "Ventura." A further 375 were ordered later that year, and its first flight was on July 31, 1941.

The Venturas weren't built in Lockheed's Burbank plant, or even by Lockheed as such. Vega Aircraft Corp., a wholly-owned subsidiary with a factory adjacent to the Lockheed-owned Union Air Terminal in Burbank, was selected to build

View from above of a U.S. Army Vega B-34, with two fixed .50-caliber machine guns and two flexible .30-caliber guns in the nose; .50-caliber guns are in the Martin powered turret and the ventral gun station.

the Ventura, hence its identity as a Vega rather than a Lockheed product. On November 30, 1943, Vega was absorbed by Lockheed, and the factory, where 2,750 Boeing B-17s were also being produced, became "Lockheed Plant 1A." Some Ventura variants for the U.S. Army were built in the main Lockheed plant.

Ventura I—These had armament of two fixed and two flexible .303-caliber machine guns in the nose; two or four more in the dorsal turret; two in the waist positions; and two in the ventral station. The Ventura I could also carry 2,500 pounds of bombs. The first Mark Is were powered with 1,850hp civil engines. Deliveries began in September 1941, and Venturas were in service by November.

Ventura II—The 487 Ventura IIs carried more fuel, 3,000 pounds of bombs and four guns in the turret, and they were powered with 2,000hp U.S. Army R-2800-31 engines.

Ventura IIA—These were 200 planes originally ordered for Britain under Lend-Lease that carried the U.S. Army designation "B-34." Only 25 were sent to the R.A.F.; others went to other Empire forces—20 to Australia, 25 to Canada with R.A.F. serial numbers, and 23 to New Zealand. The rest remained in the U.S. and were soon designated "RB-34," since they weren't considered suitable for combat missions. Most were used as trainers and for utility work.

Ventura III and IV—The Ventura III was to have been an R.A.F. version of the U.S. Army O-56 (later the B-37), but none of them were procured. No "Ventura IV" designation was assigned.

Ventura V—These were "navalized" versions of the Ventura supplied under Lend-Lease by the U.S. Navy from PV-1 orders. British forces acquired 388, and many were diverted to Australia, Canada, New Zealand and South Africa.

The prefix "G.R." was given to reconnaissance versions as in "G.R. Mark V."

American Venturas—The U.S. Army took over some of the British-contract Ventura Is, and then provided others to the R.A.F. and its own squadrons from later B-34 contracts. The Army, however, called its B-34s "Lexington" rather than "Ventura." The U.S. Navy became the major user of Venturas as "PV-1" and "PV-3," still using the British name.

Model 37—Because the drafted Ventura Is didn't meet U.S. Army specifications, they couldn't be given Army designations or serial numbers. Instead, the Army simply called them "Model 37." These became "R Model 37" in October 1942. This resulted in an interesting bit of confusion by some when they misunderstood the spoken letter "R" to mean "Our Model 37," as compared with the British Model 37.

B-34—The first 200 Lend-Lease Venturas were designated "B-34," and only 24 went to the U.S. Army. Major changes included an American Martin turret and American equipment and armament, including .50-caliber machine guns.

B-34A—A further 211

B-34s: 66 went to Britain and the others went to the U.S. Army as follows: 101 B-34A-2 bomber trainers, 28 B-34A-3 gunnery trainers and 16 B-34A-4 target tugs.

B-37—The Army ordered 550 armed reconnaissance/observation versions of the Ventura under the designation "O-56." Before they were completed, however, the Army discontinued the "O for Observation" category and redesignated the O-56s as bombers, since they fit that category and could still carry 2,000 pounds of bombs. The designation "B-34B" was to have been assigned, but be-

Top photo: an unarmed U.S. Army Ventura I that had been drafted from the British order and redesignated "Lockheed Model 37." Above: one of the 18 U.S. Army Lexingtons that had been ordered as O-56 observation planes, but were delivered as B-37 bombers.

cause the planes had 1,700hp Wright R-2600-13 Double Cyclone engines instead of Pratt & Whitneys, they were given the new bomber designation "B-37." Production was in the main Lockheed plant, but because the space was needed for other projects, the contract was cut short. Only 18 B-37s were built, and they were used as trainers.

PV-1—The U.S. Navy, with 1,600 PV-1 variants ordered as "PV-1" ("P" for Patrol; "V" for Vega), was the major Ventura user. These carried

Long-range reconnaissance version of the U.S. Navy Vega PV-1 with 155-gallon drop tanks. Note the painted-over (once transparent) bomber nose, and the oddity of the star insignia on both the nose and the aft fuselage.

additional internal fuel, plus two 155-gallon drop tanks and fittings for 10 5-inch rockets, and they could carry up to 3,000 pounds of bombs, depth charges, or a torpedo in the bomb bay. The Navy used its Venturas widely in the Pacific and in Alaska from early 1943 until the end of the war. Armament varied greatly according to the mission, including night fighters for the U.S. Marines with three-man crews, six fixed nose guns and British night-intercept radar. Some photographic conversions were designated "PV-1P."

PV-2—A greatly revised Ventura with longer wings, larger tail surfaces and extensive internal and armament changes was ordered in 1943. The revisions justified its new name, "Harpoon," and made this plane too different from the basic Ventura to be called such. Harpoons did see action late in the war.

PV-3—To get Venturas into its inventory before the PV-1s on order could be built, the U.S. Navy took the last 27 of the British Ventura IIs and designated them "PV-3" in October 1942.

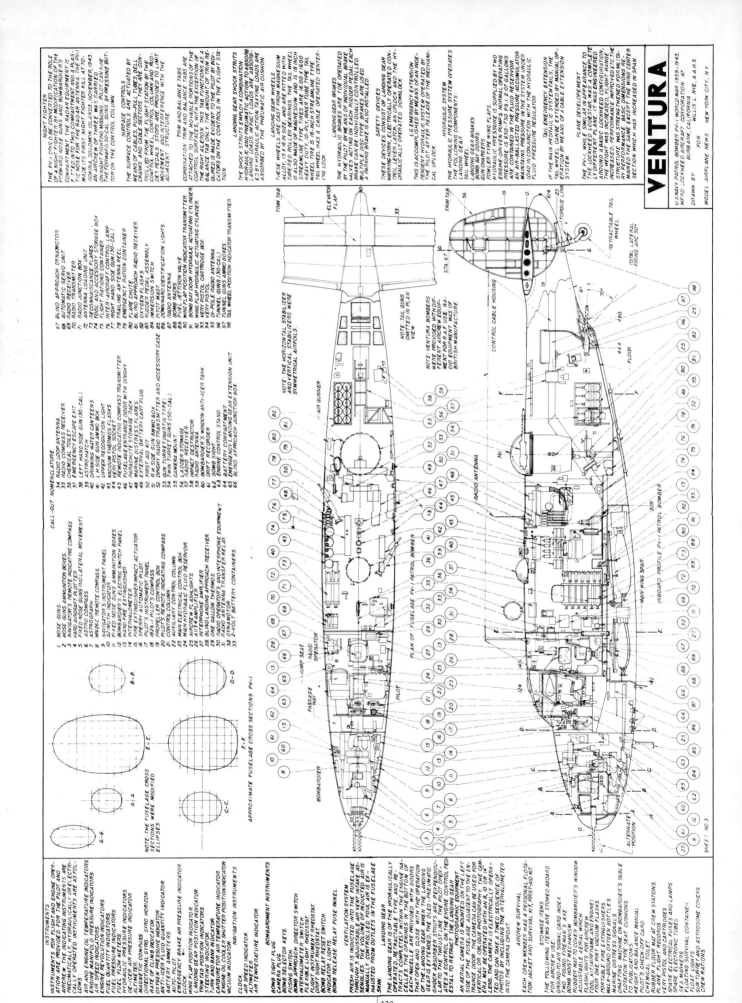

VENTURA

U.S. NAVY PATROL BOMBER PV-1 WORLD WAR 1939-1945.
MFR'D LOCKHEED AIRCRAFT CORPORATION AT
BURBANK, CALIFORNIA

DRAWN BY: FOR   WILLIS L. NYE, A.A.H.S.

MODEL AIRPLANE NEWS   NEW YORK CITY, N.Y.

SHEET NO. 3

THE VEGA VENTURA

VENTURA

U.S. NAVY PATROL BOMBER PV-1, WORLD WAR 1939-1945.
MFRD LOCKHEED AIRCRAFT CORPORATION AT
BURBANK, CALIFORNIA.

DRAWN BY: WILLIS L. NYE, A.A.H.S.

MODEL AIRPLANE NEWS   NEW YORK CITY, NY

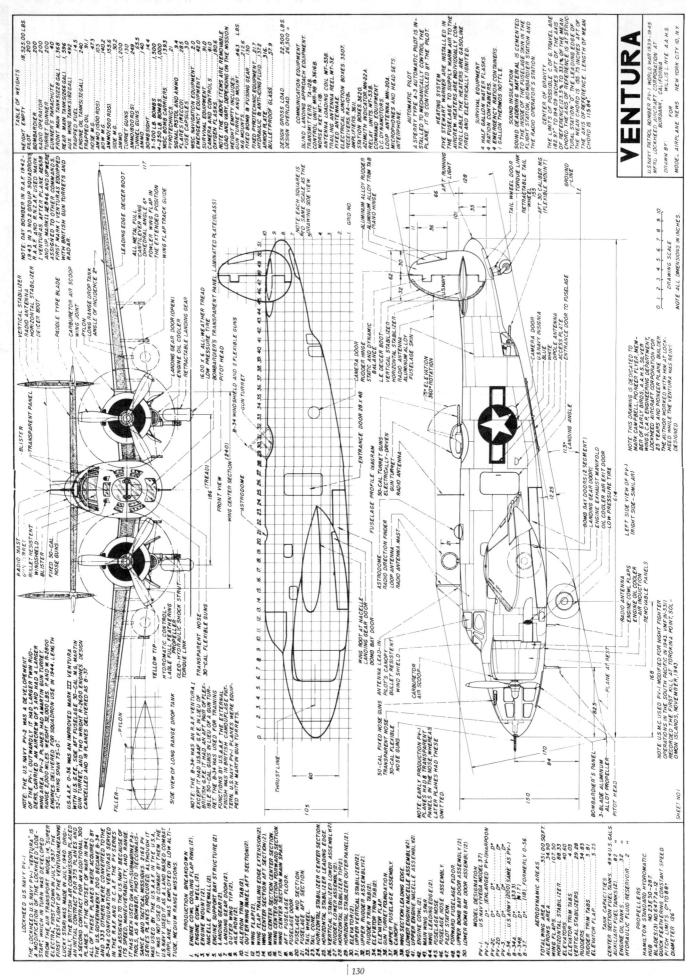

THE VEGA VENTURA

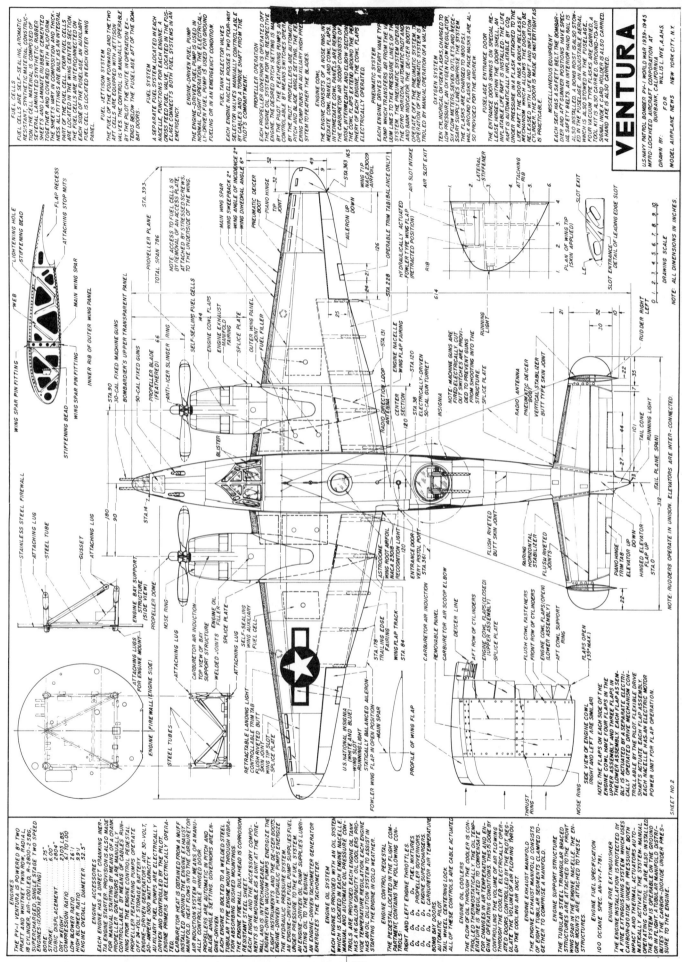

VOUGHT SB2U CHESAPEAKE / VINDICATOR

An SB2U-3 in the overall light gray adopted for tactical U.S. Navy planes in February 1941. This is Airplane No. 16 of the Marine Scouting Squadron One (VMS-1).

★   ★   ★

STARTING in the early 1920s, the Chance Vought Corporation of Long Island City, NY (later of East Hartford, CT), was the major supplier of scouting and observation planes to the U.S. Navy. Until 1934, scouting, light bombing and observation were considered separate missions, and the airplanes used separate "S," "B" and "O" designations. In 1934, some missions and designations were combined; e.g., "SB" for Scout-Bombers and "OS" for Observation-Scouts.

Vought entered the dual-designation era with the SBU-1 biplane, which started as the XF3U-1 two-seat fighter. The 124 SBU-1s and -2s were

Vought's last biplanes. Changing requirements and the Navy's final acceptance of monoplanes for use on aircraft carriers resulted in subsequent Navy monoplane designs.

Vought responded to a U.S. Navy requirement for a folding-wing monoplane scout-bomber, and they received a contract for one XSB2U-1 on October 11, 1934. Like the Hawker Hurricane, the SB2U (Vought's Model 156) carried traditional Vought tube-and-fabric structure into the monoplane age. The SBU fuselage construction and tail shape were adapted to a new, metal-frame, low-cantilever wing that contained retractable landing gear. The wing had a single spar, a closed aluminum D-tube from the spar

forward for torsional strength, and it was fabric-covered aft of the spar. The wing folded upward outboard of the flat center section by means of a manually operated screw jack that was secured to fittings on the wing and fuselage.

Its armament was two .30- or .50-caliber machine guns in the wings, and a single, flexible, .30-caliber gun in the rear cockpit. A single 500- or 1,000-pound bomb was carried on an ejector rack under the belly. Because the SB2U was a vertical dive bomber, this

device was necessary to swing the bomb clear of the propeller. Two 100-pound bombs could be carried on racks under the wing. The powerplant for the production SB2U-1s was the 825hp Pratt & Whitney R-1535-96, and 54 planes were ordered in October 1936. An odd feature (compared with previous scout models) was the great distance between the cockpits.

The SB2U-1s entered

The following figures compare the weight and performance of the SB2U-1 and the SB2U-3:

Empty Weight .. 5,049/5,620 lbs.

Gross Weight .. 7,888/8,900 lbs.

Rate of Climb .... 1,220/ 1,051 ft./min.

Service Ceiling .... 26,400/ 22,000 ft.

Fuel .... 690/2,766 lbs. *

High Speed .... 250/221mph (at 9,500 ft.)

Range .... 1,120/2,640 statute miles

*Navy specification tables for 1941 give pounds instead of gallons.

A Vought V-156F of the French Navy. Note the red, white and blue stripes on the elevators and the rudder, and the dive brakes on the wing (a feature not used on the U.S. Navy/Marine SB2Us).

This underside view of the SB2U-3 1-S-16 shows the retracted landing gear and racks for 100-pound bombs. Note the star on the lower right wing.

service in December 1937, and they were followed by 58 improved SB2U-2s that were ordered in January 1938. The final order was for 57 SB2U-3s that were delivered to the U.S. Marine Corps late in 1940. The -3s were heavier because of their increased fuel and armor and their two additional wing guns.

In 1938, the Navy allowed Vought to build 40 SB2U-2s for the French Navy as "V-156F" ("F" for France). These planes were equipped to French requirements, including the novel reverse-action French throttles that pulled back to increase power. French armament was installed in France. The V-156Fs served on French aircraft carriers and with shore-based squadrons, and they were the only SB2U types to go on the offensive (some made bombing raids from southern France into northern Italy in 1940). After the fall of France, England took over a second French contract for 50 V-156Fs, and named them "Chesapeake." Vought designated them "V-156B-1" ("B" for Britain).

The U.S. didn't adopt the British name, as it did with some other U.S. models in British service. When U.S. military planes were given "popular" names in October 1941, the SB2Us were named "Vindicator."

When the planes were re-equipped to British standards (including forward-open throttles and extra armor),

the Chesapeakes were too heavy to operate from the small British carriers to which they had been assigned. As a result, they were reassigned to

A front view of the SB2U-2 with its wings folded. Note that the turning handles on the right-hand jack are extended, and that those on the left jack are folded.

secondary shore duty and didn't see combat. It has been stated, but not verified, that the Germans used captured V-156Fs for scouting missions

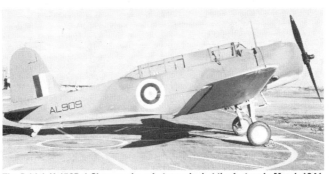

The British V-156B-1 Chesapeake, photographed at the factory in March 1941.

along the English coast.

By the middle of 1940, SB2U-1s and -2s were flying with seven U.S. Navy squadrons from four of the Navy's six big carriers. By the end of 1941, there were only four squadrons aboard two carriers. The U.S. Marines had all of their SB2U-3s at shore bases. Some of the carrier-based SB2Us that were at Pearl Harbor on December 7, 1941, were destroyed on the ground by the Japanese. Later Marine SB2U-3s were ferried to Midway Island, where they attacked Japanese ships during the Battle of Midway in June 1942.

Four SB2U squadrons served on the carriers "Wasp" and "Ranger" in the Atlantic until the end of 1942. They finished their service as trainers.

In 1939, the United Aircraft Corporation, the parent firm of both Vought and Sikorsky, merged the two into a single entity: the Vought-Sikorsky Division of United. The Vought factory was moved from East Hartford into the Sikorsky plant in Stratford, CT. The SB2U-3s that were then being built technically became "Vought-Sikorskys" instead of "Chance Voughts."

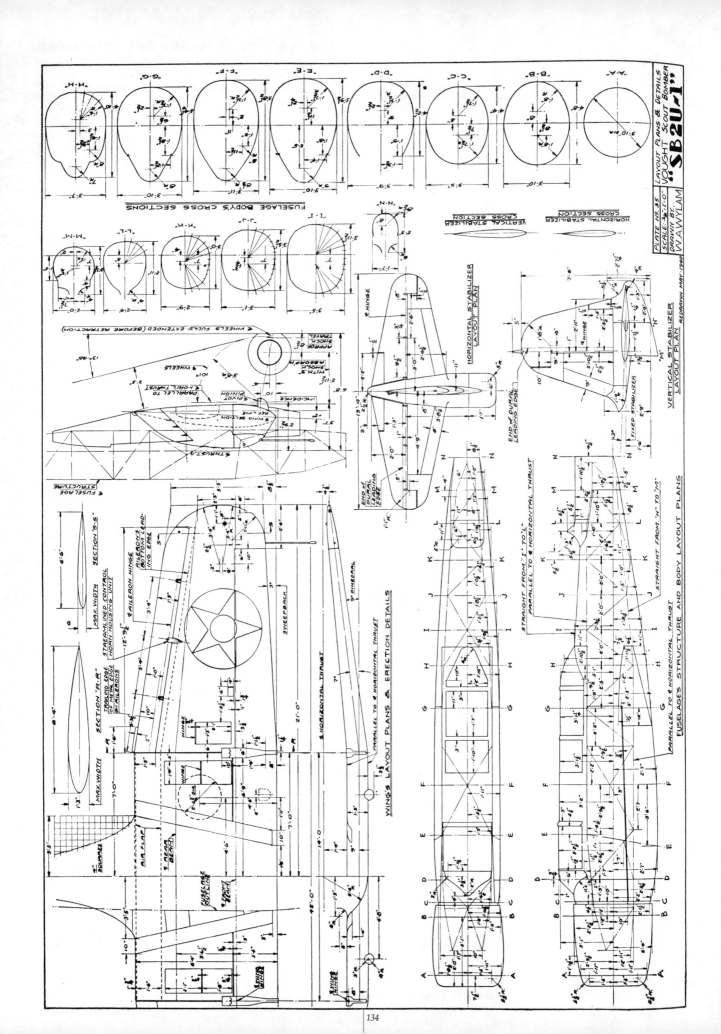

PLATE № 35
LAYOUT PLANS & DETAILS
VOUGHT Scout Bomber
"SB2U-1"
SCALE 3/4"=1'-0"
DRAWN BY
W.A.WYLAM   REDRAWN MAY-1940

FUSELAGE BODY'S CROSS SECTIONS

HORIZONTAL STABILIZER CROSS SECTION

VERTICAL STABILIZER CROSS SECTION

HORIZONTAL STABILIZER LAYOUT PLAN

VERTICAL STABILIZER LAYOUT PLAN

END OF DURAL LEADING EDGE

FIXED STABILIZER

FUSELAGE'S STRUCTURE AND BODY LAYOUT PLANS

WINGS LAYOUT PLANS & ERECTION DETAILS

SECTION "R-R"

SECTION "S-S"

MAX. WIDTH

STREAMLINED CONTROL HORN HOUSING UNIT

AILERON HINGE

AILERONS

TRAILING EDGE OF AILERONS

AIR FLAP

FUSELAGE OUTLINE

FRONT BEAM

REAR BEAM

SWEEPBACK

DIHEDRAL

WING SECTION

PARALLEL TO HORIZONTAL THRUST

VOUGHT SB2U CHESAPEAKE/VINDICATOR

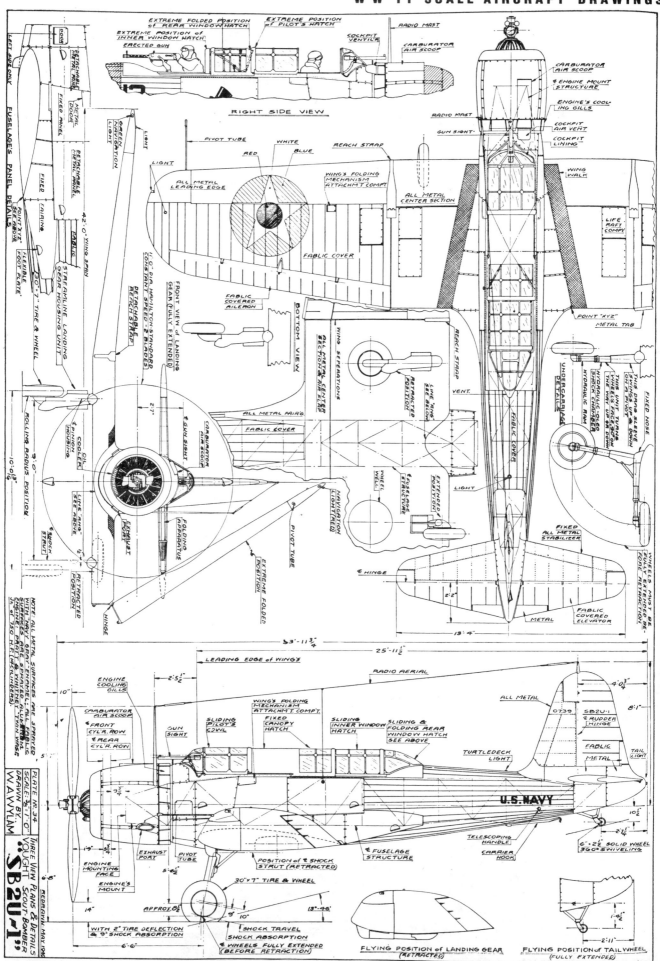

VOUGHT OS2U KINGFISHER

THE Vought OS2U King-fisher was the most widely used U.S. Navy shipboard catapult plane of the war. On March 22, 1937, the Chance Vought Company (then of East Hartford, CT) received a contract for a single XOS2U-1, which was intended as a replacement for older Vought and Curtiss biplanes that were still serving the fleet. The prototype first flew on July 20, 1938, and an order for 54 production OS2U-1s followed. The first examples, which were mostly seaplanes, reached the fleet in August 1940, while others equipped with wheels were assigned to naval air stations and reserve training bases around the country.

As an airplane, the Kingfisher had little in common with previous Vought designs, other than the SBU-SB2U tail shape. It was an all-metal monoplane with a 450hp Pratt & Whitney R-985-48 Twin Wasp Jr. engine. The distance between the pilot and the observer/gunner was unusual, even when it was compared

A Vought OS2U-3 Kingfisher seaplane, with 1943-44 dark blue-gray camouflage on the upper surfaces graduating to white undersides. The hook under the float was used to snag a retrieval net before the seaplane was hoisted aboard the mother ship.

with the SB2U. A structural innovation for a production airplane was the spot-welding (rather than riveting) of sheet aluminum.

The seaplane version used a single main float and wing-tip floats. Early floats were made by Vought, but the majority of them were built on a separate Navy

SPECIFICATIONS AND PERFORMANCE OS2U-3

Powerplant	Pratt & Whitney R-198-AN-2 or -8:450hp
Wingspan	35ft., 10⅞ in.
Wing Area	262 sq. ft.
Gross Weight	6,000 lbs.
High Speed	165mph at 5,500 ft.

contract by the Edo Corporation of College Point, Long Island, NY. The airplanes were flown from the new Vought-Sikorsky plant in Stratford, CT, to naval air stations, where the floats were installed in Navy shops.

The Navy was also involved in the manufacture of the

Kingfisher. After Vought delivered 158 improved OS2U-2s with R-985-50 engines, and was working on 1,006 longer-range OS2U-3s, the U.S. Naval Aircraft factory in Philadelphia, PA, built 300 OS2U-3s as "OS2N-1" (the Navy had built a single XOSN-1 biplane of its own design there in 1938; hence the "OS2N-1" designation).

British forces received 100 OS2U-3s in 1942, and kept the name "Kingfisher." In the U.S., Kingfishers (on wheels and on floats) served with the Inshore Patrol Squadrons. In the fleet, they operated on wheels from aircraft carriers, and catapult seaplane versions served on battleships and cruisers until the end of the war.

Although they were usually low-performance scouts and observers that were lightly armed (two .30-caliber machine guns and two 325-pound depth charges), Kingfishers earned great fame for numerous rescue missions, where they picked up downed air crews from under the guns of Japanese shore batteries, and found lost personnel. The most famous of these missions was the successful 22-day search for Captain Eddie Rickenbacker, America's WWI Ace, who was forced down in the Pacific with a B-17 crew in November 1943.

☆   ☆   ☆

An OS2U-3 ashore on its fixed landing gear. This is airplane no. 6 of Scouting Squadron Six, in the dark blue-gray top and side camouflage, and light gray underside camouflage, of 1942-43.

VOUGHT OS2U KINGFISHER

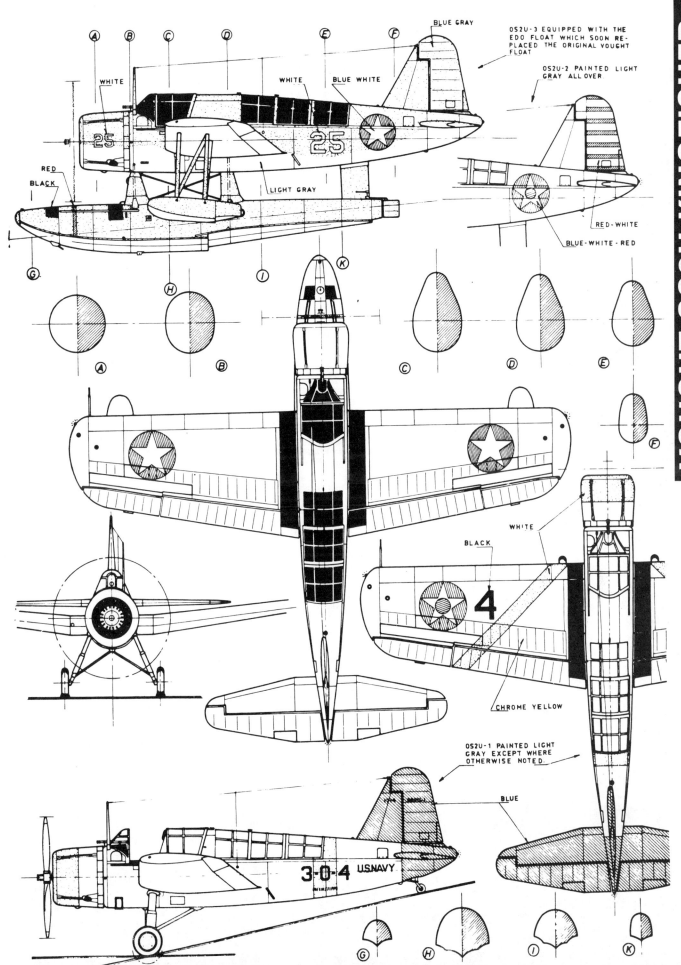

BLUE GRAY

WHITE

WHITE

BLUE WHITE

25

25

LIGHT GRAY

RED

BLACK

OS2U-3 EQUIPPED WITH THE EDO FLOAT WHICH SOON RE-PLACED THE ORIGINAL VOUGHT FLOAT

OS2U-2 PAINTED LIGHT GRAY ALL OVER.

RED-WHITE

BLUE-WHITE-RED

BLACK

CHROME YELLOW

WHITE

OS2U-1 PAINTED LIGHT GRAY EXCEPT WHERE OTHERWISE NOTED.

BLUE

4

3-O-4 U.S.NAVY

WESTLAND LYSANDER

A Westland Lysander II photographed at Kabrit, Egypt, in 1943. Note the lowered wing flaps and the very large pants (spats) over the wheels.

THE British Westland "Lysander" was developed in 1935 by Westland Aircraft, Ltd., of Yeovil, England. Westland applied latter-day technology to the traditional "Army Cooperation" airplane, which had been standardized by the major air powers as a large, versatile, open-cockpit biplane. Its mission was to work with the ground forces through observation and reconnaissance; photography; light bombing; and ground attack with machine guns. In pre-radio days, such planes could also pick up messages from ground points and drop them (and small quantities of supplies) to remote outposts.

The metal-framed Lysander retained all of the required Army Cooperation qualities, despite such major changes as a high monoplane wing, and a closed cabin in which the gunner/observer sat far to the rear, separated from the pilot by the fuel tank.

The single-wing design was much more than a simple deletion of the lower wing of a traditional biplane in the interest of improved crew visibility and streamlining. The odd planform (see photos and drawings) resulted in an overall aerodynamic forward sweep of the wing—an innovation that was many years ahead of its time. It also featured large trailing-edge flaps, and full-span, automatic, leading-edge slats that opened for slow-speed flight. Both features were relatively new to military aircraft, and they gave the Lysander unprecedented short takeoff and landing (STOL) performance.

Its initial powerplant was the 890hp Bristol Mercury XII radial engine; it had the unique Bristol-type cowling in which the leading edge of the cowling was also the collector ring for the engine exhaust. The single exhaust stack was at the lower right side. The Lysander's initial armament was a pair of forward-firing, .303-caliber machine guns in the wheel fairings outboard of the propeller arc, and a single WW I vintage, .303-caliber Lewis machine gun in the rear cockpit. Using both belly racks and racks on winglets, sixteen 20-pound bombs, four 216-pound bombs or two 250-pound bombs could be carried. Other stores, such as flares, smoke generators, supply cannisters and auxiliary fuel tanks, could also be

Lysander IIs with stub wings in place on the landing gear; the wheel covers have been removed. Note the far-aft location of the fuselage bomb racks and the early form of the narrow fin flash that was adopted in mid-1940.

SPECS AND PERFORMANCE LYSANDER III

Powerplant	870hp Bristol Mercury XX or 30
Empty Weight	4,365 lbs.
Gross Weight	6,318 lbs.
High Speed	209mph at sea level; 196mph at 15,000 ft.
Minimum Speed (at gross weight)	56mph
Takeoff Run (to clear 50-foot obstacle)	930 ft.
Landing Run (over 50-foot obstacle)	1,020 ft.

Side view of the Lysander II. Note how the rear portion of the cabin enclosure slides straight aft.

carried by the versatile Lysander.

Another innovative Lysander feature was the single-leg landing gear, which was designed for high-impact short and hard landings. It had large spats over the wheels, and it could be fitted with stub wings, called "winglets," that served as mounts for bomb racks, rescue equipment and miscellaneous supplies. Later, a large cylindrical cargo container or auxiliary fuel tank was fitted under the belly. The first flight of the prototype was on June 15, 1936.

Lysander I—Successful tests of two prototypes resulted in an order for 169 Lysander Is, and production was completed in 1939. Gross weight was 4,065 pounds.

Lysander II—This was similar to the Mk I, except for a change to a 905hp Bristol Perseus XII sleeve-valve engine. Because of size and detail differences, this wasn't interchangeable with the Mercury engine. Westland built 442 Mk IIs, and a further 75 were built in Canada. Gross weight was 6,015 pounds.

Lysander III—This plane "reverted" to an 870hp Mercury XX engine; 250 were built in Yeovil, and another 17 were built in a new Westland plant in Doncaster. The armament was increased to two flexible machine guns.

Lysander IIIA—These were improved Mk IIIs with 870hp Mercury 30 engines; 370 were built. A further 100 were completed as unarmed T.T. Mk III target tugs.

The R.A.F. had seven squadrons of Lysanders in service when the war started, and six were sent to France. Their role was traditional as long as the front remained stable in the "Sitzkrieg." When the "Blitzkrieg" began on May 10, 1940, the old Army Cooperation role was shattered; the Lysander and similar types were unable to operate in the old way. Their own troops were hard to follow in the rapidly changing scene; enemy armored columns were impervious to light machine-gun attacks and even to light bombs, and they possessed formidable firepower that was deadly to slow, low-flying aircraft. Further, the overwhelming German air power shot down many Lysanders, and destroyed others on their airfields. Of 174 Lysanders sent to France, only 50 were able to return to England—88 were lost in combat, and 36 were either destroyed on the ground or abandoned by their retreating squadrons.

Many British-based Lysanders were lost in the Battle of France, when they flew across the Channel to drop supplies to surrounded Allied troops and were hit by German ground fire.

The Army Cooperation role continued in modified form in other theaters of the war—notably in North Africa, were Lysanders had been sent before the war. After the war began, Lysanders also served in Greece, Palestine and India. The Lysanders' most famous operation—and the one best suited to their STOL characteristics—was the nighttime shuttling of French Resistance and other agents (and supplies) into and out of occupied France. Between August 1941 and late 1944, some 400 such sorties were made, with nearly 300 people flown in and 500 brought out. For this clandestine work, the Lysanders were painted overall matte black.

This view of a Lysander III with a belly-mounted auxiliary fuel tank shows the full-span wing slats open during a landing approach.

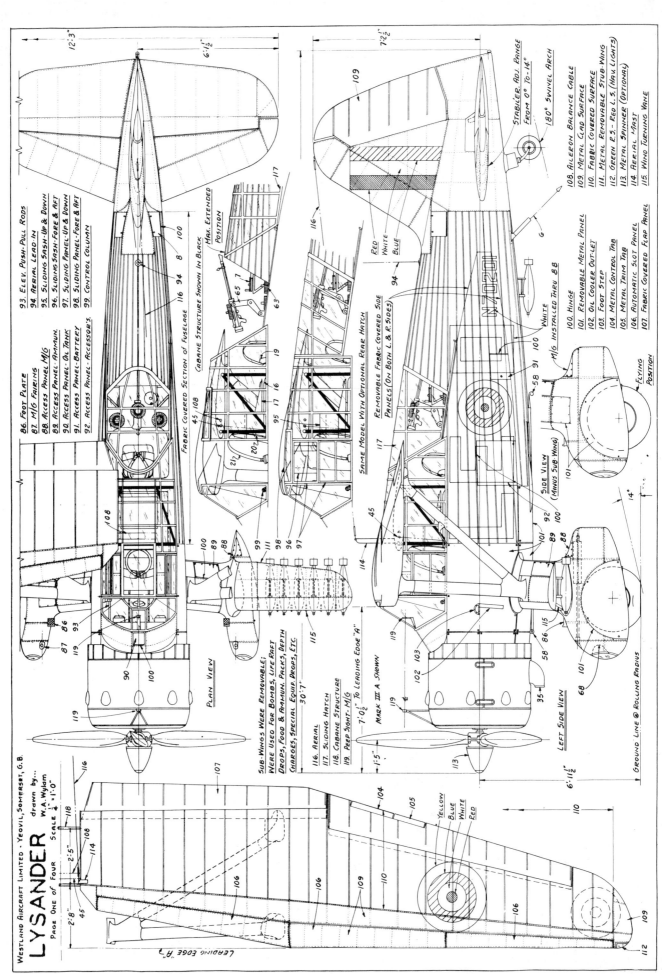

WESTLAND AIRCRAFT LIMITED · YEOVIL, SOMERSET, G.B.

LYSANDER

PAGE ONE OF FOUR

drawn by... W.A. Wylam

SCALE ¼" = 1'-0"

86. FOOT PLATE
87. M/G FAIRING
88. ACCESS PANEL-M/G
89. ACCESS PANEL-AMMUN.
90. ACCESS PANEL-OIL TANK
91. ACCESS PANEL-BATTERY
92. ACCESS PANEL-ACCESSORIES.
93. ELEV. PUSH-PULL RODS
94. AERIAL LEAD-IN
95. SLIDING SASH-UP & DOWN
96. SLIDING SASH-FORE & AFT
97. SLIDING PANEL-UP & DOWN
98. SLIDING PANEL-FORE & AFT
99. CONTROL COLUMN

100. HINGE
101. REMOVABLE METAL PANEL
102. OIL COOLER OUT-LET
103. FOOT STEP
104. METAL CONTROL TAB
105. METAL TRIM TAB
106. AUTOMATIC SLOT PANEL
107. FABRIC COVERED FLAP PANEL
108. AILERON BALANCE CABLE
109. METAL CLAD SURFACE
110. FABRIC COVERED SURFACE
111. METAL REMOVABLE STUB-WING
112. GREEN P.5 - RED L.S. (NAV. LIGHTS)
113. METAL SPINNER (OPTIONAL)
114. AERIAL MAST
115. WIND TURNING VANE

116. AERIAL
117. SLIDING HATCH
118. CABANE STRUCTURE
119. PEEP SIGHT-M/G

SUB-WINGS WERE REMOVABLE;
WERE USED FOR BOMBS, LIFE RAFT
DROPS, FOOD & AMMUN. PACKS, DEPTH
CHARGES, SPECIAL EQUIP. DROPS, ETC.

FABRIC COVERED SECTION OF FUSELAGE

CABANE STRUCTURE SHOWN IN BLACK

MAX. EXTENDED POSITION

PLAN VIEW

SAME MODEL WITH OPTIONAL REAR HATCH
REMOVABLE FABRIC COVERED SIDE
PANELS (ON BOTH L.& R. SIDES)

RED
WHITE
BLUE

M/G INSTALLED THRU 88
WHITE

SIDE VIEW
(MINUS SUB-WING)

FLYING POSITION

LEFT SIDE VIEW

STABILER. ADJ. RANGE FROM 0° TO-14°

180° SWIVEL ARCH

GROUND LINE @ ROLLING RADIUS

MARK III A SHOWN

7'-0½" TO LEADING EDGE "A"

LEADING EDGE "A"

WESTLAND LYSANDER

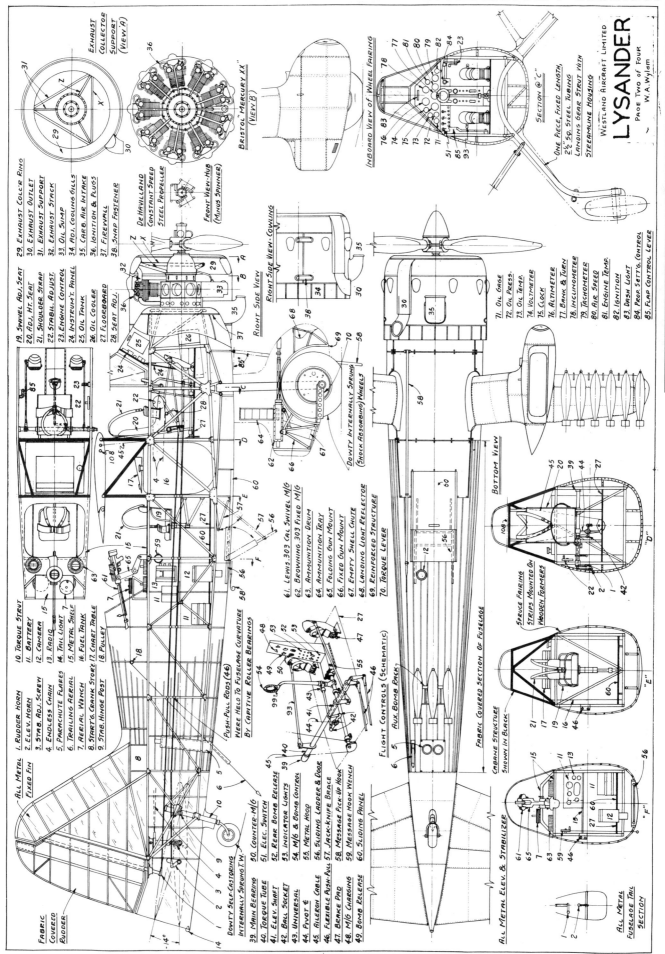

LYSANDER
Page Two of Four
W.A.Wylam

WESTLAND AIRCRAFT LIMITED

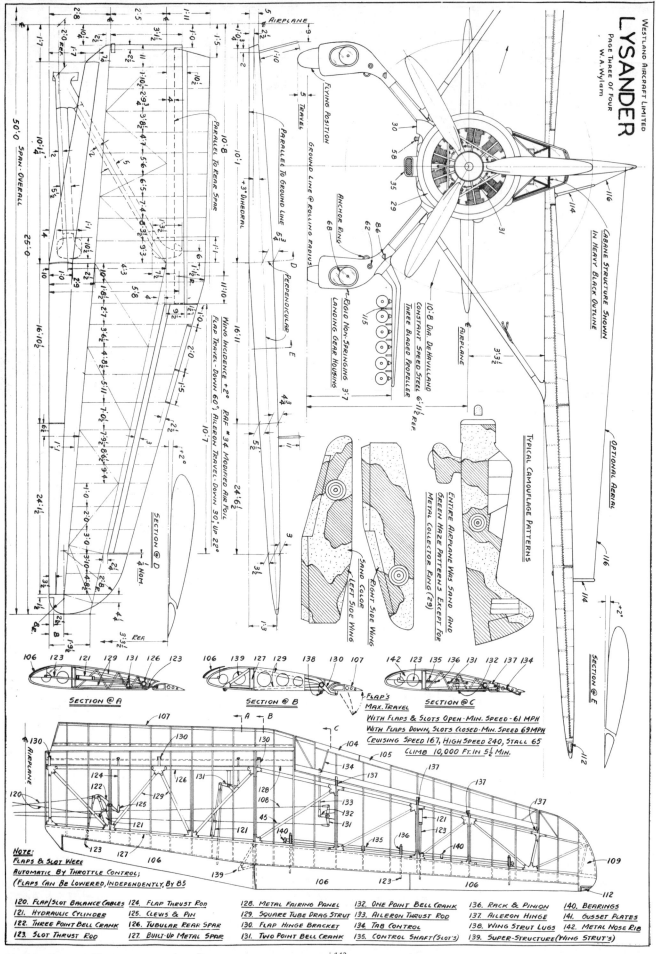

TYPICAL CAMOUFLAGE PATTERNS

ENTIRE AIRPLANE WAS SAND AND
GREEN HAZE PATTERNS EXCEPT FOR
METAL COLLECTOR RING (29)

SAND COLOR
LEFT SIDE WING
RIGHT SIDE WING

SECTION @ A

SECTION @ B

SECTION @ C

SECTION @ D

SECTION @ E

FLAP'S
MAX. TRAVEL

WITH FLAPS & SLOTS OPEN-MIN. SPEED -61 MPH
WITH FLAPS DOWN, SLOTS CLOSED-MIN. SPEED 69 MPH
CRUISING SPEED 167, HIGH SPEED 240, STALL 65
CLIMB 10,000 FT. IN 5½ MIN.

NOTE:
FLAPS & SLOT WERE
AUTOMATIC BY THROTTLE CONTROL;
(FLAPS CAN BE LOWERED, INDEPENDENTLY, BY 85

120. FLAP/SLOT BALANCE CABLES	124. FLAP THRUST ROD	128. METAL FAIRING PANEL
121. HYDRAULIC CYLINDER	125. CLEVIS & PIN	129. SQUARE TUBE DRAG STRUT
122. THREE POINT BELL CRANK	126. TUBULAR REAR SPAR	130. FLAP HINGE BRACKET
123. SLOT THRUST ROD	127. BUILT-UP METAL SPAR	131. TWO POINT BELL CRANK

132. ONE POINT BELL CRANK	136. RACK & PINION	140. BEARINGS
133. AILERON THRUST ROD	137. AILERON HINGE	141. GUSSET PLATES
134. TAB CONTROL	138. WING STRUT LUGS	142. METAL NOSE RIB
135. CONTROL SHAFT (SLOT'S)	139. SUPER-STRUCTURE (WING STRUT'S)	

WESTLAND LYSANDER

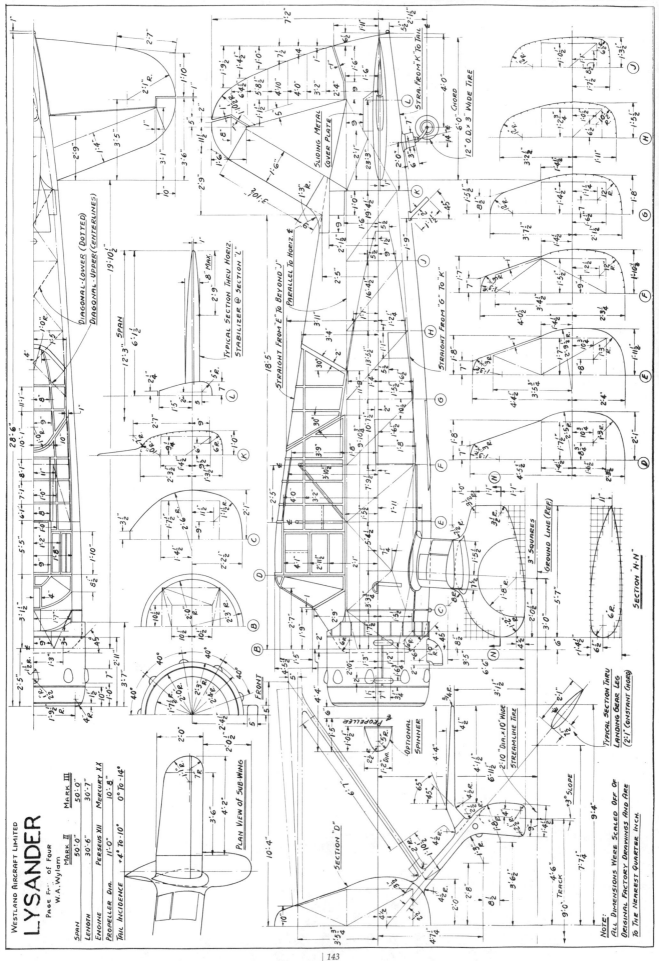

WESTLAND AIRCRAFT LIMITED

LYSANDER

Page Four of Four
W. A. Wylam

	Mark II	Mark III
Span	50'·0"	50'·0"
Length	30'·6"	30'·7"
Engine	Perseus XII	Mercury XX
Propeller Dia.	11'·0"	10'·8"
Tail Incidence	+4° To ·10°	0° To ·14°

Plan View of Sub-Wing

Typical Section Thru Horiz.
Stabilizer @ Section "L"

Sliding Metal Cover Plate

12" O.D. x 3" Wide Tire

Section "N-N"

3" Squares

Ground Line (Ref.)

Typical Section Thru
Landing Gear Leg
(2:1 Constant Chord)

2'·10" Dia. x 10" Wide
Streamline Tire

Section "D"

Optional Spinner

Propeller

Note:
All Dimensions Were Scaled Off Of
Original Factory Drawings And Are
To The Nearest Quarter Inch.

143

THE WESTLAND WHIRLWIND

Only 12 Westland Whirlwinds were built after this P7110. Note the four-cannon armament and the "bullet" at the fin-stabilizer intersection that wasn't on the two prototypes.

THE British Westland Whirlwind was the world's first production twin-engine, single-seat fighter that was designed as such. The prototype flew on October 11, 1938, beating the American Lockheed XP-38 by three months. The Whirlwinds saw extensive action in Europe during the war, but they weren't built in great numbers. There were two prototypes, and only 144 production models that equipped two fighter squadrons.

Design of the Whirlwind began in 1936, in response to an Air Ministry request for a twin-engine, single-seat fighter. Westland beat proposals from Bristol and Hawker, and received a contract for two prototypes in February 1937. The Whirlwind airframe was, in effect, a scaling-down of conventional twin-engine transports and bombers; it had a shorter nose, engines in nacelles on the wing, and landing gear that retracted into the nacelles. This led to odd proportions, because the single-seat airframe was relatively small, but the nacelles,

This view from above shows engine and radiator air intakes, located in the leading edge of the wing, between the fuselage and the nacelles. Note the 1940 Sand and Spinach camouflage, the Type A.1 roundels on the fuselage and the Type B roundels on the upper wing surface.

SPECIFICATIONS AND PERFORMANCE: WHIRLWIND

Powerplant .... Rolls-Royce Peregrine, 860hp at 2,850rpm at 13,500 ft.; 885hp at 3,000 rpm at 15,000 ft.

Wingspan .... 45 ft.

Length .... 32 ft., 3 in.

Wing Area .... 250 sq. ft.

Empty Weight .... 8,310 lbs.

Gross Weight .... 10,356 lbs. (fighter); 11,388 lbs. (bomber with two 500-lb. bombs).

High Speed .... 315mph at 5,000 ft.; 360mph at 15,000 ft.; 270mph at 15,000 ft. with two 500-lb. bombs.

with their standard-size engines, had to be as big as those on much larger aircraft.

The structure was all metal, including even the covering of the control surfaces. Its powerplants were 885hp Rolls-Royce Peregrines, which were developments of the earlier Rolls-Royce Kestrel that preceded the famous Merlin. The Whirlwind was the only airplane to use this engine, and troubles with the Peregrine hindered Whirlwind production and operations. Armament was the heaviest of any British fighter of the time; it had a battery of four 20mm cannons in the nose.

An initial order for 200 Whirlwinds was soon followed by an order for 200 more. Production began in Westland's Yeovil plant, but it suffered from the higher priority that was given to the Lysander program, and the first production Whirlwind didn't fly until May 1940. Two Whirlwinds, plus the second prototype, were assigned to No. 25 Fighter Squadron, but they were withdrawn when that unit was re-equipped with Bristol Beaufighters. The three, and other Whirlwinds, were then assigned to No. 253 Squadron, but because there were so few of them, they didn't participate in the Battle of Britain. Whirlwinds didn't engage the enemy until January 12, 1941, when two were sent up to intercept a lone German bomber over England. They scored a "probable"; and the first confirmed victory came on February 8, when a German Arado 196 seaplane was shot down.

The Whirlwind was kept secret from the public until February 1942. The Germans, however, knew of it much earlier; they had accurate silhouettes of the Whirlwind in their aircraft recognition manuals.

The short range of the Whirlwind precluded its use as an escort on long-distance bomb raids, but it did conduct escorts as far as Holland. Although it could hold its own against the Messerschmitt 109, the Whirlwind lacked high-altitude capability—a feature that wasn't considered important in a fighter when it was designed, but became very important after the war started. Whirlwinds equipped a second squadron (No. 137), and participated in low-altitude missions. They took part in attacks on German airfields and military installations in western France from their bases in England.

Bombing was added to the Whirlwind's activity in mid-1942, when racks for two 250-pound or two 500-pound bombs were added to the wings outboard of the nacelles. This version was named the "Whirlibomber."

The Whirlwind was already suffering from low priorities in its own factory, and production suffered further setbacks when the new Ministry of Aircraft Production decided to cancel Peregrine engine production in favor of increased Merlin production. As a result, the second order for 200 Whirlwinds was cancelled, and only 144 on the first order were completed. Westland then converted the Whirlwind production line to licensed production of Supermarine Spitfires.

The delivered airplanes were now "orphaned," with little support from the factory or the engine manufacturer; and the operational Whirlwinds were withdrawn from service. No. 263 Squadron was the last to use them, and 12 Whirlwinds made a spectacular attack on Cherbourg Harbor in France on October 22, 1943.

A variety of British colors and markings were used during the career of the Whirlwind. The first prototype was painted overall red with white letters and Type A roundels all over. The second prototype was all silver, again with Type A roundels. The odd arrangement of a black underside for the left wing, with a Type A.1 roundel matching a Type A roundel under the duck-egg blue right wing, is correct. This arrangement was also used by some other British fighters in 1940. Type C roundels were used on the fuselage and under the wings from July 1942 on.

This underside view of the Whirlwind shows the landing gear completely enclosed in nacelles, and Type A roundels under the wing.

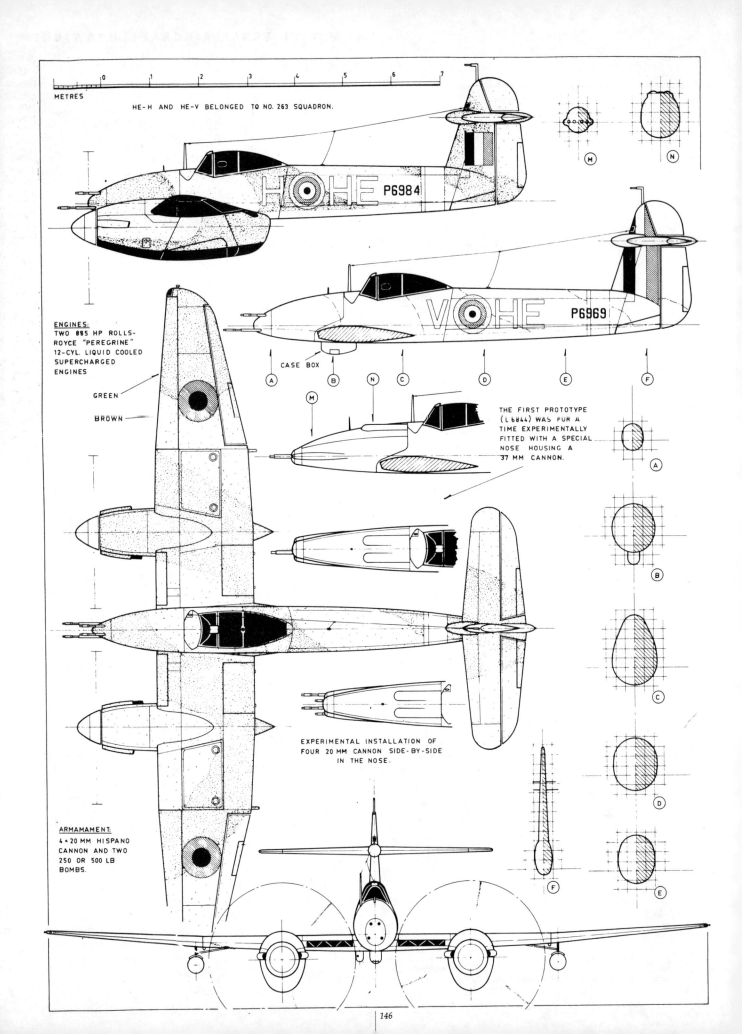

METRES

HE-H AND HE-V BELONGED TO NO. 263 SQUADRON.

P6984

P6969

ENGINES:
TWO 885 HP ROLLS-
ROYCE "PEREGRINE"
12-CYL. LIQUID COOLED
SUPERCHARGED
ENGINES

GREEN

BROWN

CASE BOX

THE FIRST PROTOTYPE
(L6844) WAS FOR A
TIME EXPERIMENTALLY
FITTED WITH A SPECIAL
NOSE HOUSING A
37 MM CANNON.

EXPERIMENTAL INSTALLATION OF
FOUR 20 MM CANNON SIDE-BY-SIDE
IN THE NOSE.

ARMAMAMENT:
4 × 20 MM HISPANO
CANNON AND TWO
250 OR 500 LB
BOMBS.

WESTLAND WHIRLWIND

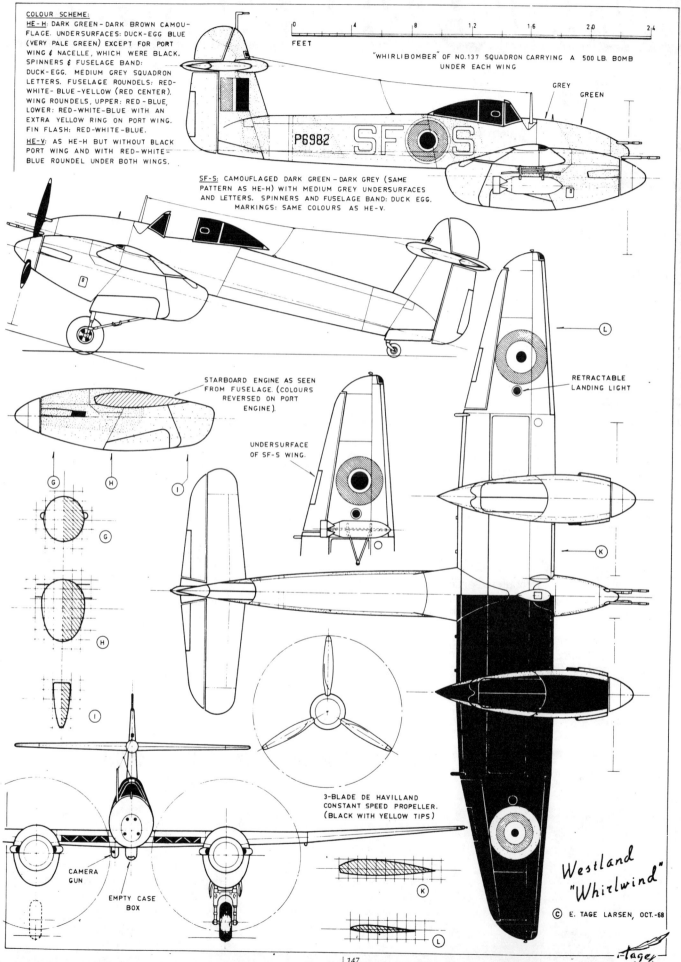

COLOUR SCHEME:

HE-H: DARK GREEN-DARK BROWN CAMOU-
FLAGE. UNDERSURFACES: DUCK-EGG BLUE
(VERY PALE GREEN) EXCEPT FOR PORT
WING & NACELLE, WHICH WERE BLACK.
SPINNERS & FUSELAGE BAND:
DUCK-EGG. MEDIUM GREY SQUADRON
LETTERS. FUSELAGE ROUNDELS: RED-
WHITE- BLUE -YELLOW (RED CENTER).
WING ROUNDELS, UPPER: RED-BLUE,
LOWER: RED-WHITE-BLUE WITH AN
EXTRA YELLOW RING ON PORT WING.
FIN FLASH: RED-WHITE-BLUE.
HE-V: AS HE-H BUT WITHOUT BLACK
PORT WING AND WITH RED-WHITE=
BLUE ROUNDEL UNDER BOTH WINGS.

"WHIRLIBOMBER" OF NO.137 SQUADRON CARRYING A 500 LB. BOMB
UNDER EACH WING

GREY

GREEN

P6982   SF S

SF-S: CAMOUFLAGED DARK GREEN – DARK GREY (SAME
PATTERN AS HE-H) WITH MEDIUM GREY UNDERSURFACES
AND LETTERS. SPINNERS AND FUSELAGE BAND: DUCK EGG.
MARKINGS: SAME COLOURS AS HE-V.

STARBOARD ENGINE AS SEEN
FROM FUSELAGE. (COLOURS
REVERSED ON PORT
ENGINE).

RETRACTABLE
LANDING LIGHT

UNDERSURFACE
OF SF-S WING.

G

G

H

H

I

I

K

L

L

CAMERA
GUN

EMPTY CASE
BOX

3-BLADE DE HAVILLAND
CONSTANT SPEED PROPELLER.
(BLACK WITH YELLOW TIPS)

K

Westland
"Whirlwind"

© E. TAGE LARSEN, OCT.-68

FEET   0   4   8   12   16   20   24

INFORMATIVE MODELING

NEW!

R/C AIRPLANE BUILDING TECHNIQUES

Item # BKP05911 $9.95

This new book contains over 100 great "how to" building and finishing techniques with step-by-step photos and illustrations. Author Randy Randolph covers it all: cutting and drilling, working with balsa, making jigs, construction, tool ideas, CG locators, Nyrod installation, building wings, covering, trimming, motor mounts, mufflers and exhausts, radios and installation, landing gear, wheels and more!

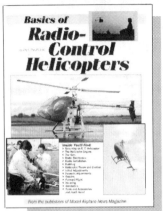

BASICS OF RADIO CONTROL HELICOPTERS

Item # BKP01880
$9.95

If you're interested in the fascinating world of R/C helicopters, here's a book by Paul Tradelius that will provide answers to all your questions—from selecting a helicopter kit and radio, through building the machine, and right up to aerobatic flying. Helicopter theory is presented in terms you can really understand, and you'll learn what kind of tools you'll need, how to make the inevitable repairs, even where to buy—all you need to know about helis!

BASICS OF RADIO CONTROL AIRPLANES

Item # BKP08900
$9.95

Ideal for beginners, this book guides readers through the difficult task of choosing the best airplane and radio equipment. It also includes helpful hints on controls, landing gear, radios, tools, adhesives, hardware, support equipment, balance and trim, maintenance, repairs and much more! Author Randy Randolph makes learning R/C easy, and no other book covers the basics of R/C airplanes better.

BASICS OF RADIO CONTROL SAILPLANES

Item # BKP11890
$9.95

Expertly written by long-time glider guider Alan Gornick, this book takes you carefully through the entire process—from choosing the type and class of sailplane that suits you, to the final step of flying it. Flying techniques are described in easy-to-understand terms, and you'll find information on the types of tools and adhesives to use during construction and finishing. All R/Cers will find this book enjoyable and informative.

NEW!

400 GREAT R/C MODELING TIPS— Vol. I and Vol. II

Volume I   Item # BKP01870 $9.95
Volume II   Item # BKP11911 $9.95

SPECIAL PRICE: Volume I & II   Item # BKP400PK
BOTH ONLY $15.95—SAVE $3.95

These books by Jim Newman contain numerous time and money-saving tips on building, tools, engines, covering and finishing, controls, landing gear, the flight box and much more—all beautifully illustrated. These 800 tips have been picked from the popular "Hints & Kinks" column featured in *Model Airplane News*. They're the innovative ideas of hundreds of modelers!

BOOKS

Air Age Book Mart

FLYING MODEL WARPLANES

Item # BKP07911
$14.95

International guide to plans and kits!

Compiled by John Fredriksen, this comprehensive reference book is an international guide to model airplane plans and kits. You'll find more than 8,500 plans, kits and semi-kits—representing over 600 types of historical aircraft. All entries in the guide are uniform and convey the following specifications: wingspan, length, motor flight mode, company, price and designer. Appendixes on documentation, model magazines and organizations worldwide are included, along with an international directory and an index of manufacturers.

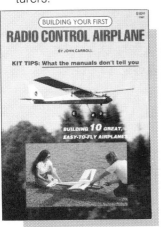

BUILDING YOUR FIRST RADIO CONTROL AIRPLANE

Item # BKP01890
$10.95

Author John Carroll built 10 of the best available R/C airplanes, and then he documented what he had learned. It's all here to help you avoid his mistakes! This book goes beyond the usual kit instructions and helps you fill the gaps found in most manufacturers' instruction manuals. Chapter topics include: Getting Started, Buying the Right Stuff, Covering and Radio Installation.

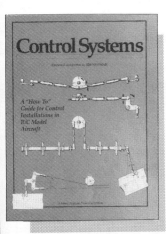

CONTROL SYSTEMS

Item # BKP01850
$4.95

Master hobby illustrator Jim Newman wrote this treatise on installing more complex control systems in R/C aircraft. It's great for new installations or for modifying your present flying machine. The illustrations are impeccable. You'll definitely want this book for your R/C library!

LEARNING TO FLY R/C MODEL AIRPLANES

Item # BKP01851
$9.95

Step-by-step instructions with detailed illustrations and photos help beginners ease their entry into the world of R/C flight. Written by John Carroll, this comprehensive book takes you from basic flight instruction through advanced aerobatics. Chapter topics include: Getting Started, Choosing Equipment, Building, The Engine, Ground Handling, Flight Basics, and Special Flying Techniques. Rank beginners will find this book a great instructional tool!

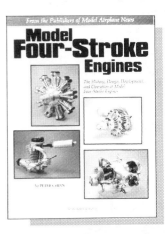

MODEL FOUR-STROKE ENGINES

Item # BKP01861
$9.95

Written by renowned model-engine expert Peter Chinn, this book covers the history, design, development, operation and maintenance of the ever-popular 4-stroke engine. This well-illustrated book will answer all your questions about 4-stroke engines, including opposed twins, radials, Wankels and conventionals. This is the definitive 4-stroke engine book that any modeler will enjoy.

SCRATCH-BUILDING R/C AIRPLANES

Item # BKP11912
$9.95

This comprehensive, illustrated guide to the successful completion of a model built from construction plans is an invaluable tool for the scratch-builder. Author Richard Uravitch guides you through the entire process, including: how to "read" plans, selecting materials, tool requirements, building and finishing, making templates, alignment methods, engine and radio installation, covering and much more!

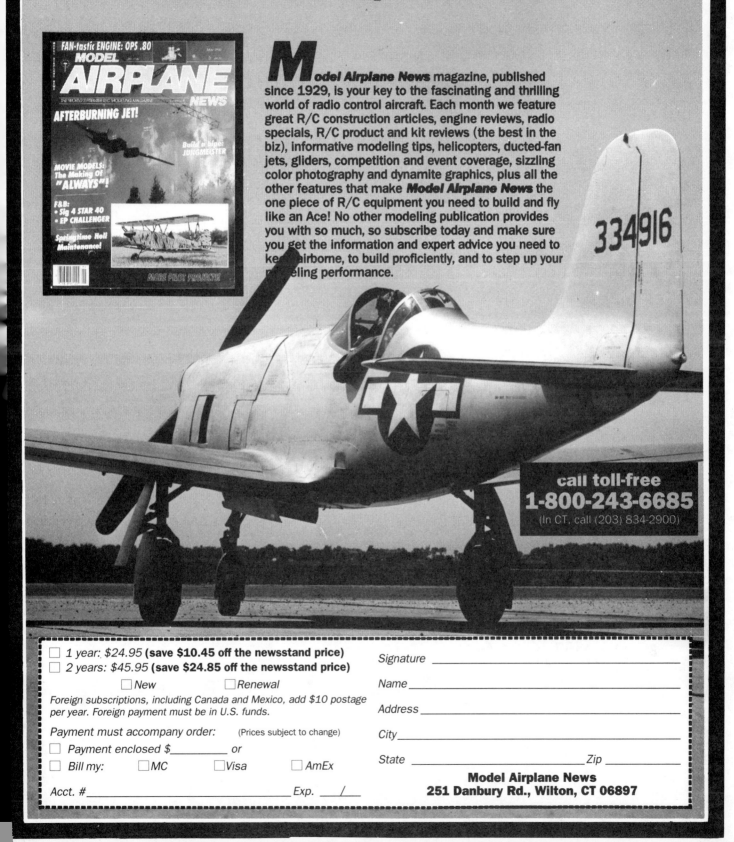

黄瑞
碧
山王
邦

08. 05. 1997
TAIPEI TAIWAN